MANIFEST DESTINY

A SHORT HISTORY OF THE UNITED STATES

Revised Edition

MANIFEST DESTINY

A SHORT HISTORY OF THE UNITED STATES

Revised Edition

KENNETH W. McNAUGHT
with
JOHN C. RICKER
and
JOHN T. SAYWELL

Maps by Robert Kunz and Tom Sankey

IRWIN PUBLISHING INC.
Toronto, Canada

Canadian Cataloguing in Publication Data

McNaught, Kenneth W., 1918-
  Manifest destiny

Bibliography: p.
Includes index.

ISBN 0-7720-1245-8

1. United States — History. I. Ricker, John
C., 1923-   II. Saywell, John T., 1929-
III. Title.

E178.M178 1980   973   C79-094868-0

© 1980 by Irwin Publishing Inc.
A Former Clarke, Irwin & Company Limited Book
ISBN 0-7720-1245-8

First edition published 1963
First published in paperback format 1965
Revised edition published 1980

    2   3   4   5   6   85

Printed and bound in Canada
by John Deyell Company

CONTENTS

LIST OF MAPS

LIST OF CHARTS

PREFACE

If Lord Bolingbroke was right when he said that "history is philosophy teaching by examples," surely the United States of America is one of the fittest subjects of historical study. Thomas Jefferson and Alexander Hamilton, formulating policies for a new nation, looked to their colonial past, to their European background, and to the vast American hinterland—and from each they chose examples to sustain their differing arguments. John C. Calhoun and Abraham Lincoln ransacked history, secular and biblical, to arrive at sharply differing conclusions about slavery and equality. The point, of course, is not that American history (or any other history) provides unimpeachable answers for everyday philosophy, but that man can only learn from his accumulated experience, and history is the record of that experience.

American history is peculiarly rich in signposts to the future. While the history of Britain and Europe commands the respect due to authority, and the accolade accorded intellectual achievement, that of the United States compensates by its breathtaking pace, its incorporation of much that is most worthy in the Anglo-European past, and especially by its twentieth-century dynamic. If the mind recoils from passages of nativist bigotry, or the advent of the "mass society" in the United States, it must also recall that the most overt forms of totalitarianism are not of American origin, but rather of European. If the face of the American twentieth century bears the disfigurement of violence, it bears also the features of vigour and of a continued commitment to the highest ideals of western civilization.

This brief account is necessarily selective in its materials. It is not an attempt either to romanticize or to castigate. Rather, its purpose is to come to grips with the inner story of the United States, not minimizing its conflicts but analyzing them. At every stage of that exciting story the clash of personalities, and the contest of men against the forces both of nature and of ideas, tempts the historian to draw conclusions. Wherever possible this temptation has been avoided in the hope that the story itself will lead the reader to his own conclusions.

The author wishes to express his gratitude to John Saywell, Ramsay Cook, and John Ricker, with whom he worked on an earlier version of this book, and from each of whom he learned much.

KENNETH MCNAUGHT

Toronto, January, 1980

MANIFEST DESTINY

A SHORT HISTORY OF THE UNITED STATES

Revised Edition

Introduction

1500-1783

THE THIRTEEN American colonies which became independent with the sundering of the first British Empire in 1783 had already amassed a considerable heritage. A part of the expanding frontier of European civilization, these colonies had begun to add to that civilization a North American experience which in many ways marked Americans as different from their European forefathers. Yet it is well to remember that American colonial life was itself an aspect of the clash of European empires and to begin any account of American history with a brief recapitulation of America's "European phase."

At the end of the fifteenth century several European states, of which Spain and Portugal were the most powerful, gave their support to maritime adventurers in the search for overseas wealth and possessions. Thus began the quest for empire and the expansion of Europe which was to last for over four centuries, and was to bring the entire world within the orbit of western civilization. For many of these adventurers the precious metals and luxurious spices of the Orient were the chief objectives. An English poet expressed this aim nearly a hundred years after the discovery of America:

> I'll have them fly to India for gold,
> Ransack the ocean for orient pearl,
> And search all corners of the new-found world
> For pleasant fruits and princely delicates.

That "new-found world" was the vast land mass that the fifteenth-century sailors had found lying in the path of a direct sea route to the wealth of Asia. Christopher Columbus, sailing under the Spanish flag of Ferdinand and Isabella, was the first adventurer to set foot on the continent later

3

christened America. Columbus' son described the scene which took place in the autumn of 1492 on the coral island of San Salvador (Watling Island):

> Presently they saw naked people, and the Admiral went ashore in the armed ship's boat with the royal standard displayed . . . [and] with the banners of the expedition on which were depicted a green cross with F on one arm and a Y on the other and over each his or her Crown. And all having rendered thanks to our Lord kneeling on the ground, embracing it with tears of joy for the immeasurable mercy of having reached it, the Admiral rose and gave this island the name San Salvador.

The Spanish laid claim to much of the then uncharted Americas, but they concentrated most on the central and southern sections of the New World where they were to have great success. The unknown areas in the north were left for the explorers, merchants, and fishermen of the countries of northern Europe. But England and France were slow to join the fifteenth- and sixteenth-century quest for empire. While Spain and Portugal were discovering America and charting the route around the Cape of Good Hope, the people of England and France were occupied chiefly with domestic political and religious conflicts. Not until the end of the sixteenth century had both countries become sufficiently united and wealthy to turn their attention to the struggle for empire, and that attention soon centred on North America.

1. FOUNDATION OF THE AMERICAN COLONIES

After a century of preliminary exploration of the St. Lawrence regions and the Atlantic seaboard France established a firm colonial base in 1608 at Quebec. One year earlier England planted her first permanent continental colony in the fever-ridden lowland at Jamestown. Virginia, like New France, was at first ruled by a company of merchant adventurers. Settlers in Virginia found life difficult;

they had expected to discover gold and acquire quick fortunes but they found instead the backbreaking labour of cultivating the soil. Tobacco, however, was soon developed into a staple export, and a lucrative source of income.

The charter of Virginia contained one clause of great significance for the development of the English colonies. All Englishmen in the colony, it said, "should have and enjoy all liberties, franchises and immunities . . . as if they had been abiding and born within this our realm of England." By 1619 a representative assembly known as the House of Burgesses had been established in Virginia. Thus from the earliest years of settlement, English colonists, unlike their French counterparts, enjoyed a form of government in which they could express their views about local matters. Even after Virginia was transformed from a chartered Company colony into a Royal colony in 1624, it was able to preserve and even strengthen the powers of the House of Burgesses.

Virginia was only one of several types of colonies that Englishmen established in America. The colony of Massachusetts was strikingly different from Virginia in both origin and organization. Primarily it grew out of the determination of English Puritans to escape the control of the Anglican Church in England and to build a society on the basis of their own religious principles, ruled by what they called "godly magistrates." In 1620 a dissenting religious group, the Pilgrims, some of whom had lived for eleven to twelve years in Holland, landed on the rocky shores of New England from their weather-beaten ship, the *Mayflower*. Nine years later the basis of a large Puritan settlement was laid when wealthy English Puritans obtained a charter for the Company of Massachusetts Bay. By 1640, 25,000 persons had joined in the "Great Migration" to New England. The arrival of these religious dissenters in New England was in sharp contrast to the exclusion of dissenters in New France which was purposely maintained as a Roman Catholic colony.

The Puritans' objective was to establish a community where they could freely practice their religious beliefs. In

Massachusetts the primary test for full citizenship became membership in the Puritan church. Within these limits—and they were narrow, for the Puritans did not tolerate differences of religious opinion—Massachusetts practised self-government free from outside control. The chief executive of the colony was the governor, elected by the board of directors. The charter, however, provided for the establishment of a "general court" which allowed for popular participation in goverment. In addition, Massachusetts pioneered in the development of local government, for each settlement had its "town meeting" where citizens gathered to discuss and settle local affairs. By the mid-seventeenth century Massachusetts was a thriving colony. While the rocky lands of New England were not well suited to farming, access to the sea meant that agricultural produce would be supplemented with fish. More important, such access gave energetic Puritan merchants an opportunity to join in the profitable trade which grew up between America, the West Indies and Great Britain.

Not everyone found the tight Puritan rule of Massachusetts to his liking. Roger Williams was one of those who resisted the strict standards of religious orthodoxy for citizenship. He insisted that the state and the church should be separated for they were concerned with quite different matters. All men, regardless of religious belief, should be allowed to participate in civil affairs, he argued, while the church should be restricted only to the chosen few, or "saints" as the Puritans called the converted. After a bitter dispute with the ruling oligarchy in Massachusetts, Williams was forced to flee and he organized a new colony at Providence, Rhode Island. In 1644 Williams obtained a charter for the colony of Rhode Island. The new colony's liberality was well described in the vigorous seventeenth-century prose of Williams himself: "We have long drunk the cup of as great liberties as any people we can hear of under the whole of heaven. We have not only been long free . . . from the iron yoke of the wolfish bishops, and Popish ceremonies. . . . We have not felt the new chains of Presbyterian tyrants, nor in this colony have we been consumed with the over-zealous fire of (so-called) godly Christian Magistrates." The separation of church and state made religious toleration possible, and this policy was accompanied by a governmental structure which permitted the popular election of the governor and barred no one from public life on religious grounds.

Protestants were not the only religious group which sought the freedom to live according to their beliefs in America. Roman Catholics found life in seventeenth-century England as insecure as did the Puritans. In 1634 the Roman Catholic nobleman, Lord Baltimore, made proprietor of a large tract of land by Charles I, began settling Catholic colonists in Maryland. Actually, the colony which was designed as a haven for Roman Catholics soon attracted settlers of various religious groups. In 1649 the Maryland Assembly passed a toleration act, which, with the exception of the years from 1654-58, remained in force throughout the colonial period. Although the act guaranteed religious toleration the Roman Catholics did suffer from political discrimination.

Thus, unlike New France, the English colonies in America exhibited a wide variation in origin, government, economic activity and religious policy. By the middle of the eighteenth century thirteen separate colonies had sprung up in America under loose British supervision. Some were founded on company charters, some were proprietary like Maryland, but most were or became Royal colonies with governors directly appointed by the Crown. Variety was equally characteristic of their economic life for tobacco, hemp, furs, agriculture, shipbuilding and overseas trade all contributed to the British colonies' well-being and economic growth. Despite these differences, however, all the English colonies had one feature in common which clearly distinguished them from their French rival. This feature was the measure of self-government which each British colony enjoyed. By the eighteenth century their assemblies, while by no means democratic in their composition, jealously guarded the rights they had been granted, and in some cases extended those rights to limit the powers of the governors and of the British government in North America. But as long as the French lay to the north and the colonies remained divided and economically dependent upon Britain, the British settlements in North America showed no desire to free themselves completely from the loose control of the motherland.

2. ANGLO-FRENCH RIVALRY

By the end of the seventeenth century Britain, as France had earlier, was showing a greater interest in her colonies, for the political and religious problems which had torn her apart in the middle years of the century had been settled by the Glorious Revolution of 1689 and Britain was free to embark on a career of commercial and territorial expansion. Yet even before the end of the century Britain had attempted to bring some order into her colonial affairs by adopting a series of laws governing Imperial commercial activities. These Navigation Acts were based on the economic theory known as mercantilism whose object was to promote the power of the mother country by developing colonies and confining their trade within the Empire thereby making the mother country economically self-sufficient. Beginning as early as 1620 and continuing into the years before the American Revolution, the British government passed laws which prohibited the colonies from selling goods to foreign countries or transporting their products in foreign ships. In the seventeenth and early eighteenth centuries these laws were undoubtedly beneficial to both Britain and the colonies for they not only ensured Britain's control over colonial commerce, but they guaranteed a market for the colonies' expanding production.

Britain's growing interest in her North American colonies during the last years of the seventeenth century was a symptom of the deepening European rivalry between France and Britain at the end of the seventeenth century. Both countries were anxious to defend and ambitious to extend their commercial and political power. Their colonies in North America quickly became part of a global competition that stretched from Europe to India; indeed, their fate depended upon the outcome of that struggle. In North America the odds against the French were higher, for their population was small and spread over a vast area that was dangerously open to attack from both land and sea. Nevertheless, throughout the latter years of the seventeenth century New France was able to defend her position. Yet the little French community was disastrously weakened not only by the increasing indifference of the mother country but by the rapidly growing power of the English colonies. Despite her heroic efforts to spread her influence westward along the St. Lawrence and southward down the Ohio valley, New France found herself increasingly hemmed in by the British in New England and New York to the south and on Hudson Bay to the north. In 1713, at the close of the War of the Spanish Succession, Britain's encirclement of New France was further extended when Acadia (Nova Scotia) was ceded to the British.

For another four decades New France managed to continue its precarious existence. Internally it developed at a quickened pace and largely on its own initiative. A high birthrate caused the population to jump from 42,000 in 1720 to around 70,000 in 1758. But the fur trade remained the lifeblood of the colony. Every year competition with the British fur-traders grew more bitter. Finally, in 1744, war in Europe between Britain and France spread to the New World. The main target of the British in North America was the impressive fortress of Louisbourg which the French had constructed on Cape Breton Island following their loss of Nova Scotia to the British in 1713. The fortress represented a serious threat to the New England fishermen and the English colonists were naturally eager to destroy it. In 1745 that objective was achieved, at least temporarily. But by the treaty of Aix-la-Chapelle, which ended the war three years later, Louisbourg was returned to France in return for Madras, a city the French had taken from the British in India. The treaty of 1748 was, however, a truce rather than a real peace settlement, and during the following decade both sides engaged in war preparations.

9

3. THE FRENCH AND INDIAN WAR

In North America during the years of uneasy peace there was sporadic warfare along the undefined border which separated French from English colonies. By 1754 this border warfare had once more exploded into open conflict, despite the existence of an official peace between Britain and France in Europe.

In 1756 the Seven Years' War was officially begun and North America became a major battleground. Indeed, William Pitt, the British Prime Minister, shrewdly recognized that France's greatest area of weakness was her American colonies and he determined to destroy the French empire overseas while Britain's European allies held France in check on the continent.

In 1756 the French commander in New France, Montcalm, had only 6,000 regulars and 10,000 militiamen under his command and he was faced with the problem of defending the long frontier of the colony. Quebec City alone was effectively fortified while the rest of the colony lay wide open to enemy attack either by the overland route from New England or down the St. Lawrence. Britain's great strength and France's great weakness in the colonial war was on the sea, for there the powerful, well-disciplined British navy was clearly master. The survival of New France depended upon massive reinforcements from the home government. But France was fighting for her life in Europe, and even when reinforcements were dispatched the troopships were turned back by the British naval blockade. Without these reinforcements the little colony of New France could not hope to defend itself successfully.

Soon after the outbreak of war, despite the courage of the French-Canadian militia, it became apparent that the struggle was hopeless. "From all sides, dear brothers, the enemy is making immense preparation, its forces at least six times greater than ours," one Church leader announced, and the parish priests were ordered to sing the psalm, *Miserere mei Deus*. At Quebec in 1759 the British General, James Wolfe, led his army up the cliffs at the Anse-au-Foulon (Wolfe's Cove). Within five days Quebec City, the colony's major stronghold, capitulated. One year later Montreal fell into the hands of the invader. The struggle for North America had ended in the British conquest of New France, but the crucial questions of who would pay for the war and who would control the vast Ohio country beyond the Appalachians had still to be settled. With the French threat removed from the north and west the Atlantic seaboard colonies quickly became impatient with English restraints.

4. THE NEW IMPERIAL POLICY

For Britain, the successful conclusion of the long war with France brought two pressing needs. First, a new governmental and administrative system for her vast new territories had to be devised. Secondly, means had to be found to pay the enormous debt incurred during the war, which had risen to £140,000,000. Since nearly half of this staggering debt had been incurred in fighting the war in North America, it was not surprising that the British government looked to the colonies for new sources of revenue. It was out of the twin needs for administrative reorganization and sources of increased revenue that a new colonial policy was born.

The outlines of the new policy were quickly revealed. The Royal Proclamation of 1763 established four new provinces in the New World, all with constitutions patterned on the experience of the thirteen colonies. The new provinces of Quebec, East and West Florida, and Grenada in the West Indies were each given a royal governor, an appointed executive council, and an elective assembly. Though the political settlement seemed satisfactory, many people in the thirteen colonies objected strenuously to the new territorial divisions, for the Proclamation drew a line running down the crest of the Appalachians, and decreed that land sales and settlement beyond that line were forbidden until an agreement had been reached with the Indian tribes in the area. To traders, land-hungry settlers and speculators in the thirteen colonies, this plan had the appearance of a plot to turn this rich area into a preserve for the British and Canadian traders working out of Montreal.

If these new political divisions were obnoxious to many colonists, the programme for financing the North American empire and controlling its trade was even more so. The Navigation Acts had been fairly easily evaded prior to 1763, but now the Royal Navy was instructed to enforce them rigidly, and new courts were established in the colonies to try smugglers. Moreover, in order to raise one-third of the cost of maintaining 10,000 regular troops in the colonies for their defence, the British government began experimenting with new revenue acts. When the colonists failed to respond to British requests for suggestions as to the best method of contributing to their own defence, the British parliament passed a Stamp Act in 1765. The Act required that in the North American colonies revenue stamps be purchased and affixed to all legal documents, pamphlets and several other categories of business paper. Compared to taxation in England, this tax was very low. On the other hand, it was the first tax to be levied directly on the colonists by the British parliament.

At once colonial lawyers, businessmen and legislators protested that as Englishmen they could not be taxed by any legislature in which they were not represented. Their ringing cry "no taxation without representation" drew much support from farmers who constituted nine-tenths of the colonial population. In fact, the customs laws had involved taxation, but the colonists argued that these had been primarily for trade regulation, and that direct taxation was a different matter. Actually, the colonists did not want representation in the British parliament where they would always have been outvoted; what they wanted was to avoid both British taxation and responsibility for their own defence.

At a Stamp Act Congress in New York, delegates from nine of the colonies drew up a list of grievances and rights which they forwarded to London with a request for repeal of the Act. At the same time, non-importation agreements became popular in the colonies and groups calling themselves Sons of Liberty intimidated anyone who purchased British imports. Many royal officials, especially customs collectors, had their houses ransacked, their belongings stolen and their bodies tarred and feathered. This violence, together with the severe financial losses suffered by British merchants as a result of the boycott, caused parliament to repeal the Stamp Act.

Another device to raise revenue was tried in 1767, when the Townshend Acts placed special though not heavy duties on imports into the colonies of paint, tea, lead and glass. Although these duties were not "direct taxes" the revenue from them was to be used to pay royal officials in the colonies. Colonists, now deeply suspicious, saw tyranny lurking in this plan which they interpreted as an effort to remove judges and governors from dependence upon colonial legislatures for their salaries. Once again non-importation agreements were arranged among the colonists and smuggling became more widespread than ever. To reinforce the law, Britain sent extra troops to Boston in 1770. When a small detachment of these troops was taunted and snowballed by a crowd of Boston townsfolk, the soldiers opened fire, killing four of their tormentors and wounding several others. At once news of the "Boston Massacre" spread through the colonies, and in London it became clear that rebellion rather than revenue would result from further attempts to collect the new duties.

The Townshend duties were repealed in 1770 except for a threepenny tax on tea. Nevertheless, enforcement of the Navigation Acts was strengthened and throughout the colonies tempers flared as royal officials used general search warrants in their tireless search for smuggled goods. Opposition to British policy, already well established, was further stimulated by the ingenious activities of Samuel Adams of Boston. Adams established Committees of Correspondence so that scattered Massachusetts towns could keep each other posted on the latest grievances as well as on methods of resistance. Soon there were intercolonial correspondence committees, then a central co-ordinating committee, and colonial leaders became accustomed to working in concert. Adams, who was genuinely dedicated to democracy, was found useful by merchants who were rather more interested in loosening trade restrictions than in political thought. Impecunious himself, he suddenly found his affluent backers ready to supply him with the elegant clothes necessary for his new intercolonial organizing work.

5. BACKGROUND TO REVOLUTION

Despite undercurrents of agitation there was relative calm in the colonies for three years following 1770. Many prosperous merchants had been worried by the outbursts of mob violence. While they were prepared to protest constitutionally they did not care to risk a rebellion which might imperil their own property or even introduce a more radical form of democracy. In 1773, however, another Imperial crisis induced many men of property in the colonies to think once again of lawless action. In that year the British government took drastic steps to save the great East India Company from bankruptcy and thus safeguard an important source of revenue. To bolster the Company's sagging finances, the government granted it the privilege of importing tea into the American colonies without paying the customs duties normally levied in England when tea was trans-shipped for the colonies. With this privilege the Company's agents could sell tea in the colonies, even after paying the threepenny Townshend tax, more cheaply than could any colonial importer. So violent was the colonial merchants' reaction to the Tea Act that not a single case of East India tea was landed. In Maryland, the Company's ship was burned. At Boston, importers organized a gang of rowdies, painted them to resemble Mohawks, and led them on board three tea ships at anchor in the harbour. All the chests were dumped into the December waters in one huge "tea party."

When news of the Boston outrage reached England early in 1774, punitive legislation—which came collectively to be

14

called the "Intolerable Acts"—was quickly enacted. The port of Boston was closed until damages had been paid, the Massachusetts charter was suspended and town meetings forbidden. In addition, officials accused of murder while enforcing the law were to be tried not in colonial courts, but in England, where they were likely to receive easy sentences. At the same time, the Quebec Act was passed by the British government. Although it had been long in preparation and was designed to reconcile French Canada to the conquest, the Act also had important meaning for the colonists south of the St. Lawrence. Indeed, their darkest suspicions were aroused by three of its provisions. The Act extended the boundaries of Quebec to include the Ohio valley; it thus seemed to make permanent the exclusion of American colonists from that area, which had been decreed as a temporary measure in the Proclamation of 1763. Furthermore, the Act established for Quebec a provincial constitution which made no provisions for a legislative assembly and thus seemed to threaten colonial liberties. Finally, colonial leaders noted with horror that the hated Roman Catholic Church was to be recognized in the huge new province of Quebec.

Although Massachusetts was the centre of opposition to the "Intolerable Acts," other colonists rallied to the cause in the belief that all colonial liberties were in question. Twelve of the colonies sent representatives to a Continental Congress which assembled in Philadelphia in 1774. This first Continental Congress debated colonial problems for seven weeks, produced a stirring Declaration of Rights, and issued appeals to the King and people of Britain for redress of grievances. The petitions were rejected in England, while in the colonies radical spokesmen such as John Adams of Massachusetts and Patrick Henry of Virginia led in establishing a tight non-importation agreement known as The Association. Other leaders such as Samuel Adams and John Hancock began organizing colonial militia soldiers as "minute-men," and collecting stores of arms and ammunition. At Lexington and Concord, near Boston, British regular troops seized some of these stores, but were driven back upon Boston by colonial snipers. Although with wiser statesmanship and better communications war might still have been averted, this skirmish was in fact the opening battle of the American War of Independence.

6. THE AMERICAN REVOLUTION

One month after the skirmish at Lexington the second Continental Congress assembled at Philadelphia in May 1775. The Congress appointed George Washington, lately a colonel in the British colonial army, to command a Continental army, and issued a Declaration of the Causes and Necessity of Taking up Arms. The Declaration recounted the sins of the British parliament in taxing without representation, denying jury trial, permitting general search warrants, suspending constitutions and sealing off the West.

Although radical leaders were already pressing for independence of the America colonies, they did not gain a majority in the Continental Congress until early in 1776. Declarations continued to profess loyalty to Britain and to depict the armed resistance as being aimed at redress of grievances only. So slight was the demand for independence that while Washington's slowly growing army skirmished with British troops at many places, a toast to the King was drunk nightly in his officers' mess. After the failure of a desperate American assault on Quebec in December 1775, colonial radicals grew more insistent that the blood already shed must be justified by the achievement of independence. The radical cause was immensely aided by the appearance in January 1776, of a fire-eating pamphlet, *Common Sense*, by an English radical named Tom Paine.

Recently arrived from England, Paine was an extreme democrat. Written with a minimum of logic and a maximum of rhetoric, his pamphlet swept through the colonies and whipped up sympathy for the independence movement:

There is something very absurd in supposing a Continent to be perpetually governed by an island. . . . Of more worth is one honest man to society, and in the sight of God, than all the crowned ruffians that ever lived. . . . O ye that love mankind! Ye that dare oppose not only the tyranny but the tyrant, stand forth!

The Continental Congress, already angered by the growing numbers of hired German mercenaries in the British army in the colonies, and aware that foreign aid would be needed by Washington's army, took the fateful step in July, 1776. Hoping to attract French support by planning complete separation from the British Empire, and anxious to build greater intercolonial unity by defining its goals clearly and dramatically, Congress adopted a Declaration of Independence on July 4. The chief author of the Declaration was Thomas Jefferson of Virginia. At thirty-three this brilliant planter-lawyer was already noted for his literary style. He couched his argument in the popular philosophical terms of the eighteenth century, the terms of natural law and natural rights:

We hold these truths to be self-evident: That all men are created equal; that they are endowed by their Creator with certain unalienable rights; that among these are life, liberty, and the pursuit of happiness; that to secure these rights, governments are instituted among men, deriving their just powers from the consent of the governed; that whenever any form of government becomes destructive of these ends, it is the right of the people to alter or to abolish it, and to institute new government, laying its foundations on such principles, and organizing its powers in such form, as to them shall seem most likely to effect their safety and happiness. . . .

At one leap the Congress removed its case from one based upon the rights of Englishmen to one based upon the rights of man. Justifying this radical position by a philosophy of government which stemmed from the Englishman John Locke, the Declaration went on to list all the grievances, real and imagined, of the preceding years and to lay *all* of these at the door of George III. Having insisted for ten years that their allegiance was to the King, not parliament, the colonists had now decided to break even their connection with the Crown. The same session that approved the great Declaration also appointed a committee to travel to France to seek an alliance against Britain, and in 1778 Louis XVI signed a Franco-American treaty which bound each party to assist the other if attacked by Britain.

The War of Independence was also a civil war. Opinion in the colonies was divided about equally three ways among the radicals, or patriots, who controlled the Continental Congress; the Loyalists, or Tories, who remained loyal to Britain; and the uncommitted. Most of the Tories hoped to ride out the storm without losing their property; the rest left for England or took refuge in Quebec and Nova Scotia.

Immediately following the Declaration of Independence, colonial legislatures adopted new constitutions as independent states. The new states continued to send delegates to the Continental Congress, which was the central body responsible for directing the military resistance to Britain. The outstanding leader in the war was George Washington who, through the most distressing days and with completely inadequate supplies, kept an army in the field. Congress, lacking direct taxing powers, had to rely on state contributions, and on bonds issued to finance the war. Few states responded fully to requests for money, supplies or men.

Fortunately for the colonists, inadequate British leadership prevented the Empire from using its vastly superior naval and military resources against the disorganized colonial forces. In 1778 the colonial cause won support from France and Spain, and Holland soon joined with them, all three countries hoping to gain revenge for earlier defeats at British hands. In 1780 the French landed an army of six thousand in Rhode Island. In 1781, with the American treasury empty, disunity and suspicion rampant among the states, and desertions from the Continental army frequent, the decisive battle of the war was launched. The British General, Cornwallis, allowed himself to become hemmed in at Yorktown on Chesapeake Bay. There he expected to receive reinforcements from the Royal Navy. Instead, the French fleet successfully blockaded the harbour, while the combined French and American armies overwhelmed the beleaguered British forces. The victory at Yorktown put the seal on colonial independence. Although the war dragged on for another year and a half, the British government, disgraced by its handling of the war, was replaced by a ministry which favoured peace negotiations with the victorious colonies.

At Paris, the scene of the peace negotiations, the British and American negotiators met secretly to arrange a settlement. The Americans, Benjamin Franklin, John Adams and the brilliant New Yorker, John Jay, knew that the terms of their alliance with France prohibited negotiation by either ally of a separate peace settlement with Britain. However, they suspected that France had designs on the trans-Allegheny West, and they therefore outmanœuvred the French by signing a separate treaty with Britain.

In the Treaty of Paris, signed in 1783, the British agreed to a generous settlement. Their magnanimity flowed from a desire to re-establish their lucrative American trade, and to prevent the Franco-American alliance from becoming a permanent feature of world politics. Moreover, the British Whig government, which was responsible for the negotiations, was composed of men who had always been critical of the unbending Tory policies which, they claimed, had led to the American Revolution. By the treaty Britain recognized the independence of the colonies and ceded to them territory reaching from the Atlantic to the Mississippi and from Florida to the Great Lakes. The Floridas were not included, only because they had been recaptured by the Spanish forces during the war. In return for these concessions the Treaty committed the independent colonies to recommend earnestly to the various state governments that steps be taken to restore property confiscated from Loyalists, as those who had retained their allegiance to the Crown were called, and to place no obstacles in the path of Loyalists who sought repayment of debts owing to them. The inability of the American Congress to fulfill this undertaking was to prove cause of serious Anglo-American friction in the future.

It remained for the Americans to organize, defend and develop their expansive continental empire. No new nation had ever benefited more from the coincidence of European rivalries, nor had any stripling state been more eager to exploit its legacy. Even before the war had ended, plans for the future were being laid, and if there was no unanimity about the shape of the future nation, the very multiplicity of plans and ambitions bespoke a formidable vigour.

1

The Supreme Law of the Land

THE TREATY of Paris in 1783 ended the American War of Independence, but the survival of an independent United States of America was still very much in doubt. Old problems remained to plague the new nation. How were the Americans going to govern themselves? Would the central government and the new state governments, all extremely jealous of their independence, be able to establish a workable relationship? Would the Americans now really have free access to the trans-Appalachian West? If so, what authority would control that vast region? Would the United States government be strong enough to deal with great powers like Britain, France and Spain in disputes over trade and territories? In short, was the United States of America genuinely a new nation or was it a collection of thirteen separate states only loosely joined together? Between 1783 and 1789 American statesmen answered most of these questions.

1. THE ARTICLES OF CONFEDERATION

The first American federal constitution had been drafted by a committee appointed by the Continental Congress of 1777. The resulting constitution, the Articles of Confederation, was described by their principal author as a "firm league of friendship." With the Articles of Confederation the Americans embarked on a new and dynamic experiment in government; for the Articles created a federal union of states in which the citizens of the thirteen states were to have two governments, one for all the states combined and one for

21

the state in which they lived. Although that constitution gave a considerable number of powers to the central government, it provided little power of enforcement. Under the Articles, there was a Congress which was composed of delegates from the states and was empowered to deal with foreign and inter-state affairs, the post office, and public lands. But Congress was given no taxing power and therefore had to rely upon state levies both for defence and general revenue. In addition, there were no national courts and no clearly defined executive branch to put the laws of Congress into effect. Moreover, since each state delegation in Congress had only one vote, and the enactment of important bills required a two-thirds majority, speedy transaction of business was almost impossible. Finally, amendments to the Articles themselves required a unanimous vote in Congress, but every proposed amendment found at least one of the thirteen states opposed.

In spite of these weaknesses, the Confederation Congress, that is, the Congress that came into being as a result of the Articles of Confederation, was not totally unsuccessful. It handled the problems of the West with efficiency and remarkable foresight. In 1785 it passed a Land Ordinance which provided that western lands should be surveyed in an orderly fashion and the proceeds from their sale be used to pay off the national debt. The surveyors were to divide the land into townships six miles square, with each township divided into thirty-six sections of one square mile each. In each township the money derived from selling the sixteenth section was to be used for founding public schools. Thus the Ordinance not only established a useful pattern for later western expansion, but guaranteed the early development of public education, and secured the land titles of the first settlers.

Even more significant for the future was the Northwest Ordinance of 1787 which dealt with the problem of government in the public domain. The 1787 Ordinance decreed that the Northwest Territory should never be open to slavery and that the pioneers should be granted self-government

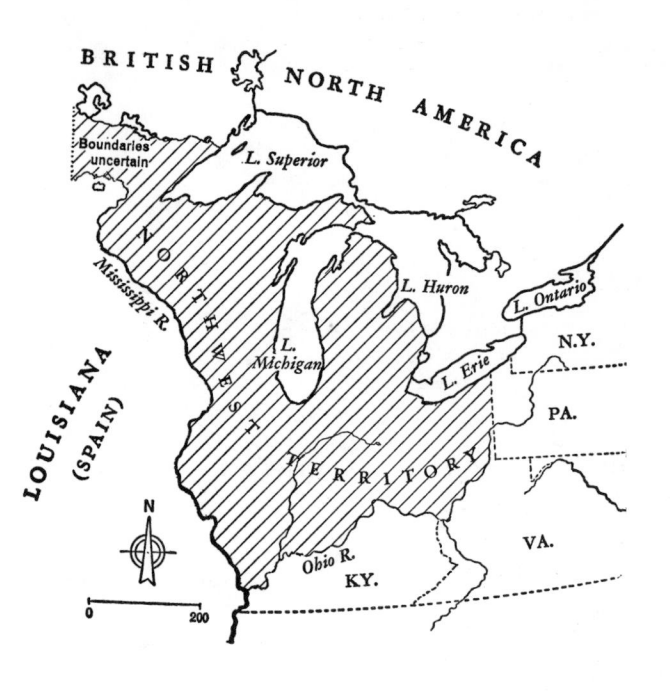

THE NORTHWEST TERRITORY IN 1787

as soon as the population was sufficiently large. Not more than five nor less than three states were to be created there, and Congress might admit any of them into the Union "on an equal footing with the original states in all respects whatever," whenever the population of the particular region reached 60,000 free inhabitants. The Ordinance, which was the American answer to Britain's old Imperial problem of how to govern weak, unsettled areas, continued to be upheld by succeeding American governments.

But despite its successful western settlement policy, the

Confederation Congress could not provide security against Indians on the frontiers, or against the threat posed by Spanish territorial claims to the south or the presence of British traders and troops in American fur-trading areas. Nor was it able to offer any naval protection for American commerce on the high seas. It could not effectively regulate trade between the states and foreign countries, or even among the various states themselves. Moreover, since Congress lacked the power to control currency, and since any bank could issue its own currency, money values fluctuated wildly and it became difficult to plan interstate business. While most farmers were satisfied with the slow economic growth which was inevitable under these conditions, businessmen were deeply concerned about the missed opportunities for expansion. Many blamed too weak a national government for the country's troubled and slow economic development. Some men even feared that without a stronger central government the entire federal experiment would collapse.

People who entertained such fears were particularly concerned about the public credit. Since first the Continental and later the Confederation Congress lacked taxing power, each had had to borrow large amounts of money. The bonds which represented the government's promise to repay these loans were held by merchants and bankers. By 1784 the government had issued more than $40,000,000 worth of bonds, but was unable to pay even the interest on them. In addition, state governments, which had issued $20,000,000 worth of bonds, were also in financial difficulties. In Massachusetts the problem produced a serious crisis, and an armed uprising.

At the centre of the crisis was the conflict between debtors and creditors over "hard money." The value of a dollar was measured by its gold or silver content, but the amount of coinage, or hard money, in circulation was very limited. Thus, gold and silver dollars were in short supply and of high value. Most people found it difficult to secure enough hard money to meet their obligations and argued for expansion of the money supply. In the absence of fresh gold and silver discoveries this could only be done by printing paper money which, because it did not have to be entirely redeemable in specie, made possible an expansion of the money supply. It also, however, had an inflationary effect, that is, it lowered the purchasing power (or value) of the dollar.

When the Massachusetts legislature levied a tax of twenty dollars a household (a considerable sum of money in the eighteenth century) to pay off the bonded debt, the conflict over hard money burst into the open.

Facing mortgage foreclosures and loss of their property, the already hard-pressed farmers argued that paper money should be issued to allow them to meet their debts more easily. But creditors hated the idea of printing paper money because they would have to accept payments in currency of less value than that in circulation when they had advanced their original loans. With the Massachusetts jails full of debtors, a rebellion formed under the leadership of Daniel Shays, a captain in the War of Independence, who now spoke for the western counties of Massachusetts. The farmers believed that the Boston businessmen who dominated the government had no right to tax them, and many decided to resist the tax collection. Fighting between the rebels and state militia lasted from October 1786 to February 1787 when the rebellion was finally suppressed. Although it had failed, Shays' rebellion had shocked the men of property in all the states, who realized that rebellion had a way of spreading. To these men, a stronger national government seemed more desirable than ever.

Other matters like western expansion, trade problems, and foreign relations also seemed to require a strong central power. American land speculators wanted the western frontier to be made secure against the Indians. There was uneasiness also because in the southwest and the northwest Spain and England still maintained posts in territory that had been ceded to the United States by the treaty of 1783. Manufacturers wanted protection against British goods

25

which were flooding the American market, and merchants wanted a government strong enough to bargain with England for entry of American trade into the British West Indies. Always present, too, was the problem Benjamin Franklin voiced when he said: "We should I think be constantly on our guard and impress strongly upon our minds, that though Great Britain has made peace with us, it is not in truth reconciled either to us, or to its loss of us." Historians have called these years the "critical period" of American history, and many contemporary Americans talked in a similar vein. As one of them put it in 1787: "The American war is over; but this is far from being the case of the American revolution. On the contrary, nothing but the first act of the great drama is disclosed."

2. THE NEW CONSTITUTION 1787

The second act of the great drama was the formulation of a new constitution under which Americans could more effectively rule their new nation. In 1786 George Washington, Alexander Hamilton, John Jay, James Madison and others issued an invitation to the states to send delegates to a national convention at Philadelphia in May 1787 to discuss the problems of disunity in the country, for by 1787 the federal union was floundering. The Confederation Congress reluctantly endorsed the invitation, stating that the convention would be "for the sole and express purpose of revising the Articles of Confederation." The Philadelphia Convention, however, was to achieve far more than that "sole and express purpose."

Delegates to the Philadelphia Convention were generally conservative. Among them there was only one farmer; most were lawyers, plantation-owners, merchants, and bond-holders. Well aware of the immense wealth and power that might be developed in North America with the help of a strong and purposeful central government, the conservative businessmen and lawyers were determined to equip their country with the framework of government that would enable it to secure the West, guard its own markets, and provide a native mercantilist system to replace that which had been lost by withdrawal from the protective British Empire. Their economic interests and sense of nationalism thus demanded a strong central government. So did their political philosophy, for most of the Fathers of American Confederation feared democracy and believed that the central government would be less likely to yield to popular demands than state governments, and, therefore, should have more power. As George Washington put it:

> It is much to be feared, as you observe, that the better kind of people, being disgusted with the circumstances will have their minds prepared for any revolution whatever. . . . Would to God, that wise measures may be taken in time to avert the consequences we have too much reason to apprehend.

For economic, national and political reasons, then, the Founding Fathers quickly agreed not just to amend the Articles of Confederation, but to write a new constitution.

The Virginia delegates, led by George Washington, were the first to arrive at the dignified Georgian State House in Philadelphia. They brought with them a plan for a strongly centralized government, which was not unlike that proposed for the later Canadian Confederation. It provided for a Congress of two houses to which the states would elect representatives in numbers proportionate to the size of the free (non-slave) population of each state. The great power which this "large state" plan obviously gave to the most populous states was further increased by the provision that the central government could disallow any law passed by a state legislature. Delegates from the smaller states were naturally not enthusiastic about the Virginia plan. In fact many of them (such as those from the state of Delaware which had a population of only 60,000) had been specifically instructed to oppose any plan that departed from the principle of equal representation and voting power for each state as such, regardless of is population.

27

The small states countered the Virginia plan with a proposal put forward by William Patterson, leader of the New Jersey delegation. The New Jersey plan retained the existing Congress with its equality of representation for states, but gave the central government power to regulate the tariff, levy its own taxes, and create an executive and judicial branch.

During the steaming June days debate on the two plans rose to fever pitch. A delegate from Delaware underlined the bitter suspicions aroused by the struggle over the issue of "equal versus proportional representation" when he warned: "The large states dare not dissolve the Confederation. If they do the small ones will find some foreign ally, of more honour and good faith, who will take them by the hand and do them justice." One delegate wrote of those days: "We were on the verge of dissolution, scarce held together by the strength of a hair."

Solution of the problem of representation in the central government came in the form of the "Great Compromise," which was worked out by a small committee along lines proposed chiefly by the aged and revered Benjamin Franklin. The compromise provided for a legislature of two houses. The lower house, or House of Representatives, was to be composed of members elected from each state on the basis of population; these members were to vote individually in the House, rather than on the old basis of one vote per state delegation. To mollify the small states, the compromise provided that the upper house, or Senate, was to be composed of two members from each state, regardless of population. In addition, the Senate was given almost as much legislative power as the House of Representatives, as well as certain special powers of considerable importance so that the small states would be assured of an effective voice in the government.

To some extent James Madison, one of the Virginia delegates, was right when he noted that the real division among the delegates of the Convention of 1787 "did not lie between the large and small states; it lay between the Northern and the Southern." This division was between people who drew their wealth from different kinds of property. Many Northern businessmen wanted the central government to be able to foster industry by protective tariffs, and to regulate and encourage trade by other means. Southern planters, however, wished to remain free to buy and sell in whatever world markets were most advantageous to them, and felt that tariffs would restrict rather than extend their trade. Moreover, they were fearful that the federal government would use its powers over trade and commerce to interfere with the Southern slave trade. After bitter and prolonged debates on these topics, the delegates reached another compromise. The South agreed to give Congress control over commerce in return for a guarantee, written into the Constitution, that the slave trade would not be interfered with before 1808.

The Southern slave owners argued that slaves should be counted as property rather than as people for purposes of assessing direct federal taxes, which were to be levied in the states according to population. But state representation in the House of Representatives was also to be in proportion to population, and for this purpose the Southerners wanted the slaves to be counted as people. Here again a compromise saved the day. In any state, three-fifths of the slave population were to be used in determining both taxes and congressional representation. By another compromise the South secured a clause requiring free states to return fugitive slaves to their masters. These clauses were to become extremely important in later disputes, for they enabled Southerners to claim that the Constitution recognized slaves as property and thus that the federal government had a duty to safeguard the Southerner's right to hold slaves.

Most important, perhaps, of all the debates at Philadelphia were those concerning the nature of the American federal system. Every federation must be a compromise between those who desire a strong centralized government to serve the national interests and those who favour decentralized government to protect local interests. As the long debate over the Articles of Confederation had already revealed, on this question the American people were sharply divided. The bitter debate on the power of the central government was continued in Philadelphia.

To establish the Constitution's new and fundamental authority, its framers wrote:

> This Constitution, and the laws of the United States which shall be made in pursuance thereof; and all treaties made under the authority of the United States, shall be the *supreme law of the land.*

Despite the reservations held by many people, then and later, all else, including state laws and constitutions, were to rank below the Constitution in authority. All public officials and judges, both state and federal, would be bound by this "supreme law of the land." Under the Articles of Confederation the central government had had no real power over states or individuals. The new federal constitution provided

THE FEDERAL DIVISION OF POWERS

FEDERAL POWERS	SHARED POWERS	STATE POWERS
• Foreign relations, war and peace	• Taxation	• To establish local government
• Regulation of foreign and interstate commerce		
• To legislate on citizenship and immigration	• Borrowing of money	• To conduct elections
• To coin money		• Public education
• To operate postal system	• Establishing courts and penal laws	
• To control patents and copyrights		• To regulate business within state
• To maintain armed forces		
• To establish federal courts	• To charter banks	• Control of marriage and divorce
• To govern federal territories and admit states to Union		
• To enact laws "necessary and proper" to carrying out its powers	• Expropriation of property in the public interest, with the just compensation	• Any power not granted to the federal government nor specifically prohibited by the Constitution

that the states would give up many of their powers to the central government. These powers, together with the powers already possessed by the old Congress, were then "enumerated" in the Constitution as belonging exclusively to the central government, thus giving it direct power over the people of the various states. The central government was empowered to direct foreign affairs, matters of war and peace, and to regulate all commerce between the states and foreign countries as well as among the various states themselves. In addition, Congress was given sole authority to regulate the issuance of money, to raise money by taxation for federal purposes, to administer all non-state territories of the Union, and to regulate the admission of new states. To underline the amplitude of the new central powers, the Constitution declared that congressional revenues could be employed not only for the common defence and other enumerated powers, but, in a section often called the elastic clause, it provided that Congress could "make all laws which shall be necessary and proper for carrying into execution" the enumerated powers and "all other powers vested by this Constitution in the Government of the United States or in any department or office thereof." Interpretations by the courts of the elastic clause and the interstate commerce clause have frequently been used to expand the powers of the central government beyond any point envisaged by even the most nationally-minded Fathers of the Constitution.

It was impossible, as it is in any federal constitution, to define beyond a shadow of a doubt the line separating central and local powers. Moreover, it was necessary to conciliate the defenders of states' rights, those men inside and outside the Convention who feared the growth of a distant central authority that might prove as despotic as they believed the British government in London to have been. Thus each state retained control over voting qualifications, education, intrastate businesses, criminal law within the state, marriage and divorce, local government institutions, and general "police powers" involving the safety and health of its citizens. Further, the Tenth Amendment to the Constitution, ratified in 1791, stated: "The powers not delegated to the United States by the Constitution, nor prohibited by it to the States, are reserved to the States respectively, or to the people." This Amendment lent weight to the views of those who, in later disputes over the balance of power within the Union, argued that the states remained sovereign and had merely delegated some powers to the federal government.

3. THE CONGRESSIONAL-PRESIDENTIAL SYSTEM

Within the central government itself no one branch was given supreme control; the system created in 1787 is said to be one of "checks and balances" or "separation of powers." One of the delegates from Massachusetts, and later President, John Adams, summed up the theory of checks and balances thus:

> A Legislative, an executive, and a judicial power comprehend the whole of what is meant and understood by the government. It is by balancing each of these powers against the other two, that the efforts in human nature toward tyranny can alone be checked and restrained, and any degree of freedom preserved in the constitution.

To achieve this balance the Constitution divided the various powers within the jurisdiction of the central government among the three branches, made some powers (such as treaty-making) the joint responsibility of two branches, and created different sources for the authority of each branch—direct election, indirect election, and appointment.

The power to make federal laws was given to a Congress composed of the Senate and House of Representatives. To ensure the influence of the states in the federal government and to protect the states' rights, each state was given two members in the Senate. To make certain that the Senators would really represent the states, the Senators were to be elected by the members of the state legislatures. Senators were to remain in office for a term of six years, but to guard against too sudden changes in the Senate the terms of office

CHECKS AND BALANCES IN THE AMERICAN CONSTITUTION

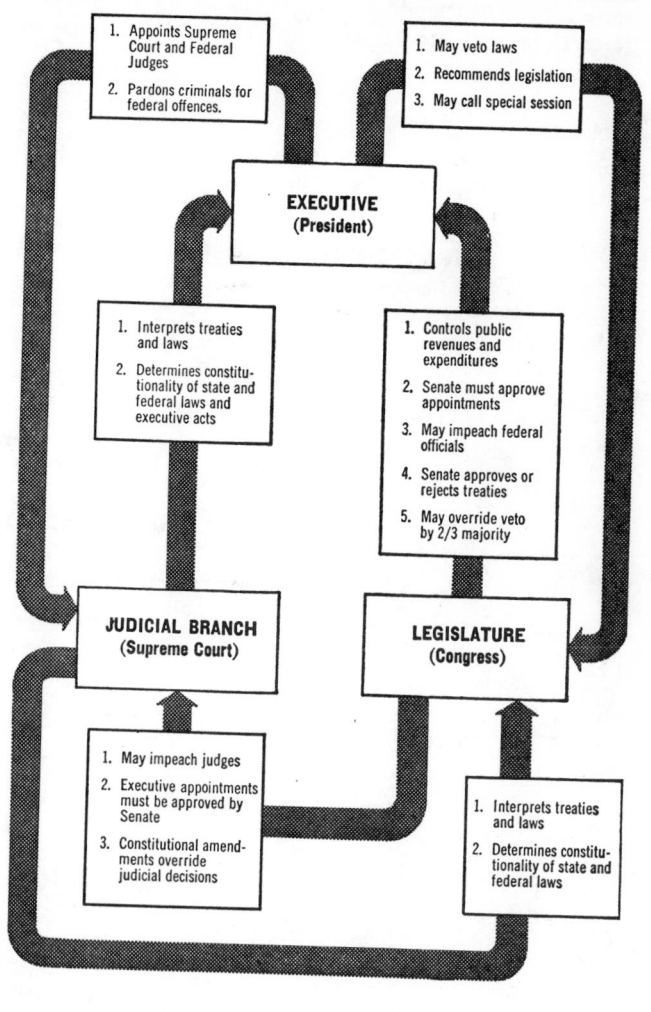

1. Appoints Supreme Court and Federal Judges
2. Pardons criminals for federal offences.

1. May veto laws
2. Recommends legislation
3. May call special session

EXECUTIVE (President)

1. Interprets treaties and laws
2. Determines constitutionality of state and federal laws and executive acts

1. Controls public revenues and expenditures
2. Senate must approve appointments
3. May impeach federal officials
4. Senate approves or rejects treaties
5. May override veto by 2/3 majority

JUDICIAL BRANCH (Supreme Court)

LEGISLATURE (Congress)

1. May impeach judges
2. Executive appointments must be approved by Senate
3. Constitutional amendments override judicial decisions

1. Interprets treaties and laws
2. Determines constitutionality of state and federal laws

were staggered, with one-third of the Senate retiring every two years. Members of the House of Representatives were to serve for two years only, and the number of Representatives for each state was to be in proportion to the population of the state.

To become law, a bill had to receive a majority vote in each House, as well as the signature of the President. Bills that required the expenditure of public money had to originate in the House of Representatives, but all other bills could origin-

THE LEGISLATIVE PROCESS

(A bill, after being drafted by a member of Congress or a committee, is introduced either in the Senate or the House of Representatives. If it involves the raising and spending of money it must originate in the House as does the bill in this chart.)

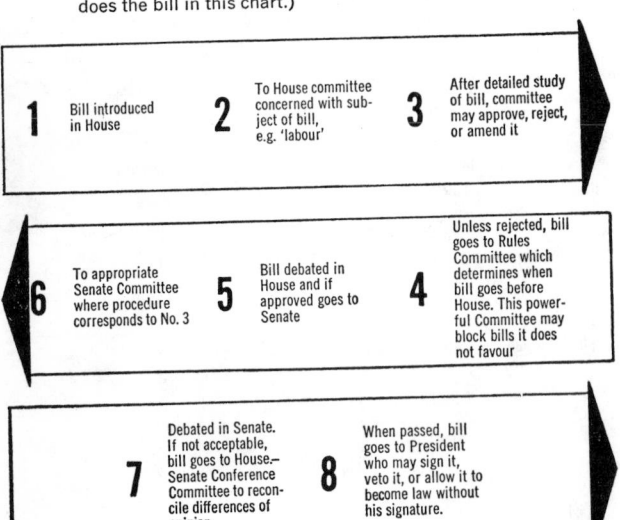

1 Bill introduced in House

2 To House committee concerned with subject of bill, e.g. 'labour'

3 After detailed study of bill, committee may approve, reject, or amend it

6 To appropriate Senate Committee where procedure corresponds to No. 3

5 Bill debated in House and if approved goes to Senate

4 Unless rejected, bill goes to Rules Committee which determines when bill goes before House. This powerful Committee may block bills it does not favour

7 Debated in Senate. If not acceptable, bill goes to House.—Senate Conference Committee to reconcile differences of opinion

8 When passed, bill goes to President who may sign it, veto it, or allow it to become law without his signature.

ate in either the House or the Senate. While the House of Representatives alone had the right to initiate money bills, the Senate also had its important special powers. It could refuse to endorse Presidential appointments of judges, diplomats and cabinet members, and no treaty could go into effect without approval by two-thirds of the Senators. Moreover, since the Senate could amend money bills it gradually came to exercise powers equal to those of the House in controlling public expenditures.

The separating and balancing of powers is most clearly seen in the office of President and in his relations with Congress. The Constitution made the President chief executive of the nation and charged him specifically with carrying out the laws of Congress and upholding the Constitution in all aspects. The President was to be chosen by state "electors" who were referred to collectively as the electoral college. The voters in each state elected a number of electoral college members equal to the number of Senators and Congressmen from that state. The electors then met in each state to ballot for a President. This provision had two objects: first, to prevent popular passions from being directly reflected in Presidential elections; and second, to enable the voters to select men from their state whom they could know and trust to charge with electing a President, because with the size of the country and the slow methods of transportation it was impossible for all the voters at that time to know and judge between rival Presidential candidates. After the establishment of political parties, however, it became the practice for candidates for the electoral college to run on "party tickets," which meant that they were committed to vote for the Presidential candidate nominated by their party.

The President's term of office was to be four years and as chief executive his powers were very great. He was commander-in-chief of the United States armed forces. He was to appoint the heads of the various executive departments of government which were charged with carrying out congressional laws: for example, he appointed the Secretary of State to head the State Department, and the Secretary of the

Treasury to manage national finances. Each departmental head was to be responsible directly to the President, and collectively these men have come to be known as the President's Cabinet. The separation of powers is emphasized in the provision that neither the President nor anyone appointed to public office by the President could be a member of Congress. Thus, American cabinet members were not to be able to defend their policies personally in the legislature. The President was also given large powers in defence and foreign affairs, since as well as commanding the army and navy he appointed all ambassadors and authorized the negotiation of treaties. But this power was also checked by the treaty-approving power of the Senate and by the Senators' right to withhold approval of Presidential appointments. The House, too, could severely limit any of the President's powers by refusing to vote the money to implement his policies. At the same time, the President was given the power to veto a congressional bill by returning it unsigned to the House in which it originated within ten days of receiving it. If he merely refuses to sign, the bill becomes law automatically after ten days, unless the congressional session ends in less than ten days. The latter case is known as a "pocket veto." However, if Congress repasses the vetoed legislation with a two-thirds majority in each House, the bill could become law despite the President's veto and without his signature.

The great authority of the President was enhanced by the fact that he was the only federal official in the nation to be chosen by "all the people." Furthermore, he could be removed from office before the expiration of his normal term only by the extreme procedure of impeachment. In order to do this, an indictment of the President for grave misdemeanours first had to pass the House of Representatives. Then a committee of the House would present the case before the Senate, which would act as a court to try the case. This drastic procedure has been attempted only once, in 1868, and on that ocassion it failed.

The careful checking, balancing and separating of the federal government's powers reflected the determination of the framers of the Constitution to prevent any individual or "vested interest" from usurping power. Although many American observers, including some Presidents, have felt that this system inhibits effective use of national powers, most attempts to change it by amending the Constitution have failed. Succeeding generations have generally hesitated to lay hands on a system which, despite its admitted imperfections, has generally protected their basic liberties.

To judge legal cases involving the interpretation of the Constitution, and to clarify the meaning of congressional legislation, the Constitution authorized the establishment of a federal court system presided over by a Supreme Court. Under the Articles of Confederation, the central government had had to rely upon state courts, which were frequently hostile to federal policy, for the enforcement of its laws. The Supreme Court was the answer to this problem. While state courts were obliged to enforce federal laws, their decisions could now be appealed to the Supreme Court whose members were to be appointed by the President. The Supreme Court, however, could not give advisory opinions on problems referred to it by government; rather, it was to judge only in actual cases arising under existing law.

While the Constitution was the supreme law of the nation, it was far from inflexible. Usage later changed many original provisions, and the document itself prescribed procedures for its own amendment. An amendment could originate as a resolution in Congress. If it passed by a two-thirds majority it was then to be sent to the various states for consideration. If three-quarters of the states ratified it, the amendment then became a part of the Constitution equal in strength to the original clauses. Although a great many amendments have been proposed over the years, only twenty-three have been ratified. The first ten of these are really a part of the original Constitution since they were promised as part of the campaign to ratify the Constitution in 1787-88. The party system has been more important than the amending procedure in making the Constitution flexible. By having representatives in both Houses of Congress, in state governments and in the

Presidency, parties have considerably modified the original separation of powers. While a cabinet member may not sit in Congress, other members of his political party do sit there and, if liaison is good, help to implement Presidential policies.

At Philadelphia it was decided that the new Constitution would take effect as soon as it was ratified by at least nine of the thirteen states. At once, supporters and opponents of the Constitution began to organize their forces. In each state a convention was summoned to discuss ratification of the Constitution. The differences of opinion in these conventions were to produce two political parties whose membership was further clarified by later differences over financial and foreign policies. The supporters of ratification were called Federalists and their opponents were known as Antifederalists. The Antifederalists included supporters of states' rights, small farmers from the frontier townships, and artisans. In addition, some businessmen, worried about debts they had contracted, feared that the Federalists were conspiring to keep money in short supply and to impose heavy taxation, both of which policies would work to the advantage of creditors. The Federalists, who generally drew their supporters from the more well-to-do classes, mostly living in the older settled areas close to the seaboard, argued for stability, law and order, and the sacredness of contractual debts which they felt could be achieved only through a strong central government.

For years historians have differed about the reasons for the adoption of the Constitution. A famous American historian, Charles Beard, in his book *An Economic Interpretation of the Constitution,* argued that the men of property had triumphed over the majority of common people. It is now generally believed, however, that, as the ratification debates developed, the division of opinion reflected not only property interests but also local and sectional interests and ideas which were not necessarily the result of a person's class in society.

This was not in fact a particularly democratic age, and even those people who opposed the Constitution did not necessarily do so because it seemed to favour the rich. Nevertheless, the majority of Americans seemed to be Anti-federalists and their position was well put by a farmer delegate to the Massachusetts ratifying convention:

> These lawyers and men of learning and moneyed men, that talk so finely, and gloss over matters so smoothly, to make us poor illiterate people swallow down the pill, expect to get into Congress themselves; they expect to be managers of this Constitution, and get all the power and all the money into their own hands, and then they will swallow up all us little folks, like the great leviathan, Mr. President; yes, just as the whale swallowed up Jonah. This is what I am afraid of.

Patrick Henry of Virginia typified another form of opposition to the proposed Constitution. He suspected that the Constitution was simply a device to seize power from the states, where the people were more directly influential in government, and centralize that power. "Who," he cried, "authorized them to speak the language of We the People instead of We the States?" This was the "states' rights" cry that was to be heard down through American history and which would eventually help to produce the bloody Civil War.

Ratification of the Constitution came largely because the Federalists had precisely the powers and advantages that the Massachusetts farmer had feared. Newspapers carried lengthy arguments in favour of the Constitution, ministers preached its virtues, and hundreds of pamphleteers supported it. The most famous of the pamphlets, known as *The Federalist*, was a collection of newspaper articles containing penetrating arguments in favour of a strong central government. The authors of *The Federalist* were John Jay, Alexander Hamilton and James Madison. Because all were "Fathers of the Constitution" and wrote from inside knowledge of the Philadelphia debates, their work has often been cited by American courts in later years to prove or disprove various interpretations of clauses in the Constitution.

In addition, the fact that very few poor men attended the ratifying conventions aided the Federalist cause. Even so, in several states the division was very close and in an effort to gain more votes for ratification some of the Federalists promised that if their conventions were to ratify the Constitution, a Bill of Rights would be added to it during the first session of the new Congress. This Bill was to be in the form of amendments to the Constitution guaranteeing specific rights to both individuals and states. The amendments would be introduced at the first session of the new Congress.

Despite the bitterest opposition, nine of the thirteen states had ratified the Constitution within four months after the Philadelphia Convention had ended in September 1787. Resistance in the key states of Virginia and New York gave way while North Carolina and Rhode Island followed soon after. While the Constitution was not, perhaps, what an English Prime Minister, W. E. Gladstone, later called it, "the most wonderful work ever struck off at a given time by the brain and purpose of man," it was a document of monumental importance. As decade followed decade, and generation succeeded generation, the work of the Philadelphia Convention assumed ever wider significance, until today it affects the destiny of the world itself.

2

Federalists and Republicans

THE CHOICE of George Washington as first President of the United States was unanimous, indeed almost automatic. By the time of his inauguration on April 30, 1789 the new President could look back on a most distinguished career in the British frontier military service, in planting and land speculation, in the long and arduous struggle to keep an army in the field during the Revolutionary War, and in the Philadelphia Convention. He was not a brilliant man, but what he lacked in intellect he more than compensated for in his quiet wisdom and devotion to his nation's welfare. Washington would have preferred to remain on his peaceful estate on the Potomac rather than to accept the office of President. As he said:

> My movement to the chair of government will be accompanied by feelings not unlike those of a culprit who is going to the place of his execution; so unwilling am I in the evening of a life nearly consumed in public cares to quit a peaceful abode for an ocean of difficulties.

It was certainly fortunate for the nation that a man of Washington's temperament and lack of ambition was elected as its first President; for Washington resisted every opportunity the novel republican experiment offered him to become the Cromwell or Napoleon of the American Revolution.

In the spring of 1789 the United States was in a truly critical position. The nation owed large debts both to Americans and foreigners, its trade was excluded from all British ports, pirates preyed on its ships, and its Indian frontiers were turbulent. Yet despite these problems the new government was launched with surprising leisure. On March 4, 1789 the church bells of New York rang out and the battery guns at the tip of Manhattan Island boomed their acclaim of the day appointed for the opening of the first Congress. It was a false start. Not until the first week in April had enough Senators and Representatives clattered and bumped their way to New York to provide quorums for both Houses.

Once established, however, the administration took a firm grip on the country, created governmental machinery and adopted major national policies, with a speed calculated to make up for lost time. Washington chose Thomas Jefferson as Secretary of State to deal with foreign relations, Alexander Hamilton for the Treasury, Henry Knox for War and Edmund Randolph of Virginia as Attorney-General. Although the department heads at first corresponded with the President by letter, they soon felt the need to meet together to exchange ideas and co-ordinate departmental policies. A Presidential cabinet thus came into being, although no mention was made of such a body in the Constitution.

1. HAMILTON AND THE FEDERALISTS

The thirty-three-year-old Hamilton was a dominant figure in Washington's first administration. Born in the West Indies, the illegitimate son of a French Huguenot mother and a Scottish father, he was brought to New York by an uncle who provided for his education. There, he achieved rapid success and some fame in college and at the bar. As an army colonel he had been Washington's aide during the last phase of the Revolutionary War. He was already well known as a lawyer and a student of public affairs by the time he helped organize the movement for the Constitutional Convention at Philadelphia in 1787. His share in writing the influential Federalist Papers had further enhanced his reputation. Although his faith in what he called "the rich and well-born" sat oddly on one of his origin, he nevertheless became the most eloquent spokesman in the United States of the right of the rich to govern. Always suspicious of democracy, he declared that "the people is a great beast" and that the common man "seldom determines aright." Democracy, to Hamilton, was chiefly a means of persuading the common man that the decisions of the natural leaders, or men of wealth, were best for the nation. Some years after 1789, reflecting on the Constitution, for whose adoption he had worked so hard, he described it as "a frail and worthless fabric" which would probably not last a generation, because it did not concentrate power sufficiently in the hands of the central government. In one or two crises, in exasperation, he even advocated a monarchy for the United States on British lines, and on occasion was tempted to return to the army and lead it to glory and quick power against the Spanish in the lower Mississippi valley.

Hamilton's personal code was as rigid as that which he advocated for the nation. In 1804, he was challenged to a duel by Aaron Burr, a bitter political enemy; he accepted the challenge although he disapproved of duelling. Refusing to fire, he allowed Burr's shot to end his life. Despite his premature death, Hamilton had lived long enough to leave an indelible mark on the political constitution and economic life of the United States, for this handsome and enigmatic man had formulated the major Federalist policies during George Washington's Presidency.

The most important of these policies arose from the need to deal with the huge legacy of debt from the revolutionary and confederation period. To establish the national credit, which he felt was necessary to the country's independence, he recommended paying the full value of the national debt, twelve million dollars of which was owned by foreign investors and forty million by Americans. This proposal had a two-fold aim: it would strengthen the financial credit of the United States abroad and at home, and it would secure the loyalty of the nation's businessmen to the central government. But at home most of the bonds were no longer held by their original purchasers. As the credit of the Continental and Confederation Congresses had declined, and as debtors found it more difficult to get money to repay their creditors, the bonds had been sold to speculators at a fraction of their value. Thus Hamilton's proposal to have the national treasury redeem them at their full value would enrich the bond speculators, some of whom knew in advance of Hamilton's proposal and had hard-riding agents scouring the back country, buying up bonds at less than twenty-five cents on the dollar. Despite the vehement opposition of many Antifederalists who argued that the government should redeem the bonds only at their market value, Congress approved Hamilton's plan.

The Secretary of the Treasury also recommended that the twenty-five million dollars of state debts, incurred during the Revolutionary War, be assumed by the federal government. This measure too would increase the support given to the central as opposed to the state governments. States like Georgia and Virginia with small debts, or states which had already paid much of their own debts, bitterly resented the fact that they would be taxed to help pay off the larger debts of states like Massachusetts and they strenuously opposed the proposal. To ensure the success of his measure in Congress, Hamilton made a bargain with Jefferson. Many Southern Congressmen who were followers of Jefferson wanted the nation's capital to be in the South. In return for a promise to move the capital from New York to Philadelphia and after ten years to the banks of the Potomac River, Jefferson secured enough votes from his followers to ensure the passage of Hamilton's Debt Assumption Act.

Hamilton next recommended the creation of a Bank of the United States to help the government safeguard its funds, sell bonds, and stabilize currency values. After another fiery debate, with Northern votes carrying the bill, Congress agreed to charter the new Bank for a period of twenty years. The Bank was to have a capital of ten million dollars and a bank-note circulation of seven and a half million dollars. While the Bank was to be privately owned, the government was required to purchase one-fifth of the stock and to ensure the Bank's stability. Not only could the Bank issue paper money, it could establish branches throughout the country which would have the same functions as the National Bank. Once again, Hamilton's opponents cried "special privilege" and "centralization." The private owners of Bank stock, they argued, would have a splendid guaranteed investment and great influence over credit throughout the nation; moreover the Bank would still further buttress the central government.

The differences of opinion over the Bank issue were so deep and so strong that Washington asked for opinions on the constitutionality of the Bank Bill from his Cabinet. The written opinions prepared by Hamilton and Jefferson clearly defined two opposing points of view on the interpretation of the Constitution. Jefferson voiced the "strict construction" argument: nowhere, he argued, did the Constitution empower the central government to charter a National Bank, and for that government to move beyond its specific constitutional powers was "to take possession of a boundless field of power, no longer susceptible of any definition." Hamilton stuck closely to his idea of the "executive impulse," that is, to the belief that a strong national executive must guide Congress and compel the "lesser" state governments to accept policies for "the good of the nation." Thus he argued for a "loose construction" of the Constitution by which the central government would possess powers "implied" by the elastic clause of the Constitution. He felt that since the Constitution gave the federal government control of currency it *implied* the right to charter a bank for the carrying out of that power. But Jefferson believed that to accept such "implied powers" in connection with the Bank would provide a precedent for the central government to expand *all* of its enumerated powers. This, he thought, would demolish states' rights, and since state governments were "closer to the people," would further limit democracy.

Washington signed the Bank Bill principally because he agreed with Hamilton that the central power should be strengthened. But tension steadily mounted as the rest of Hamilton's programme appeared, tension which rose to fever pitch over the excise tax question.

In order to raise revenue to pay the interest on the new

government bonds which were being sold to replace the old debts, Hamilton decided to levy an excise tax on various products, including liquor. Congress passed the necessary act, and by the spring of 1791 tax collection was in full swing. But popular opposition was fierce; the tax was called "odious, unequal, unpopular, and aggressive." In the hills of western Pennsylvania, where farmers converted their bulky grain into distilled whiskey in order to reduce transportation charges across the mountains, the opposition broke into violence. Tax collectors and even federal marshals were tarred and feathered. Rebellious frontiersmen were in complete agrreement with their representatives who hurled this challenge at the federal government.

> It [the excise] shall not be collected. We will punish, expel, and banish the officers who shall attempt the collection. . . . The sovereignty shall not reside with you, but with us. If you presume to dispute the point by force, we are ready to measure swords with you, and if unequal ourselves to the contest, we will call in the aid of a foreign nation [Britain]. We will league ourselves with a foreign power.

In this resistance Hamilton saw a golden opportunity to prove the strength of the new government and to show businessmen that the ghost of Daniel Shays had really been laid. Into the West rode Hamilton at the head of 13,000 soldiers whom he had persuaded President Washington to mobilize. Although there was no organized rebellion to crush, a hundred people were arrested and two of them sentenced to death. Hamilton had clearly demonstrated that the federal government could and would use force to collect revenue, the very thing that had been impossible under the Articles of Confederation.

The excise taxes were but one part of Hamilton's revenue programme. In 1789 he had persuaded Congress to place tariff duties on imported goods. Three years later he argued successfully that these duties should be increased enough to protect American manufacturers against foreign competition. Farmers and merchants protested that this was unfair assistance to one small group, but again Hamilton won his point. Clearly, he wanted to establish a republic whose society and government would very much resemble English models: one which would rapidly become an industrial nation with real control situated in the Eastern cities. Since nine-tenths of the American people in the 1790's lived on farms, plantations or in very small towns, his plan was bound to run into serious opposition.

Two political parties emerged out of the effort to organize and express public opinion on these issues. The first of these was the Federalist party. The Federalists had been the chief promoters of the Constitution and they had won a majority of seats in the Congress. Once in power, they formed caucuses or party conferences in both Houses, made sure that their supporters received appointments to the courts and other lucrative offices, and extended their influence into the electoral districts. Both their power and their policies stimulated the growth of an opposition party.

2. JEFFERSON AND THE REPUBLICANS

Led by Thomas Jefferson and James Madison, the Democratic Republican party, often simply called the Republican party, also had very definite ideas about what was best for the nation. Madison's support of Jefferson gave the opposition party particular strength since Madison had been a principal author of much of the Constitution and of some of the most brilliant essays in the Federalist Papers. Both men were gravely alarmed as they saw the unfolding of Hamilton's full plan of centralized government.

Thomas Jefferson, unlike Hamilton, was born an aristocrat. Like George Washington, he was a Virginia planter with extensive estates. He had been an ambassador to France during the Philadelphia Convention and thus had had no direct influence on the framing of the Constitution. As the author of the Declaration of Independence, however, and as a political theorist in his own right, he was welcomed in the Paris salons and witnessed the first enthusiastic phases of the French Revolution. He deeply distrusted Europe and England, and deplored the early manifestations of the industrial revolution in those countries and the growth of ugly industrial towns. He believed that farms bred the most virtuous men while the great cities, about which Hamilton dreamed, debased men by depriving them of contact with nature and making them dependent upon others for the right to work. Moreover, Jefferson despised Hamilton's low view of human nature and believed that men were essentially good and trustworthy. He felt that evil and fickle men were largely the product of vicious social and political institutions, of systems which denied to them their natural independence and freedom of growth. As a legislator in Virginia and as its Governor from 1779 to 1781, he regularly assaulted the "artificial aristocracy of wealth and birth." Desiring an intelligent democracy he worked for a system of public education for all, a wide franchise and legal reform. Jefferson regarded an established church as one of the bulwarks of a privileged class and he campaigned vigorously for separation of church and state. While he did not think that a movement for abolition of slavery would gain sufficient public support to succeed, he did argue that "the day is not distant when [the public] must bear and adopt it, or worse will follow."

It was natural that this broadly cultured man should not remain quiet in the face of Hamilton's assault on the liberal principles in which he believed. In particular he opposed Hamilton's centralization of power and advocated a strict interpretation or "construction" of the Constitution and the upholding of the powers of the states. Jefferson believed that all governments tend to be interested in increasing their own power; that they should therefore be held in the closest check by an active and well-informed democracy. On one occasion he remarked: "If left to me to decide whether we should have a government without newspapers, or newspapers without a government, I should not hesitate for a moment to prefer the latter." Later in life he declared that he would not wish to live in a community in which there was not an attempted rebellion at least every twenty years.

It is small wonder that inside Washington's Cabinet, Jefferson and Hamilton were constantly at loggerheads. In Congress the Republicans began their own caucus which quickly became even more disciplined than that of the Federalists. Throughout the country Jefferson and Madison developed permanent organizations of support for the party and enlisted such prominent men as Governor Clinton of New York, Albert Gallatin of Pennsylvania and Aaron Burr of New York. The party organization thus built up, and particularly the congressional caucus of the Republicans, was to control the Presidency from 1801 to 1825, under Jefferson, Madison and James Monroe respectively.

Curiously, although Washington sympathized with Hamilton's views in most matters, the Jeffersonians supported Washington for President in 1792 and he was thus unopposed and returned unanimously for a second term. The same year, however, saw the first open demonstration of party politics. Governer Clinton, the Republican candidate for Vice-President, took fifty electoral votes while John Adams, the Federalist, won with seventy-seven. In an election in the same year, however, the Republicans gained the majority of seats in the House of Representatives.

As the parties took shape, issues over which they were bound to disagree were plentiful. One of the most important of these concerned America's relationship to Europe and to European power in the New World, a problem which was to remain central to American party politics for a long time.

3. FOREIGN AFFAIRS AND PARTY STRIFE

The beginning of the French Revolution coincided with the launching of the American Constitution, and at first Americans welcomed "the end of French tyranny" wholeheartedly. The leading Federalist lawyer (and future Chief Justice) John Marshall wrote: "In no part of the globe was this revolution hailed with more joy than in America." Even in conservative Boston, Royal Exchange Alley was renamed Liberty Street, while throughout the United States there were popular celebrations and feasts to observe the fall of the Bastille. But by 1790 many Americans, and all Federalists, took a different view. They took note of Edmund Burke's *Reflections on the French Revolution* and agreed that the new ideas of the French democracy were more dangerous to men of property than was the *ancien régime*. They saw the single-chamber Assembly of the 1791 French Constitution as an attack on the checks and balances they themselves had erected against "unbridled democracy" in the United States.

With news of the execution of Louis XVI and the Jacobin Reign of Terror, the Federalists turned against France and showed a growing sympathy for England when France declared war on the British. Most Jeffersonian Republicans, on the other hand, continued to support the French drive for greater democracy and applauded *The Rights of Man,* a pamphlet by the political philosopher, Tom Paine, which argued vehemently for complete democracy, agnosticism in religious matters, and the levelling of social distinctions. In the spring of 1793 Republicans welcomed Citizen Genêt who arrived from France as ambassador of the new government. Genêt's main job was to organize American support in the war against England. He was a personable and confident young man and soon had commissioned a number of American ship captains to attack British merchantmen. Hamilton and his Federalist colleagues in the Cabinet pointed out that Genêt's behaviour was highly irregular, and that he had not even bothered to present his credentials to the President before launching his campaign to whip up enthusiasm for France. Jefferson agreed that Washington should ask the French government to recall him. Genêt himself, however, decided that life was too precarious in France. He married a daughter of the Governor of New York and settled into a Hudson Valley estate. But his short career as France's ambassador had raised the temperature of American politics and led to a significant decision.

The French government wanted the United States to

honour the Franco-American treaty of 1778, in which the United States had promised to help defend the French West Indies should they be attacked by Britain. Hamilton wanted to disavow the treaty because of the guillotining of Louis XVI. Jefferson, however, argued that the treaty should be honoured, or at least that the United States should bargain for commercial concessions from England as the price of repudiation. Washington finally decided to ignore the treaty and to declare the United States neutral in the European struggle. Jefferson argued that the President's action was unconstitutional. Since Congress had the exclusive power to declare war, he said, it must also have the sole authority to declare neutrality. As a result of this dispute, Washington lost confidence in Jefferson, and Hamilton's power increased proportionately.

As the French revolutionary war dragged on, relations between the United States and Great Britain grew steadily worse. Since 1783 American merchants had been excluded from all the ports of Great Britain and her colonies; in 1793 the British government issued an order to seize all ships of any nation trading with France or French colonies. In the United States the Republicans called for a stern response and open support of France, but the Federalists refused to make a break with Britain for they owned most of the shipping and would pay most of the taxes if war were to break out. Moreover, almost ninety per cent of United States imports were produced in Britain. Finally, Federalists felt that Britain stood for the same kind of government and society that they wished to build up in America, while France stood for revolution, anarchy, terror and atheism. At the peak of this clash over foreign policy, Jefferson resigned and was succeeded as Secretary of State by Edmund Randolph, a leading Federalist, thus strengthening the Federalist party's hold on the executive and emphasizing the growing strength of the party system.

Meanwhile, events in the interior of the continent further damaged Anglo-American relations. In 1783 the British had agreed to surrender all their western fur-trading posts in American territory, including Detroit, Oswego, Niagara and Michilimackinac. The fur-traders in Canada naturally objected to such a course, for it would mean their exclusion from much of their traditional western trade. In the treaty of 1783 the Americans had promised to compensate the Loyalists for the damages the latter had suffered during the Revolutionary War, and when they delayed doing so the British used the default as an excuse to retain the western posts. The Americans believed that the British in the West encouraged and supported the Indians in their fierce opposition to the advancing American settlement south of Lake Erie.

Anxious to remove these causes of conflict with Britain, Washington sent John Jay to London in 1794 to arrange a treaty. The British were sympathetic, for they had no desire to force the United States into the arms of revolutionary France. Nevertheless, they proved to be hard bargainers. In the end Jay's Treaty provided that Britain would withdraw from the western posts and remove her troops by 1796; that the United States could trade with some parts of the Empire, but not with the British West Indies; and that joint commissions would discuss the questions of debts and boundaries. The British adamantly refused to abandon their policy of seizing American ships trading with France. While war had been averted and the troublesome western question temporarily solved, Jay's Treaty was unpopular in the United States. Jay was burned in effigy, flags were flown at half-mast, and Hamilton was stoned in the streets of New York. Republican strength increased rapidly. Even the defeat of the Indians by General "Mad Anthony" Wayne at the Battle of Fallen Timbers in 1794, which cleared the way for settlement westward from Lake Erie, did little to quell growing criticism of the Federalists.

Jay's Treaty, however, did encourage Spain to make concessions to the United States in the south, where Spain controlled Florida and the mouth of the Mississippi. Fearful that with the British threat removed in the north the United

States might attack her possessions in the south, Spain signed the Pinckney Treaty in 1795 adjusting the boundary of West Florida as the United States wished and permitting the Americans to use the port of New Orleans and the lower Mississippi River.

Although they wanted much more, settlers in the trans-Allegheny West were encouraged by these treaties. By 1800, Kentucky, Tennessee and Vermont had been admitted to the Union as states and the Ohio country was being occupied. In the Northwest Territory there were already 45,000 settlers. Most of the Americans who were thus busy forming new societies in the West were Jeffersonian in politics. They distrusted the distant central government and the business leaders of the Federalist party. Interested in cheap or free land, easier credit and military help to hasten the reluctant Indian withdrawal along the frontiers, they looked to the Republicans as the party most interested in the frontiersmen and western expansion.

In the midst of the party struggle Washington decided not to run for a third term, thus establishing a precedent not broken until 1940. His farewell address, delivered in the face of a mounting attack on the Federalist leadership, advised the nation to keep neutral in foreign affairs and to avoid party politics.

> I have already intimated to you the danger of parties in the State. . . . Let me now . . . warn you in the most solemn manner against the baneful effects of the spirit of party. . . . The great rule of conduct for us in regard to foreign nations is, in extending our commercial relations to have with them as little political connection as possible.

4. ADAMS AND FEDERALIST DECLINE

In 1796 John Adams, a scrupulously honest man, was elected the second and last Federalist President. Adams was concerned about the democratic tendencies of the age as well as with threats to American national interests. When he saw that the French were trying to bribe American ambassadors and were seizing American ships in retaliation for the Jay Treaty and American repudiation of the Franco-American treaty, he supported military preparations in anticipation of a war with France. While a settlement was arranged with the French in 1800 and the war scare passed, the tension it had created was exploited for political purposes.

In 1798, alleging a dire threat of subversion by pro-French opinion in the United States, the Federalists passed the harsh Alien, Sedition and Naturalization acts. The latter prescribed fourteen years instead of the previous five as the period an immigrant must wait before naturalization. The Alien Act gave the President power to arrest and deport undesirable aliens, while the Sedition Act empowered the executive to imprison anyone who spoke or wrote in such a way as to bring the government into disrepute. Federalist judges decreed fines and imprisonment for seventy people brought to trial under the Sedition Act, while men like Judge Samuel Chase took the trials as occasions to preach violently against the Republican party. Many of the convicted men were Republican editors and one was a Republican Congressman from Vermont.

James Madison called the Sedition Act "a monster that must forever disgrace its parents." Across the country protest against the arbitrary acts mounted. Republicans declared that the acts violated the Bill of Rights and the legislatures of Virginia and Kentucky passed opposition resolutions, prepared by Madison and Jefferson. These "Virginia and Kentucky Resolves" defined the Republican position on states' rights by asserting that the Union was a compact. Since the sovereign states entered a voluntary compact to establish a central government for certain common purposes, it was argued that if the central government violated the agreement the compact would be broken. The resolutions declared that the powers of the central government were merely delegated to it by the various states and that the states had the right to declare any federal law "unauthoritative, void and of no force." While the resolutions did not specifically say how a state might make its veto effective they did give additional prestige to the doctrine of states' rights.

As the election of 1800 approached, opposition to the Federalist programme of centralization of power in the federal government and the arbitrary use of that authority increased in strength. The Federalist candidates for the Presidency and Vice-Presidency, John Adams and Charles Pinckney, lost to Jefferson and Aaron Burr. Jefferson was clearly the man the country wanted for President, but the electoral college did not distinguish between the votes for President and Vice-President, and Jefferson and Burr had both received the same number of electoral votes. Thus the decision was made by the House of Representatives, which reflected the will of the people and the electors by selecting Jefferson as President and Burr as Vice-President. To avoid a similar problem in the future the Twelfth Amendment, passed in 1804, provided that the electors would vote separately for the two offices.

The election of 1800 plainly showed that Republican and Jeffersonian ideas had the support of the great majority of ordinary Americans as well as of Virginia planters and some of the leading families of New York and Pennsylvania. The Federalists were disheartened. As one commented pessimistically after the election: "I cannot describe how broken and scattered your federal friends are! We have no rallying point; and no mortal can divine where and when we shall again collect our strength. Shadows, clouds and darkness rest on our future prospects."

Thomas Jefferson referred to the election as "the Revolution of 1800." It remained to be seen what new directions would be given to American government, business and society by the Republicans.

3

Nationalism and Sectionalism

IN HIS first inaugural address Thomas Jefferson appealed
to his countrymen to unite in defence of their institutions
and principles. Referring to the bitter conflict between
Federalists and Republicans, he declared that "every difference of opinion is not a difference of principle. We are all
Republicans, we are all Federalists. If there be any among
us who would wish to dissolve this Union or to change its
republican form, let them stand undisturbed as monuments
of the safety with which error of opinion may be tolerated
where reason is left free to combat it."

1. THE REPUBLICAN PROGRAMME

Jefferson's inauguration took place in 1801 in Washington,
which had now become the capital of the United States.
Although Hamilton was right in saying that the new President was "as likely as any man I known to temporize" rather
than to attempt a drastic change, Jefferson did implement
many of his election promises. In this he was ably assisted
by James Madison whom he appointed Secretary of State
and Albert Gallatin, a Pennsylvanian of aristocratic Swiss
birth and great financial ability, who served as Secretary of
the Treasury.

Jefferson dropped many Federalist customs which he believed had a flavour of monarchy. Instead of appearing before Congress to read his messages, like the king opening
parliament, Jefferson communicated them in writing. Frequent informal levees at the White House replaced the

occasional formal receptions at the "President's Palace." The conviviality of Jefferson's popular evenings was enhanced by the huge cellar of excellent wine which he had acquired while he was in France. The Republican administration repealed excise taxes, eliminated many public positions and allowed the Alien and Sedition laws to lapse. Jefferson not only curtailed government expenditures, but also allotted government funds for specific purposes, rather than have Congress provide lump sums to be spent at executive discretion.

All of this programme was "Jeffersonian" in that it reduced the growth of the central government's influence and power, and within the central government appeared to give more power to Congress and less to the executive. But in other ways the Republican President fulfilled Hamilton's prediction that he would temporize. Jefferson did not in fact touch the central core of the Hamiltonian system, satisfying himself, rather, by modifying its operation. Indeed, as a practical politican, Jefferson actually increased the power of the Presidential office, and through personal contacts he kept control over the Republican majority in Congress; for by keeping in close and friendly communication with Republican leaders in House and Senate he was able to get favourable legislative action on policies desired by himself and his cabinet. His predecessor, Adams, who had not had a majority following in Congress, had been unable to overcome the "separation of powers," and like many later Presidents had encountered grave difficulties as a result. In appointing men to the hundreds of public positions, from the foreign service down to postmasters, Jefferson took care to strengthen his party. The courts, however, remained mostly under Federalist judges. As Congressman William Giles of Virginia remarked: "The revolution of 1800 is incomplete so long as that strong fortress is in possession of the enemy."

A direct clash between the Federalists entrenched in the Supreme Court and the Republicans came in 1803 when Chief Justice John Marshall, Jefferson's cousin, delivered his judgment in the case of *Marbury versus Madison*. The significance of this decision was Marshall's assertion of the Supreme Court's power to invalidate federal legislation. He consistently upheld the principle that both state and federal laws were subject to constitutional review by the Supreme Court, and defended this assertion of judicial independence in these words:

> The particular phraseology of the constitution of the United States confirms and strengthens the principle, supposed to be essential to all written constitutions, that a law repugnant to the constitution is void, and that courts, as well as other departments are bound by this instrument.

The Jeffersonians were furious, and asked who was to check the courts and to whom the judges were responsible. They asserted that the executive could enforce laws even if they had been declared unconstitutional by the Supreme Court. The Judiciary Act passed in 1789, establishing the federal court system, had empowered the Supreme Court to interpret the Constitution but nowhere had the Constitution itself specifically given the Court this power. Thus, argued the champions of states' rights and a strict construction of the Constitution, the Supreme Court did not have the right of judicial review over state or federal legislation. They even argued that the legislature could impeach judges, relying on the will of the people as expressed in succeeding elections to decide who was right. There could be no final solution to this question, but in Marshall's thirty-four years as Chief Justice the claims of the Supreme Court to judge the constitutionality of both federal and state laws were steadily entrenched.

Despite his opposition to centralization and executive power, Jefferson was to take one step which would increase the power of both the central government and the President. In 1800 Napoleon Bonaparte had acquired the vast Louisiana territory from Spain and two years later prohibited Americans from using the port of New Orleans. Americans were alarmed by the closure of a port which handled forty per cent of their exports. They also suspected that Napoleon planned to re-establish a powerful French empire in North America and permanently exclude them from the trans-Mississippi West. Jefferson at once instructed his minister in Paris, Robert Livingston, to try to purchase New Orleans, and sent James Monroe of Virginia to assist him. A nervous Congress voted two million dollars for diplomatic expenses. While the Federalists called for war against France, Jefferson sent a secret note to the French government, warning it that the French move "completely reverses all the political relations of the United States, and will form a new epoch in our political course. . . . There is on this globe one single spot, the possessor of which is our natural and habitual enemy. It is New Orleans, through which the produce of three-eighths of our territory must pass to market. . . . The day that France takes possession of New Orleans . . . we must marry ourselves to the British fleet and nation."

2. WESTERN EXPANSION

War between Britain and France was once more on the horizon, and Napoleon did not want to have the extra and heavy burden of defending distant Louisiana, which he felt the British would undoubtedly try to seize. To everyone's surprise he offered to sell all of Louisiana to the United States for fifteen million dollars. The two American ambassadors hastily concluded a treaty with Napoleon. Jefferson now faced a serious problem. He had argued for a strict interpretation of the Constitution; was he now to use a power of acquiring new territory which was not mentioned in the Constitution? Jefferson would have preferred to have waited for an amendment to be added to the Constitution giving the President this power. But he knew that the amending process was very slow and he feared that Napoleon might change his mind in the interim. Supported by his closest advisers he decided to throw caution to the winds and placed the treaty before the Senate for ratification. Ironically, in the debate that ensued the Federalists, in opposing the treaty, argued

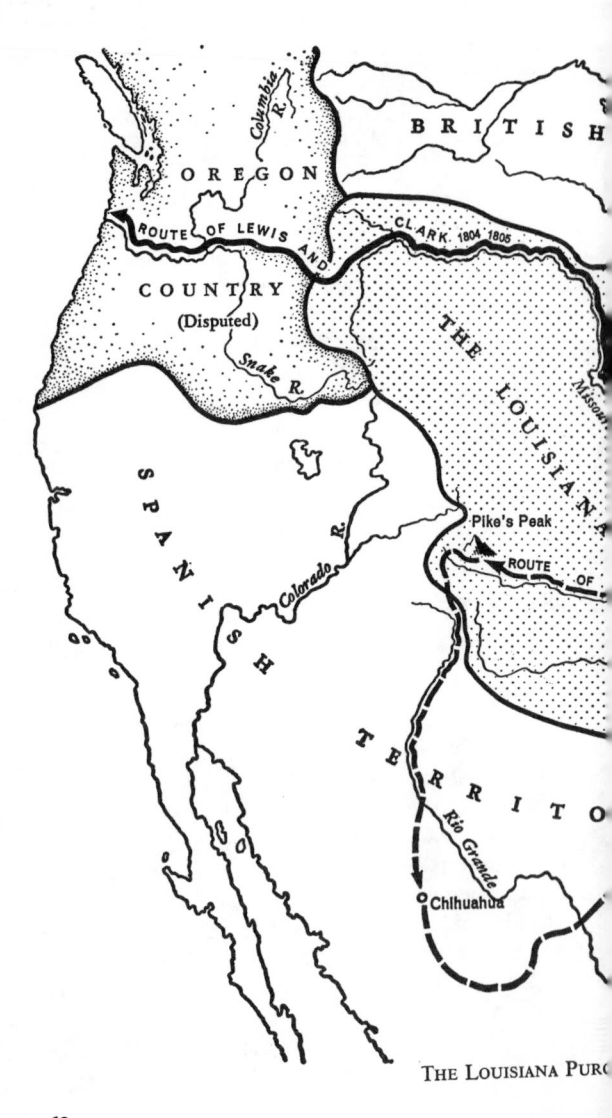

THE LOUISIANA PURC

NORTH AMERICA

Boundaries uncertain

Red River

Mississippi R.

1806

INDIANA TERRITORY 1800

L. Superior

L. Michigan

MICHIGAN TERRITORY 1805

L. Huron

L. Erie

St. Louis

...RCHASE

Arkansas R.

KENTUCKY

TENNESSEE 1796

MISSISSIPPI TERRITORY 1804

WEST FLORIDA (SP.)

New Orleans

Cleveland

OHIO 1803

Washington

VIRGINIA

NORTH CAROLINA

SOUTH CAROLINA

GEORGIA

EAST FLORIDA (SP.)

L. Ontario

St. Lawrence R.

DISPUTED TERRITORY

VT.

N.H.

NEW YORK

MASSACHUSETTS

R.I.

CONN.

PENNSYLVANIA

Pittsburgh

N.J.

DEL.

MD.

N

United States 1803

Louisiana Purchase 1803

0   200

that the Constitution did not give the executive the power to buy new territory, while the Republicans argued that the joint treaty-making power of President and Senate covered the situation. The fact that the West was predominantly Republican in politics and that the acquisition of Louisiana would greatly increase the Republican party's future political strength, plus the Eastern Federalists' innate distrust of the West, helps to explain why the Federalists opposed the treaty. Nevertheless, the Senate ratified the treaty and on December 20, 1803 Louisiana was formally transferred to the United States.

Behind the obvious temptation of the offer lay another reason for Jefferson's decision to accept the treaty immediately. Jefferson believed deeply in what succeeding generations of Americans were to call "Manifest Destiny," a belief that United States influence must be felt in every part of the North American continent. Two years before the Louisiana Purchase he had written:

> However our present interests may restrain us upon our own limits, it is impossible not to look forward to distant times, when our rapid multiplication will expand beyond those limits and cover the whole northern, if not the southern, continent with a people speaking the same language, governed in similar forms and by similar laws.

The Republican Congress had already eased the terms on which settlers could buy lands in the public domain and the population of the Northwest Territory grew so rapidly that Ohio was admitted as a state in 1803. Similar growth occurred in the Southwest. But it was the trans-Mississippi West that really fired the imaginations of Jefferson, his advisers and the settlers of the mid-continental valley. The negotiations with France for New Orleans had just begun when Jefferson obtained from Congress a secret vote of money for an expedition to collect information on the Far West. Under Jefferson's secretary, Meriwether Lewis, and Lieutenant William Clark, the expedition finally set out in May 1804. Crossing prairies, foothills and mountains the explorers reached the Pacific at the mouth of the Columbia River. The Journey established a tenuous claim by the United States to the huge Oregon country which, at that time, was largely the preserve of the British Hudson's Bay Company but was claimed also by Spain and Russia. While the expedition's report underestimated the worth of the intervening prairies, which it thought were mostly desert, the information about the fur trade, lumber, and mining possibilities of the Rocky Mountains gathered by the explorers greatly stimulated the Easterners' ambitions to acquire the whole continent and gave impetus to the idea of "Manifest Destiny." This American sense of nationalism was further strengthened by the course of the Napoleonic Wars.

3. FOREIGN AFFAIRS AND THE WAR OF 1812

In 1803 the war between Britain and France that Napoleon had anticipated when he offered to sell all of Louisiana to the United States had begun. Napoleon's power was supreme in Europe. To strike a blow at Britain's trade, he issued a series of decrees, called the Milan and Berlin decrees, forbidding neutral ships to visit British ports. In retaliation Britain issued orders-in-council forbidding neutral ships to trade in French-controlled European ports. Since British seapower was dominant, she was able to enforce her orders-in-council. The principal group to suffer from this double blockade was the booming American merchant marine. From 1804 to 1807 the British confiscated hundreds of American ships and searched nearly all United States merchantmen for deserters from the British navy. Over-eager British captains often "impressed" Americans, whom they claimed were British deserters. In 1807 a British warship, the *Leopard*, halted an American frigate, the *Chesapeake*. After inflicting several American casualties, the captain of the *Leopard* removed from the American ship a British deserter and three Americans who had served in the British navy. A loud cry for retaliation echoed throughout the American press and Congress.

Jefferson responded to the *Chesapeake* affair by obtaining from Congress an Embargo Act in 1807 which in effect prohibited American trade with Europe. Although Jefferson hoped thus to keep the United States out of a costly war, his policy had two major economic results. It created a widespread commercial depression along the American seaboard, which spread quickly to farm areas, and it stimulated American domestic manufacturing to replace the loss of imports from Europe.

Despite a growing uneasiness along the eastern seaboard the Republican candidate, James Madison, won the Presidential election of 1808. Madison, although he was both learned and respected, lacked the human managerial skills by which Jefferson had controlled Congress. This weakening of the executive influence was compounded when the congressional elections of 1810 returned a group of fire-eating Republican expansionists from the South and West. Soon known as the War Hawks these men, led by Henry Clay of Kentucky and John C. Calhoun of South Carolina, pressed for war with Britain. In their bellicose speeches they tempted many people with dreams of the easy acquisition of Canada, and Florida, the property of Britain's Spanish ally. At one time Calhoun boasted: "In four weeks from the time that a declaration of war is heard on our frontier the whole of Upper Canada and a part of Lower Canada will be in our possession."

In the years before the War of 1812 the War Hawks both responded to and exploited the strong sense of American nationalism which deeply resented Britain's control of the United States economic life. The continuing British interference with American shipping began to swing some Eastern businessmen towards support of the tough War Hawk line. In 1810 Congress enacted the Macon Bill, which ended the embargo, and added the proviso that if either France or Britain lifted its commercial decrees, the United States would stop trade with the other. Napoleon seized the opportunity and announced the revocation of his decrees against neutral shipping. Madison at once gave Britain three months' notice;

at the end of that time Congress prohibited trade with Britain. The action was a double trap for the President. France did not really change her policy, and yet had induced the United States to join the French blockade against British trade. It also strengthened the War Hawk position by stirring up support for war with Britain.

Westerners were not averse to war with Britain on other grounds also. They wanted to clear the Indians from the path of westward settlement. Already there had been a series of bloody battles and forced treaty-concessions between the Indians and the American frontiersmen. In 1811 an Indian confederacy under the Shawnee chief, Tecumseh, was engaged in a very indecisive armed struggle at Tippecanoe in which no one was quite sure who was winning. Yet in one way Tippecanoe *was* decisive. The War Hawks claimed that the British weapons used by the Indians in this battle and others were proof that Britain would have to be driven from North America. In addition, many Westerners felt that their exports out of New Orleans were imperilled by Britain's orders-in-council.

Responding to all these pressures, President Madison asked Congress to declare war on Great Britain in June 1812. The best summary of the reasons for the war was given in a private letter by Andrew Jackson, who was later to be President of the United States, written three months before the congressional declaration of war:

> We are going to fight for the re-establishment of our national character . . . for the protection of our maritime citizens impressed on board British ships of war . . . to vindicate our right to a free trade . . . in fine to seek some indemnity for past injuries, some security against future aggression, by the conquest of all British domains upon the continent of North America. . . . In reviewing the conduct of Great Britain toward the United States our attention is necessarily drawn to the warfare just renewed by the savages on one of our extensive frontiers —a warfare which is known to spare neither age nor sex and to be distinguished by features peculiarly shocking to humanity.

The War of 1812 had grown out of a welter of bungled diplomacy and strident nationalistic ambition. Perversely, while it was a supreme example of nationalism it greatly intensified sectional feeling. Although many Americans saw the war as a second war of independence, many others firmly opposed the war with Britain. While some Eastern businessmen agreed that it was necessary for the United States to assert her rights against British "domination," others felt that the war was principally an expression of anti-British republicanism and radical frontier democracy. Still others feared further disruption of their trade. Most of New England opposed the war, and the region continued to trade with British North America throughout the hostilities. New England Federalist leaders in December 1814 met in Hartford to declare the right of any state to nullify federal legislation. Using language oddly similar to that of the Virginia and Kentucky Resolves of 1798, they proposed seven amendments to the Constitution, all aimed at strengthening the Northeast at the expense of the Southern and Western expansionists.

The actual conduct of the war was tragic and farcical. Both the government and the armed forces were totally unprepared for war and remained in that condition throughout most of the hostilities. Enlistments lagged far behind requirements and several states refused to let their militia serve outside the state. During an attack on Queenston Heights in Upper Canada in October 1812, this policy was embarrassing for the United States and fortunate for Canada, as New York militiamen remained firmly on the American side of the Niagara River. Loans were under-subscribed, generals were incompetent and the navy often inadequate. By the end of the war much of Maine and Illinois territory was in British hands and most of the Atlantic coast was under effective blockade by the Royal Navy. Nevertheless, while the British hemmed in the Atlantic seaboard and burned Washington, individual American ships performed brilliantly and captured thirteen hundred British craft of different types. In January 1815, just before news of the peace treaty arrived, General Andrew Jackson decisively beat a British invasion force at New Orleans. Such events tremendously reinforced American nationalism. Furthermore, although American commerce had suffered heavily, the scarcity of imported European goods had stimulated American manufacturing.

The Treaty of Ghent, signed after lengthy negotiations on December 24, 1814, ended the war, but changed nothing. It provided for the return "of all territory, places and possessions whatsoever taken by either party from the other during the war." The British government had decided that the European situation at the end of the Napoleonic Wars was too unstable to permit longer, heavier efforts in North America. The American negotiators, because of the steadily deteriorating military situation in the United States, were unable to gain any assurances about neutral rights at sea and failed also to secure their other objectives of territorial gains in Canada and Florida. Definition of the Canadian-American boundary was left to future negotiations while nothing at all was said about the future of Florida. As a later President, John Quincy Adams, who helped to negotiate the Treaty, put it, "We have obtained nothing but peace."

4. ECONOMIC NATIONALISM AND THE "AMERICAN SYSTEM"

One intangible gain for the United States was a new sense of national purpose. With the Federalists discredited by their foot-dragging wartime attitude, the National Republican party absorbed the leading national politicians and all eyes turned to problems of economic growth and westward expansion. The vibrant post-war nationalism was reflected in vigorous economic policy, territorial expansion and diplomacy.

The chief architect of economic policy in these years, Henry Clay, an ex-War Hawk Senator from Kentucky, liked to talk of the "American System." Clay's "System" meant the very positive use of government to encourage the growth of industry and trade as well as to extend American political control over the western hemisphere. Supported by another ex-War Hawk Senator, John Calhoun of South Carolina, Clay carried forward his pre-1812 expansionist ideas. But now expansionism was endorsed by most businessmen, attracted not only by dreams of American-controlled hemispheric trade but by plans to use the government to protect them against foreign competition and furnish them with a stable banking system and "internal improvements" such as better roads, bridges, canals and harbours and, by the 1830's, railways. To guard against the tendency of local banks to over-issue both credit and paper currency Clay and Calhoun secured an act of Congress in 1816 to charter a second Bank of the United States to replace the first National Bank whose charter had not been renewed in 1811. Four-fifths of its stock was bought by private businessmen and one-fifth by the government. The policy of the Bank of the United States was to compel state banks to limit their issues of paper money in an attempt to stabilize the nation's finances.

In the same year Congress passed another Hamiltonian measure, a new tariff act. Even Southerners, following Calhoun, put aside their free trade convictions to vote for the 1816 tariff which was designed to protect infant American industries. Some Southerners and most Westerners hoped to see factories built in their own localities as a result of protection such as the new act afforded against cheap English goods, which had begun to swamp the American market in 1815 once the war was over.

With these foundations of the "American System" laid, and with the National Republicans again winning the Presidency in 1816, Clay's aims seemed well advanced. Booming prosperity in the United States after 1814 created opportunities which lured thousands to the trans-Allegheny West. In the decade from 1810 to 1820 the population west of the Appalachians more than doubled to reach a total of 2,200,000, which was greater than that of New England. Through the tortuous river valleys piercing the Appalachian barrier flowed unbroken streams of settlers, merchants and land speculators. The most heavily travelled route was along the federally built National Road which by 1818 reached from Cumberland in Maryland to Wheeling on the Ohio River. William Cobbett, an English observer in 1817, was amazed by this western spectacle: "The rugged road, the dirty hovels, the fire in the woods to sleep by, the pathless ways through the wilderness, the dangerous crossings of the rivers"; all this he wrote in order "to boil their pot in gypsy fashion, to have a mere board to eat on, to drink whiskey or pure water, to sit and sleep under a shed far inferior to English cowpens, to have a mill at twenty miles distance, an apothecary's shop at a hundred, and a doctor nowhere."

Yet it was done; and both the demands of the West and the profits to be made produced a frenzied economic growth. More roads were built with federal assistance and many were added by private companies which charged tolls for their use, and were frequently subsidized by state legislatures. Even so, transportation costs for importing and exporting from the West were high, either by road or by the hundreds of keelboats which had to be rowed when travelling upstream. Steamboats and canals helped to reduce costs. The first successful steamboat, the *Clermont*, was built by Robert Fulton, and in 1807 this formidable little vessel, spewing forth sparks and dense smoke from the black column of its single funnel, made the one-hundred-and-fifty-mile trip up the Hudson River from New York to Albany in thirty hours. One trembling witness observed: "Fishermen became terrified and they saw nothing but destruction devastating their fishing grounds, whilst the wreaths of black vapour and rushing noise of the paddle wheels, foaming with the stirred-up water, produced great excitement." By 1830 over two hundred steamboats were plying trans-Appalachian rivers, and upstream freight rates had been more than halved.

To supplement the river systems came the canals in the 1820's and 1830's. The greatest of these was the Erie Canal, finished in 1825 and linking Albany with Buffalo three hundred and sixty miles away. This startling achievement gave the Americans a continuous navigable water route from New York City to Toledo at the western end of Lake Erie. It

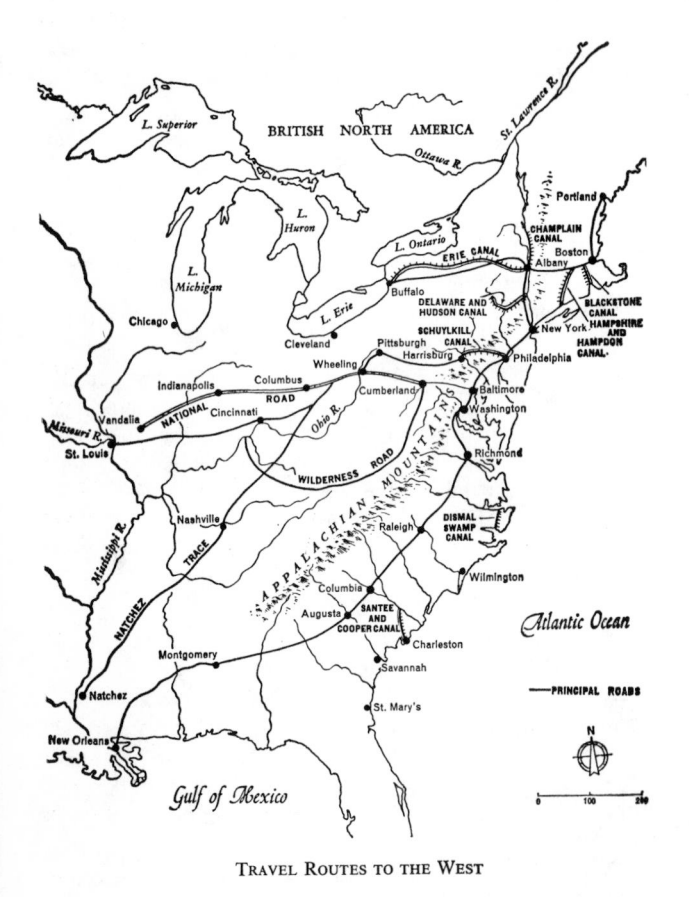

TRAVEL ROUTES TO THE WEST

cut the cost of east-west freight by nine-tenths and the time consumed in travel by more than one-half. The new commercial tie with the West made New York City the greatest trade centre on the seaboard and stimulated a tremendous export of grain, lumber and other produce from the West. It also encouraged Eastern manufacturers to produce for the mushrooming Western market. From the Canadian point of view completion of the Erie Canal was a critical blow to Montreal merchants in their long competition with New York to be the centre of trade between Europe and the American mid-continent.

5. JUDICIAL NATIONALISM

The new post-1812 nationalism was also reflected in the judgments of the Supreme Court where Chief Justice John Marshall firmly upheld the powers of the federal government against the claims of the states. The most important statement of judicial nationalism came in 1819 in the case of *McCulloch versus Maryland*. This legal dispute involved the validity of an act passed by the state of Maryland taxing a branch of the Bank of the United States. Since the Bank was founded upon a charter granted by the federal government, Marshall regarded the Maryland action as an attempt to limit or even to destroy the federal power. In effect, the question before the Court was once again whether the federal government had the power to charter the Bank. Marshall, repeating the arguments used by Alexander Hamilton in 1791, declared the Maryland statute unconstitutional. The federal government, he claimed, had "implied powers" which could be used to achieve legitimate national objectives. Speaking of the elastic clause of the Constitution, Marshall maintained:

> Let the end be legitimate, let it be within the scope of the Constitution, and all means which are appropriate, which are plainly adapted to that end, which are not prohibited, but consist with the letter and spirit of the Constitution, are constitutional.

71

Other decisions prohibited the states from interfering with interstate commerce, regulation of which Marshall declared rested exclusively in the hands of the federal authority. By 1835 when Chief Justice Marshall died, he had given added dignity and judicial support to the Hamiltonian view of the federal government's authority.

6. THE GROWTH OF SECTIONALISM

By 1820, however, the prosperity of the "era of good feelings" ended and an economic recession set in. With it sectional tensions revived. The South was not sharing equally with the North in the growth of industry and Southerners grew suspicious of the "American System." Many Westerners blamed the depression of 1819-24 on the Eastern businessmen who controlled credit and currency through the Bank of the United States.

By 1820, also, slavery had emerged as the most ominous focus of sectional disagreements. Since the end of the seventeenth century the proportion of Negro slaves in the Southern plantation labour force had been steadily increasing. At the end of the eighteenth century, just as liberal feeling had seemed ready to accept a gradual termination of the slave system, a single mechanical invention produced a cataclysmic economic development, which quickly smothered pro-emancipation opinion in the South. That mechanism was the cotton gin invented by Eli Whitney in 1793, which increased a slave's output of cleaned cotton from one to fifty pounds a day. When it was harnessed to water power or steam a cotton gin could turn a thousand pounds daily. Almost at once the farmers of Georgia and South Carolina deserted the cultivation of indigo and rice, Virginians restricted their tobacco acres and, together with Tennessee and North Carolina planters, turned to cotton. Within a very few years cotton had become King in the South.

But cotton-growing is hard on the soil and the search for fresh land was intense as Southerners poured across the territory north of the Gulf of Mexico. By 1820, advocates of slave emancipation in the South were few and far between. To have asked a large Southern planter to emancipate his slaves would have been almost the same as asking a New England businessman to turn over half his factory for some worthy public purpose.

In these same years, Southerners' suspicions of the Northeast grew rapidly. Because of the greater employment opportunities in the growing industry of the Northeastern states, immigrants from the British Isles and Europe flowed into the North and threatened to give that section a majority in the Senate. This would have mattered little had it not been that Northern business was pressing for greater tariff protection while the South, as it became increasingly a staple-producing region, disliked even the existing tariff. In addition, many Northerners wished to eliminate slavery from the Union, as an institution contrary to the spirit of the Declaration of Independence. Moreover, the Northern majority in the House of Representatives was growing steadily, especially since only three-fifths of the large slave population in the South counted for purposes of representation in the House of Representatives. Since the South could not hold its own in the lower house it became more important to maintain its voting power in the Senate. Each state possessed two Senate seats regardless of state population, and if the South were to control the Senate it had to keep pace with the North, state by state, in westward expansion, ensuring that as many slave as non-slave states were admitted to the Union.

In 1819, when there were eleven slave and eleven non-slave states, the people of Missouri applied for admission to the Union as a slaveholding state. Lying beyond the Mississippi, Missouri was not covered by the slavery prohibition clause of the old Northwest Ordinance. In the North, public meetings and legislatures passed resolutions opposing the admission of Missouri as a slave state. Southerners argued that all states had equal rights and that it was unconstitutional to place a condition upon one of them. One Southerner wrote: "We have kindled a fire which all the waters of the

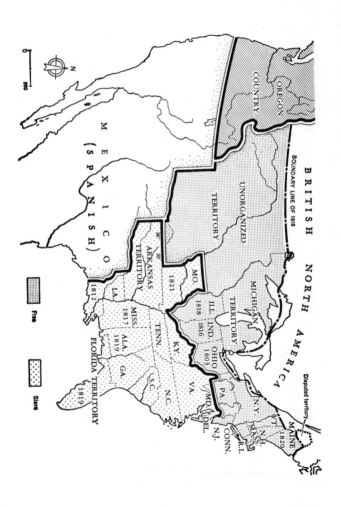

ocean cannot put out, which seas of blood can only extinguish."

As the clash of opinion reached the danger point several
congressional leaders, of whom the most prominent was
Henry Clay, sought a compromise. In 1820, North and
South finally agreed to several measures, known collectively
as the Missouri Compromise, designed to maintain equal
balance of slave and non-slave states in the Senate. By the
Compromise, Missouri was admitted as a slave state; Maine,
hitherto a part of Massachusetts, was granted a longstanding
wish for statehood, as a free state; slavery was prohibited
"forever" in all federal territory north of latitude 36° 30′,
the southern boundary of Missouri. Although the Missouri
Compromise solved the problem temporarily, the crisis had
deepened sectional feelings. Future difficulties arising from
the slavery problem were foreshadowed when the last Virginian President, James Monroe, elected in 1816, nearly
refused to sign the legislation of 1820 because the Constitution did not specifically empower Congress to exclude
slavery, a form of property rights, from the territories.

7. NATIONALISM AND DIPLOMACY

While growing sectional differences threatened the domestic unity of the United States, the country continued to expand westward. Nearly unanimous support was given to that
aspect of the "American System" which proclaimed that the
destiny of the United States was to incorporate the whole of
the continent within the American political system. To a
large extent this was an economic ambition. But many
Americans also believed that the proper role of the world's
greatest republic was to liberate "subject areas" such as the
Spanish and British colonies from the corrupt control of
monarchical Europe. While economic motives have always
loomed large in the history of American expansion so too
has the conviction that the "Great Experiment" in democracy is a genuinely superior form of society and government.

In the years immediately following the War of 1812 there

was general agreement both about the need for expansion and for a more permanent political settlement with Britain, the dominant maritime power in the world. Thus in 1817 the United States and Britain signed the pact known as the Rush-Bagot Agreement which grew out of the "unfinished business" of the Treaty of Ghent. This agreement provided that neither nation would ever maintain more than four small armed vessels on the Great Lakes. Although the pact did not exclude the later construction of such defensive military works as the Rideau Canal and Fort Henry in Upper Canada it did cut down the cost of naval defence for both nations and it helped to establish a tradition of settlement by negotiation rather than by war. This tradition was further developed in 1818 when the United States and Britain accepted the conclusions of the four commissions provided for by the Treaty of Ghent to settle problems of boundaries and fisheries. The 1818 agreements granted limited fishing rights to Americans in the inshore waters of Labrador, Newfoundland and Nova Scotia. They also fixed the western boundary between the United States and British North America at the forty-ninth parallel from the Lake of the Woods to the Rocky Mountains, and settled some disputed parts of the boundary line from the St. Croix River to the St. Lawrence. The Oregon country was left "free and open" to Americans and British subjects.

In the south Spain, its power declining, was unable to resist American expansionist pressure. Between 1810 and 1813 the United States occupied West Florida. In 1818 General Andrew Jackson invaded East Florida to subdue Seminole Indians who had been raiding across the border. Despite a violent Spanish protest, the Secretary of State, John Quincy Adams, persuaded President Monroe to be firm in attempting to secure East Florida. The result, after long negotiations, was the Transcontinental Treaty of 1819, by which Spain ceded Florida to the United States and withdrew her claims to Oregon and the Pacific coast north of the forty-second parallel. In return the United States relinquished its claim to the huge Spanish province of Texas.

Another indication of Spain's declining power in the Americas was the development of a movement for independence in the Spanish American colonies. Inspired by French revolutionary ideas, the Spanish colonies in America took advantage of Spain's troubles during the Napoleonic Wars and staged a series of revolts beginning in 1810. The new republics so formed immediately sought diplomatic recognition from Britain and the United States. Since one-fifth of United States external trade was already with the Latin American region, Henry Clay pressed for quick recognition in 1818, but Congress delayed doing so. By 1823, however, the scene had changed. A revolution in Spain had overthrown the Spanish monarchy and the Holy Alliance of Russia, France, Austria and Prussia had sent a French army into Spain, re-established the monarchy and was contemplating recovery of the lost Spanish American empire. Since Britain had dissociated herself from the European alliance and her commerce with Latin America was booming with the ending of Spanish imperial restrictions, there was no real danger that the Royal Navy would permit European intervention. Nevertheless, George Canning, the British Foreign Secretary, sought from the American minister to Britain, Richard Rush, a joint Anglo-American declaration against the Alliance's intervention in Latin America, adding to his proposed joint statement: "We could not see any portion [of Latin America] transferred to any other power, with indifference." John Quincy Adams believed that this was a British device to prevent the United States from acquiring areas such as Cuba or Texas in the future. Convinced that Britain would safeguard the independence of the American republics in any case, Adams thought that recognition of the republics by the United States should be accompanied by a separate American declaration against intervention. Further, he had a particular reason for wishing to assert United States' claims right across the continent to the Pacific. Russian fur-traders were active along the Pacific coast and claimed to own not only Alaska but the Pacific coast as far south as the fifty-first parallel.

In addition to these material and territorial considerations, Monroe and his Cabinet thought that the United States, on principle, should assert strong support for republican régimes. All these reasons together moved the President to include in his December 1823 address to Congress a number of statements which later became known as the Monroe Doctrine:

> The political system of the allied powers [the Holy Alliance] is essentially different . . . from that of America. . . . We owe it, therefore . . . to candour and to the amicable relations existing between the United States and those powers . . . to declare that we should consider any attempt on their part to extend their system to any portion of this hemisphere as dangerous to our peace and safety. . . . With the governments who have declared their independence and maintained it, and whose independence we have . . . acknowledged, we could not view any interposition . . . by any European power in any other light than as the manifestation of an unfriendly disposition toward the United States.

The President also asserted with obvious reference to Russia that the United States could not tolerate any new colonization in the Americas and in turn that the United States would not concern itself in wars which related only to Europe. Since American power was relatively slight, the Monroe Doctrine was little more than a pretentious and rather annoying statement in 1823. It was, however, significant for the future, a future in which the United States was to move steadily towards the position of a world power.

4

Andrew Jackson's America

ANDREW JACKSON was called many things in his time; King Veto, Andrew I, and a demagogic tyrant by his enemies; "Old Hickory," anti-monopolist and friend of the "common man" by his supporters. Jackson was an unsophisticated product of the Indian-fighting frontier, with little formal education. Born in the back country of South Carolina, he served in the Revolutionary War and then studied law and settled in Tennessee. He later represented Tennessee in Congress. He was described at this time as "a tall, lank, uncouth-looking personage, with long locks hanging over his face, and a cue down his back tied in an eel skin; his dress singular, his manners and deportment that of a rough backwoodsman." In office his native abilities seemed to grow and he appeared to take on considerable personal dignity.

Jackson began his term of office with the Southerner's traditional concern for states' rights, but he ended by greatly strengthening the power of the Presidency. He had failed in business as a land speculator, and this strengthened his belief that money should have a fixed value to prevent banks from cheating small businessmen and farmers; yet his own bank policy intensified the effects of a major depression and caused widespread misery among the common people. In spite of all his contradictions, however, "Old Hickory" stood for democracy, and in general the Age of Jackson was an age of reform.

1. POLITICAL BACKGROUND

Before Jackson's election there had been turbulent changes

in the political alignment of sections and leaders. During their long tenure of office the Republicans had become increasingly conservative. Beginning as an alliance of Southern planters, New York merchants and farmers, with small businessmen and settlers in the West, the Republicans drew increasing support from Eastern business interests, and in the end their version of economic nationalism, with its growing emphasis on government assistance to business, was challenged by the very people whose interests they had originally championed.

Rifts in the National Republican party in the early 1820's produced four "favourite sons," or regional candidates, one of whom was Jackson, to contest the Presidential election of 1824. While each was nominally a Republican, none could rightly claim to have the endorsement of the whole party. None of them secured a majority in the electoral college and the choice between Jackson and his three opponents had therefore to be decided by the House of Representatives. Henry Clay, Jackson's rival as a Western candidate, threw his support in the House to John Quincy Adams, the nominee of the Northeast, who was thus named President. It had been a very bitter struggle and when Adams immediately appointed Clay Secretary of State, Jackson's supporters cried "corrupt bargain." This charge hung over the entire Adams administration and Jackson's supporters used it to draw more people into what they were already calling the Democratic party. As the remaining National Republicans became increasingly identified with Eastern business interests, a number of their leaders deserted and joined the Jacksonian Democrats.

Jackson especially made much of the "corrupt bargain" charges against the Adams-Clay administration and managed to convey to his followers his personal bitterness at being "cheated" out of the Presidency. Stump speakers and Jacksonian editors carried the message effectively to the people. A four-year campaign of vicious vilification of the honest, if conservative, John Adams produced an overwhelming electoral victory for Jackson and the Democrats in 1828. Although the Jacksonians won few votes in New England they drew strong support in every other region of the country. The South and the West supported Jackson because he was identified with both those sections and because he was a "democrat." The middle class and artisans of the middle Atlantic states voted for him in opposition to control of the government by "aristocrats." Jackson thus succeeded in being all things to most people, and in this laid down an enduring pattern for Presidential aspirants.

Leadership changes and personal politics alone, however, do not explain the rise of the Democratic party. More important were state constitutional reforms which increased the political importance of the "common man." By the 1820's Westerners, Eastern farmers, wage-earners and small businessmen violently resented the dominant position occupied in the republic by the "aristocratic" men of wealth. Such resentment was reflected in the adoption of manhood suffrage in a large number of states. By 1825 the general adoption of white manhood suffrage had produced many changes in American politics. The need to attract support among the newly enfranchised voters of town and country led to more emotional appeals and to what the austere old families of Boston and Philadelphia called the rule of demagogues. To the working class and small farmers the franchise meant a chance to influence government more directly. They used their new power to establish the rule that party candidates should be named by elected party conventions rather than by legislative caucuses (meetings of party representatives in Congress). They also shifted the power of naming Presidential electors from the state legislatures to the qualified voters of the state.

The flurry of political reform had its counterpart in the tenor of excitement which existed in American society throughout the Jacksonian era. Experimentation in social relationships, and demands for economic reform filled the air. Groups of liberals campaigned for repeal of closed-Sunday laws, while others joined with more radical "utopians" to experiment with ideal communities in which property would be owned in common and the results of labour equally divided. An early but futile experiment in desegregation was made at a plantation in Nashoba, Tennessee, where whites and Negroes lived on terms of equality. Small organized groups of skilled workmen in the North pressed vigorously for free education, the end of imprisonment for debt, the protection of workers against irresponsible contractors, and recognition of the right to strike and bargain collectively. Writers proclaimed that American democracy was on the march in every area of life.

Symbolizing the "arrival" of the common man, or the triumph of King Mob as the anti-Jackson people called it, was the Presidential inauguration in 1829. Rather than hold a staid and formal reception, Jackson staged a wide-open party at the White House, with everybody welcome. The result was a scene of incredible confusion with costly crystal smashed and trampled into Brussels carpets, and elegant brocades ripped and stained beyond repair. Eventually the crowds were drawn out of the White House by the ingenious device of placing huge vats of spiked punch on the lawns. Respectable Washington was horrified.

2. POLICIES AND PROBLEMS

Jackson's belief in social equality and equality of opportunity led to other controversial policies, one being the expansion of what was known as the "spoils system." He dismissed a thousand of the ten thousand federal civil servants and replaced them with Democratic supporters. Previous administrations had also acted upon the assumption that "to the victor go the spoils," but they had been rather more circumspect in their methods. Jackson acted quickly and openly. Worse, he defended the system, calling it "rotation in office," and declaring that it was necessary in a democratic country. Like contemporary advocates of complete democracy in England, he argued that this "reform" would prevent any group from developing a vested interest in office. Jackson's supporters argued that while their wealthy opponents, who came to be known as Whigs, could reward their election workers in other ways, the Democrats could only offer the rewards of public office. Jackson's statement in praise of the system also reveals a striking difference between the complex government of today and that of his time:

> The duties of all public offices are, or at least admit of being made, so plain and simple that men of intelligence can readily qualify themselves for their performance; and I cannot but believe that more is lost by the long continuance of men in office than is generally to be gained by their experience. . . . In a country where offices are created solely for the benefit of the people, no one man has any more intrinsic right to official station than another. Offices were not established to give support to particular men at the public expense. No individual wrong is, therefore, done by removal, since neither appointment to, nor continuance in, office is a matter of right.

Jackson regarded himself as the tribune of the people and did not hesitate to use the executive power with vigour if he thought special interests inside or outside Congress were ignoring the general welfare. In his two terms he vetoed more legislation than had all his predecessors together—hence the nickname, King Veto. His concern for the general welfare, however, did not extend to the welfare of the Indians. He gave full support to the policy of forcing all Indians to move beyond the Mississippi. When the Cherokees and Seminoles presented evidence in the Supreme Court that the state of Georgia was treating them with extreme injustice, including corruption, force and fraudulent treaties, the President refused to order troops to support the court order restraining the state in its Indian policy. "Chief Justice Marshall has made his decision," Jackson declared, "let him enforce it!" Land-hungry Westerners were overjoyed by this open flaunting of the executive over the judicial power.

In other ways Jackson showed his nationalism both negatively and positively. In May 1830 he vetoed a bill to provide federal aid in the construction of an important road from Maysville to Lexington in Kentucky. He argued that since the road would be entirely within one state it did not qualify for federal funds. This negative use of the executive power pleased the people of New York, Pennsylvania and other Eastern states who had financed most of their own transportation routes. On other occasions, Jackson showed less concern both for states' rights and for economical government and, with positive use of executive influence, secured more funds for internal improvements than had his conservative predecessor, Adams.

Such issues caused a growing turmoil inside the Jackson cabinet, in Congress, and in the nation. The political and social changes which had brought Jackson to the White House were also increasing the suspicion and rivalry among the geographic sections of the republic. While Southerners were delighted to have a man from Tennessee in the Presidency, they were also alarmed by the growing influence of the North in Congress. In particular they feared the steady increase in the tariff. In 1816 the South had approved a protective tariff, but the years had shown that such protection not only failed to foster Southern industry, but forced Southerners to pay more for manufactured goods. When the tariff was raised once again in 1828, the South Carolina legislature approved a document known as the South Carolina Exposition and Protest which maintained that the 1828 tariff was unconstitutional because it had for its purpose not the raising of revenue, but the protection of one section of the country at the expense of another. The anonymous author of the Exposition was John C. Calhoun, then Vice-President of the United States. Sensing that the South could never again out-vote the North in Congress, Calhoun advocated the Doctrine of Nullification, which reiterated the "compact theory" of the Virginia and Kentucky Resolves, but also went much further. If a state believed that the compact had been broken by an act of the federal government, announced Calhoun, a state convention could declare such act to be null and void within its borders. South Carolina's

Doctrine of Nullification plainly spelled trouble for the future.

Conservative New Englanders such as John Quincy Adams and Daniel Webster, Senator for Massachusetts, whose followers were coming to be known as Whigs, also expressed sectional grievances. Above all they feared a too rapid western expansion both because it might involve heavy federal expenditures and because Westerners tended to support Democrats who proposed lowering the price of one dollar and twenty-five cents an acre for public lands. Whigs favoured sale of western public lands at reasonable prices and distribution of the resulting funds to the states. Such a policy was designed to slow down emigration from the East and thus, by retaining a plentiful labour supply, to keep wages low in Eastern towns; also, by distributing the proceeds to the states the federal treasury would not accumulate so much money from land sales. This, in turn, would strengthen Whig arguments for high tariffs as a source of federal revenues.

Southern leaders detected political possibilities in the reluctance of the East to grant Western demands for cheap public lands. The people of the Southeast were suffering hard times. Their soil was exhausted from prodigal use and they had to pay tariff-inflated prices for imported British manufactures. Calhoun and other Southerners hoped to align the South and the West politically against the North and with this alliance pull down the obnoxious tariff wall.

Out of this sectional friction came one of the greatest debates in American history. In January, 1830 Senator Robert Hayne of South Carolina delivered a speech charging that Eastern Senators were working to keep both tariff and land prices high in order to discourage the working class from westward migration. He was answered the following day by Daniel Webster. In flowery but powerful oratory the Massachusetts Senator denounced Hayne as threatening nullification and secession. He called upon the Senate to rally to the Union, with all that was implied by obedience to federal law, including tariff law. With his eyes fixed steadily on John C. Calhoun who, as Vice-President, presided in the Senate, Daniel Webster stated, during the Webster-Hayne debate:

> When my eyes shall be turned to behold for the last time the sun in heaven, may I not see him shining on the broken and dishonoured fragments of a once glorious Union: on States dissevered, discordant, belligerent; on a land rent with civil feuds, or drenched, it may be, in fraternal blood! Let their last feeble and lingering glance rather behold the glorious ensign of the republic, now known and honoured throughout the earth, still full high advanced, its arms and trophies streaming in their original lustre, not a stripe erased or polluted, not a single star obscured, bearing for its motto no such miserable interrogatory as "What is all this worth?" nor those other words of delusion and folly, "Liberty first and Union afterwards"; but everywhere, spread all over in characters of living light, blazing on all its ample folds, as they float over the sea and over the land, and in every wind under the whole heavens, that other sentiment, dear to every true American hear, "Liberty *and* Union, now and forever, one and inseparable."

Inside Jackson's cabinet the conflict of sectional opinion was further complicated by personal animosity, particularly between Jackson and Calhoun. In 1831 the President reorganized his administration, bringing Calhoun's influence to an end, and shortly thereafter Calhoun resigned as Vice-President. He was immediately elected to the Senate to represent South Carolina and lead the growing Southern resistance to Jackson's leadership. With the passage of another high tariff law in 1832 South Carolina was convinced that protection had become a permanent feature of American policy; the state accordingly decided to experiment with the Doctrine of Nullification.

Following the procedure suggested by the Exposition and Protest in 1828, a special state convention declared that the tariff law of 1832 and all other protective legislation were null and void in South Carolina. It forbade federal and state officers to collect duties in the state. The convention showed its teeth by threatening secession from the Union should the federal government try "to reduce this State to obedience" by force. Faced with actual nullification, Jackson acted decisively. He announced publicly that the State Ordinance was "incompatible with the existence of the Union" and privately referred to its promoters as "wicked demagogues" who deserved the gallows. The Congress passed a Force Act authorizing the President to use the army and navy to uphold federal law, and Jackson dispatched warships to Charleston harbour, artillery units to Fort Moultrie, and ordered troops to be ready for service.

In 1833 a compromise solution averted the immediate danger of civil war. A compromise tariff was arranged by Henry Clay and John Calhoun, who wished to avoid armed conflict, which provided that over a ten-year period all customs duties would be substantially lowered. Conflict was avoided, both sides declared victory, and South Carolina got in the last word by nullifying the Force Act. The split in the nation, however, was deepening.

In addition to the nullification struggle Jackson launched open war against the Bank of the United States. Under the management of Nicholas Biddle of Philadelphia the Bank had become a careful regulator of credit and the value of money. By granting or refusing loans to smaller, independent banks, the Bank of the United States controlled the amount of loans and credit that could be extended to businessmen. Throughout the nation, dozens of state-chartered bank owners and small businessmen, looking for easier credit, resented the power of the National Bank. Small bankers and businessmen charged that the Bank was a privileged Eastern monopoly because while one-fifth of its stock was owned by the government, the rest was owned by private Eastern investors. They asserted that the profit on its loans, made mostly in the South and West, went to enrich the Eastern bankers and those Europeans who owned some of its shares. What the Bank's opponents sought was a loose banking system under which they could gamble in land and money values without regard for the actual welfare of the farmer or worker.

Sensing in the rising Democratic criticism of the Bank an issue on which Jackson might be defeated in the 1832 election, Henry Clay induced Nicholas Biddle to apply for renewal of the Bank's charter, although the existing charter would not expire until 1836. This was a calculated gamble which proved to be a major political blunder. When the Bank Bill passed both Houses of Congress, Jackson at once vetoed it and accompanied his veto with a strongly-worded summary of all the arguments against "the Monster," as the Bank was sometimes nicknamed:

> Distinctions in society will always exist under every just government. . . . But when the laws undertake to add to these natural and just advantages artificial distinctions, to grant titles, gratuities and exclusive privileges, to make the rich richer and the potent more powerful, the humble members of the society—the farmers, mechanics and labourers—who have neither the time nor the means of securing like favours for themselves, have a right to complain of the injustice of their government.

Biddle and Clay so misread popular feeling that they actually reprinted the veto message and used it as part of their own election campaign in 1832. The message, however, inspired fears among frontiersmen, Eastern workers and small businessmen, and actually helped Jackson to be relected with a handsome majority.

In turn, Jackson committed a grave error. He decided to kill "the Monster" without waiting for its natural death in 1836, and wrote: "Until I can strangle the hydra of corruption, the Bank, I will not shrink from my duty." He instructed Roger B. Taney, his Secretary of the Treasurery, to withdraw all government deposits from the Bank of the United States and to distribute them among a large number of state banks, which were quickly dubbed "pet banks." This curtailed the ability of the Bank of the United States to control credit. Without the restraining power of the Bank of the

United States, local banks expanded their credit and loans. Speculative fever produced a boom in land sales and other "investments." In 1836, western land sales were ten times greater than the average of the preceding ten years. As bank notes became less stable in value, even the Jacksonians began to worry and in 1836 Jackson issued a Specie Circular which required government land offices to accept only gold or silver in their sales. Since local banks had issued much more paper money than they could redeem in specie, credit collapsed at once, and state bank notes fell sharply in value. Thus the prosperity of Jackson's second term was pricked, and soon after "Old Hickory" left office in 1837 the country was deep in depression.

3. DECLINE OF THE DEMOCRATS

Yet Jackson was at the peak of his popularity in 1836 and was able to name Martin Van Buren as his successor. The Democratic convention confirmed his decision and the electorate endorsed it in November. But Van Buren soon aroused widespread opposition. Suave, elegant, and an ardent lover of fashionable horse-racing, he lacked the common touch of his rough-hewn predecessor. Within a short time there were accusations that Van Buren had transformed the White House into a veritable Versailles with extravagent silver decorations and gold service for the table. Stories of the Democratic President delicately sipping champagne from the dainty shoe of a female guest did little to increase his popularity.

But the President's personal unpopularity was only one reason for the declining fortunes of the Democrats. More important was the onset of world-wide depression in 1837, which struck the United States with particular severity. American banks had borrowed heavily from British banks to finance the economic expansion of the 1830's. Faced with financial ruin, the British banks began to recall their loans from American banks. Without credit factories shut down, unemployment soared, and many workers suffered semi-starvation. Thousands of farmers, unable to meet interest payments, lost their lands as banks foreclosed on mortgages. For three years America looked little like the land of opportunity. Bread riots broke out in New York City, and political agitation reached a fever pitch. For these grave national ills Van Buren had no effective remedy.

Under the circumstances, the new Whig party easily won the election of 1840. The Whigs astutely refrained from producing a platform, contenting themselves with blaming the depression on the Democrats. In choosing a Presidential candidate the Whigs ignored Henry Clay who, despite his brilliance, had made too many enemies, and selected a political unknown, General William Henry Harrison. The "victor" in the indecisive battle of Tippecanoe, Harrison would appeal to the frontier, while Vice-Presidential candidate John Tyler of Virginia would attract Southern states' righters. The Whigs organized hundreds of torchlite processions highlighted by floats bearing model log cabins to symbolize Harrison's humble birth as opposed to Van Buren's "aristocracy." Prominent in the processions were kegs of hard cider, whose purpose was more practical than symbolic. Slogans such as "Tippecanoe and Tyler too," or "Harrison, two dollars a day and roast beef" replaced more serious campaigning. Such appeals proved irresistible and the conservative Whig party swept the country.

Inauguration day, 1841, was so cold and wet that the new President caught pneumonia. Within five weeks he was dead and the Virginian, Tyler, was President. Almost at once the Whig party split as the Southern President vetoed two bills pressed by Northern Whigs to recharter a Bank of the United States, and strongly opposed bills to increase the tariff. The followers of Henry Clay resigned from the Cabinet and were replaced by Tyler-men. Yet in spite of these divisions the country resumed its extraordinary industrial and agricultural expansion as the Age of Jackson gave way to that of the industrial revolution.

5

America and the Industrial Revolution

THE SPLIT in the Whig party revealed the growing strain placed upon national institutions by the basic economic and social differences among the three major sections of the United States. The Northeast passed through an industrial revolution which transformed it into an urban industrial society. The South, also prosperous and expanding, retained its agricultural base in a cotton economy. The Northwest, like the South, was agricultural, but it developed an economy radically different from the Southern plantation economy. Not only were the products of the two sections different, but the independent farmer of Northwest did not need and had no sympathy for the South's slave system. Thus, while all parts of the American economy expanded in the 1840's, this growth intensified rather than reduced the sectional differences within the nation. In politics the basic conflict was between Northeast and Southeast, each of which hoped to establish an alliance with, or control over, the expanding trans-Allegheny West. During the 'forties the North gradually won out in this competition because the canals and railways constructed by Northern finance bound the West economically and politically to the Northeast. As this development progressed, the South became more fearful of losing its control of the federal government and more insistent upon protecting its rights and maintaining the slave system.

Perhaps the most striking difference between North and South in the 1840's lay in the social organization of the two sections. The South was a rigidly structured society with plantation masters at the top of a social pyramid which broadened down through small farmers, poor whites and, at the bottom, Negro slaves. Classes in Northern society were much more fluid. Although there were striking economic distinctions between the rich mill-owner and the poverty-striken immigrant labourer, the spirit of Northern society was egalitarian. European visitors to the United States often saw the combination of the egalitarian and commercial spirit as the most pronounced characteristic of society in the Northeastern states.

1. THE RISE OF INDUSTRIALISM

The period was marked by revolutionary changes in farming and industry that would one day transform the United States into the most powerful nation in the world. Like the earlier political revolution, the basic patterns of the industrial revolution in the Northeastern states were imported from Britain. One incident may symbolize this relationship. An English textile worker named Samuel Slater accepted the offer of Moses Brown, a wealthy Rhode Island merchant, to smuggle to the United States the plan of an English factory loom, in spite of laws forbidding emigration of Britain's skilled factory workers, and so became the father of the American factory system.

Factory production of textiles expanded rapidly in New England during and after the War of 1812. By the 1830's there were textile factories on nearly every stream in the region. In 1846, the sewing machine invented by Howe revolutionized the making of shoes, clothing and leather articles. They, too, could now be made most profitably in factories rather than home workshops. The resulting expansion of the Eastern factory system meant markets for the growing stream of raw materials—wool, timber, coal, iron—flowing back from the new West. By 1850, with the development of steam power and the discovery of new midwestern coal and iron deposits, the middle states were beginning to catch up with the East in factory growth. And everywhere in the North the cities and towns grew like mushrooms.

The factory system required better forms of business and financial organization. Since individual businessmen usually lacked sufficient capital to establish factories, organizers formed an increasing number of public companies and corporations to bring together investors who bought shares in the enterprises. The new type of business organization produced a distinct capitalist class. It also meant changes in the life of the working class. Employees began to have fewer contacts with the factory managers, who in turn simply carried out the decisions of remote owners and stockholders. With the increasing use of the principle of "limited liability" whereby stockholders were responsible for company debts only up to the value of their stock, businessmen felt secure in investing widely in a variety of industrial undertakings. The limited company with large numbers of stockholders also made it possible for small groups of men, in combination, to control several companies while actually owning only a fraction of the total stock. Such groups were the forerunners of the huge trusts that have come to dominate North American business in our own day.

Impersonal industrial relations of this kind seemed to intensify the investors' itch for profits. The result was the lengthening of the work day, the decline of real wages, the growth of child labour, and the spread of slums in many Northern cities. The United States, in short, reproduced many of the same evils which attended the industrial revolution in England. During the 1840's there were protests against these conditions but they were usually futile. Workers in some highly skilled trades managed to form unions, which conducted several long and bitter strikes in the 1850's. But the mass of industrial workers had no unions, and the employees who tried to organize soon found themselves unemployed. The courts and middle-class opinion strongly supported the employers in their suppression of attempts to unionize. In 1815 Judge Roberts in Pittsburgh had handed down a typical decision. Roberts refused to recognize the legality of labour unions and declared that any organization of labour was a conspiracy, a threat to both employers and employees. In 1842, however, in the case of *Commonwealth versus Hunt,* the Massachusetts Supreme Court declared that while trade unionism might diminish an employer's profits, it might also be "highly meritorious and public spirited." This decision entertained the possibility of legality for trade unions, but it had very little effect at this time, for most courts continued to decide in favour of employers. In such circumstances was the urban wealth of the North forged.

The social changes are perhaps best described by novelists. Charles Dickens' Martin Chuzzlewit, disembarking in New York from the packet-ship *The Screw*, recorded the first sights and sounds:

> "Here's this morning's *New York Sewer!*" cried one newsboy. "Here's this morning's *New York Stabber!* Here's the *New York Family Spy! . . .* Here's full particulars of the patriotic loco-foco meeting yesterday, in which the Whigs was so chewed up; and the last Alabama gouging case . . . and a full account of the Ball at Mrs. White's last night, where all the beauty and fashion of New York was assembled; with the *Sewer's* own particulars of the private lives of all the ladies that was there!"

America had become a brash, unsophisticated and commercial society whose values were assessed mainly in commercial terms. The "loco-foco" meeting reported by the *New York Peeper* was a meeting of working men to protest against their poverty and miserable working conditions. Conversely, Mrs. White's ball indicated the growth of a social hierarchy based upon the wealth accumulated by Eastern merchants and bankers.

Industrial growth was accompanied by the spread of railways to link the markets of North and West. Railways used the corporate form of organization and soon became the chief means of transportation. For some time after the fourteen-mile Baltimore and Ohio Railway opened in 1830, however, the lower costs of water transport enabled canals to compete effectively with railways. Passengers on the early woodburning trains saw other advantages in canal or sea travel. On the Albany and Schenectady Railway:

> They used dry pitch for fuel, and there being no smoke or spark catcher to the chimney or smoke stack, a volume of black smoke strongly impregnated with sparks, coals and cinders came pouring back the whole length of the train. Each of the passengers who had an umbrella raised it as a protection against the smoke and fire. They were found to be but momentary protection, for I think in the first mile the last umbrella went overboard, all having their covers burnt off from the frames, when a general mêlée took place among the deck passengers, each whipping his neighbour to put out the fire.

But with such improvements as iron rails, covered passenger and freight cars, and standard gauges, the railways were soon carrying the great bulk both of freight and passengers. By 1860 there were 30,000 miles of track, much of which was interconnected for through freight. Governments assumed much of the financial risk involved in building the American railway network. States made loans to railway companies, bought equipment for them and guaranteed their bonds. The federal government gave them free grants of land. However, promoters and construction companies, often controlled by American or British bankers, retained the profits from building and operating the railways. Thus the railways, too, played a part in the transformation of the industrial and corporation pattern that was sharply changing the class structure of the United States.

There were comparable advances in other forms of transportation and communication. Within six years of the building of Samuel Morse's first telegraph line in Maryland in 1844, the major American cities could communicate by wire. By 1860 all cities east of the Rockies were linked by telegraph, and in 1861 the network was extended to San Francisco. American shipbuilding reached its peak in the 1850's when the New England clipper ships were the swiftest sailing-ships afloat. Although Britain's development of propeller-driven steamers with iron hulls established British

95

supremacy in ocean transport, American vessels plied a vigorous trade in the world's ports. And it was the American Commodore Matthew Perry who in 1854 first secured a treaty from Japan opening Japanese trade to Americans.

The opportunities presented by American industrial expansion attracted not only European capital but a steady stream of eager immigrants. In 1840 the United States population stood at seventeen million; by 1860 it was thirty-one million because of immigration and a high birth-rate. The United States was also moving toward urbanization. In 1840 one-twelfth of the people lived in cities of eight thousand or more; by 1860 the percentage of urban dwellers had almost doubled. At the same time the United States was becoming a more continental nation; by 1850 nearly fifty per cent of all Americans lived west of the Appalachian Mountains.

Most immigrants in the first half of the nineteenth century came from the United Kingdom and northwestern Europe. The majority of them found work in factories or on railways, canals or farms where they provided much of the labour required for America's economic expansion. Although Americans generally liked to think of their nation as a refuge for oppressed Europeans, thousands of native-born citizens deeply resented the influx of immigrants. Eastern workers feared that the abundance of cheap labour would result in lower wages. Conservative Whigs deplored the tendency of immigrants to vote for the Democrats, particularly in the big cities where Democratic political machines like New York's Tammany Hall often found jobs for the newcomers. Protestants were distressed because many of the Irish and German immigrants were Roman Catholic. The native-born expressed their opposition to immigration by emphasizing their "Americanism" and by forming associations designed to prevent Roman Catholics and foreigners from holding public office. In 1845 agitation of this kind culminated in the formation of the Native America party whose platform called for sweeping changes in the naturalization laws. The party was later referred to as the Know-Nothing party because its members were sworn to secrecy about its purposes and answered all questions with a curt "I know nothing."

Between 1825 and 1850 new methods and inventions made farming more efficient and more profitable. Wooden ploughs gave way to metal ones, and in the 1830's McCormick's mechanical reaper took much of the backbreaking labour out of harvesting. New interest in livestock breeding, crop rotation, and fertilizing the soil, increased productivity just as vast new farming areas were coming under cultivation. Much of the produce from the farms of the old Northwest, especially pork and wheat flour, found a market in the one-crop areas of the South. This commerce was largely carried on the Ohio and Mississippi river systems and created an economic bond between the South and the West. In politics this intersectional commerce often led Southerners and Westerners into an alliance to protect their mutual interests, especially with respect to the tariff which both farm sections wished to keep low.

2. THE GROWTH OF SECTIONALISM

Northern leaders were very much aware of the importance of sectional economic interests. One of their main concerns in building canals and then railways was to establish closer economic ties by providing easy export routes for Western farmers into the Northeast. In what amounted to a race between Northeast and Southeast for economic control of the West, the Northeast had several important advantages. Its financial institutions were stronger and it had more business-men who were interested in railways both as investment opportunities and as marketing systems. Also, while the South purchased considerable quantities of Western farm produce, the Northeast was rapidly becoming the commercial centre for shipping Western grain and flour to transatlantic markets. As Western grain production increased, so did the import-ance to the West of Northern railways, commercial services and shipping lines. Moreover, it was from Northern manu-facturers and importers that Westerners bought the equip-ment necessary to develop their thriving farm economy.

Helping to cement the economic bond between the Northeast and the West was an increasingly tense conflict between Western farmers and Southern planters over the question of land settlement in the West. The farmers, frequently supported by Northeastern factory workers and newspaper editors, demanded a policy of free land grants to anyone who would undertake to establish a homestead in the West. Southerners were bitterly opposed to such a policy, fearing that it would simply encourage the flow of small "free" farmers to the Mississippi valley and thus impede the spread of the Southern plantation economy which was based on slave labour. Behind their fears lay a complex pattern of social and economic facts.

While King Factory established his sway in the North, King Cotton held triumphant court in the South. Eli Whitney's cotton gin had ensured the expansion of cotton culture into Virginia, North Carolina and Tennessee. By 1840 the Southern states were producing seven-eighths of the world's supply of cotton, and cotton exports accounted for fifty-one per cent of the value of the total American export trade. As cotton planters relentlessly moved across the Deep South, through Georgia, Alabama and Mississippi, their demand for slaves, as well as for new lands, became voracious. In the 1840's and '50's Southern prosperity was augmented by bumper crops of tobacco, hemp, sugar and indigo. Producers of these commodities gave full support to the claims of the Cotton Kingdom for a generous share in westward expansion.

Although the South provided considerably more than half the total exports of the United States and was thus extremely important to the nation's economic life, its social structure, politics and customs were so different from those of the other sections as to make it almost a nation within a nation. Southerners despised the way of life that was developing in the North almost as much as did the English travellers who visited the United States in these years. Claiming to be democratic, the South really reserved political and social leadership to an aristocracy of the great planters. Some planters revelled in a romantic dream in which they saw themselves recreating an almost medieval society where the aristocratic values of chivalry, military valour and leadership would live again. Favourite reading for the Southern aristocrat, sitting with a mint julep under his white-pillared portico, was Sir Walter Scott.

But such romantic dreaming could be enjoyed only by a few. The social structure in the South was as sharply divided as in the North. There were about seventeen hundred planters who owned over one hundred slaves each. Ten times as many, however, owned less than half a dozen. And of the total population of seven million, six million whites belonged to non-slaveholding families. Many of these "poor whites" lived on small farms and dreamed of the day when they could enlarge their holdings and buy slaves. Others were simply degraded hangers-on of the plantation system. Yet virtually all of the lower-class whites supported the institution of slavery, hoping either to become slave-owners or fearful that emancipation of the Negro would depress their own social and economic position.

Southerners believed that slavery was essential to the Cotton Kingdom. Although importation of slaves from Africa had been legally ended in 1808 under the Constitution, many were smuggled in after that date, and in some states slave-breeding became a business in itself. Competition in the slave market forced the price of the first-class field worker up to eighteen hundred dollars, a large sum in the early nineteenth century. By 1860 there were four million Negro slaves in the South, representing an immense capital investment. To keep the slaves "in their place" the Southern whites constructed a complex system of laws forbidding anyone to teach Negroes to read and write or for whites and Negroes to intermarry. Planters encouraged their slaves to attend Negro religious services on the plantations where all teaching was focused on the rewards of the after-life. Stringent punishment was meted out to anyone assisting an escaped slave. Although many Southerners must have been secretly conscience-stricken if they reflected upon the glowing words of the Declaration of Independence, "all men are created equal," they felt obliged in public to defend their "peculiar institution" of slavery. Southern slaves, they declared, with some justification, were better cared for than Northern factory workers. The slave huts on the great plantations were scarcely luxurious, but the Negro knew that his master would look after him in sickness and old age, and many Negroes appeared happy under the system. On the other hand, no Negro family was secure from the possibility of being broken up by the sale of one or more of its members. The result of slave trading was graphically described in a letter written by a woman slave in 1852:

> Dear Husband: I write you a letter to let you know my distress. My master has sold Albert to a trader on Monday court day and myself and other child is for sale also and I want you to let [me] hear from you very soon before next cort [sic] if you can. . . . I don't want a trader to get me. . . . I am quite heartsick.

As the soil in the Southeast became exhausted and many planters moved to the rich black soil of the Gulf states more and more slaves were "sold down the river" to overseers who frequently manacled the unfortunate Negroes in gangs as they marched to the fields. Furthermore, the slave system encouraged immorality by making light of marriage and by brutally corrupting white owners who came to accept whipping and branding without personal qualms.

With more and more deeply etched distinctions between the Cotton Kingdom and the North, sectionalism became an increasingly perilous feature of the American political scene. While many Northerners considered the South to be a morally decadent society the "slavocracy" in these years was by no means lethargic. Enjoying highly disciplined political leadership in its race with the North for control of the West, the South also maintained a very strong position in the total economic life of the nation. Perhaps the chief competitive failures of the Cotton Kingdom were its refusal to diversify its farming, and its reluctance to invest in industrial development, commercial services, or shipping. As a result the planters not only saw more and more of their profits eaten up by Northerners and Europeans, but also became increasingly dependent on the cotton economy.

3. CULTURAL DEVELOPMENT

While this period of unprecedented growth produced tension and conflict between sections and classes within the nation, it also produced a vigorous American literature. American writing in this period had its roots in England, but it was influenced by American problems and had a distinctive American flavour. James Fenimore Cooper, Edgar Allen Poe and Washington Irving were deeply romantic in feeling, and wrote about American subjects, but frequently in a European style and with European audiences in mind. Poe, in particular, castigated Americans for their provincialism and often experimented with novel rhythms and strange themes in his poetry and short stories. Cooper celebrated in popular style the romance of the frontier, while Walt Whitman wrote boisterously of the strident American democracy. Herman Melville's great novel *Moby Dick* grew out of an essentially American experience. Some writers like James Russell Lowell reflected the nationalist feeling of expansion, while others like Emerson and Thoreau were highly critical of the loss of individuality in the urban, democratic developments of their day.

The growth of democracy also produced great changes in American journalism. The 1830's saw the beginning of such penny newspapers as the New York *Sun*, the New York *Herald* and Horace Greeley's New York *Tribune*. Although these dailies catered to the tastes of the masses, they also contained much more serious political comment and reporting than is usual today and their editors played a prominent part in American political life.

The rise of literacy which made such newspapers possible was the result of the spread of free public schooling. By 1850 most children in non-frontier areas of the North could attend public schools, although many were deprived of an education because of the necessity to work. Even in the South public education for whites advanced rapidly. As early as 1821 Massachusetts established the first public high school. There was often widespread opposition to these developments, especially by the wealthy who regarded tax-supported education as an unwarranted interference with individual rights by the government.

On this complex basis of class fears and ambitions, sectional suspicions, economic growth, beckoning opportunity and unexampled natural resources, the young American giant moved forward to gain control of its western empire. In doing so it brought the nation to the greatest crisis in its history.

6

The Failure of Compromise

THE WESTWARD course of empire in America not only provided exciting opportunities for individual Americans but
brought great questions of public policy more clearly into
focus. Would expansion be gradual and guided by patient
diplomacy or would it be urgent and forceful? Would
Northerners or Southerners control the trans-Mississippi
West? Would the "peculiar institution" of slavery move inexorably across the continent? Failure to find permanent
answers to these questions eventually precipitated the nation
into a great civil war. Historians still debate the causes of the
American Civil War. Some feel that the conflict was "irrepressible" while others blame a "blundering generation" that
failed to produce adequate leadership. Whatever its causes,
the war was a mixture of high ideals, rampant ambition, and
stark tragedy.

1. MANIFEST DESTINY AND TERRITORIAL EXPANSION

By the 1840's the American conviction that it was their
"manifest destiny" to expand across the entire North American continent was deeply rooted. A vociferous delegate
to the Democratic Convention in 1844 expressed a widespread sentiment when he exclaimed:

> Land enough—land enough! Make way, I say, for the
> young American Buffalo—he has not yet got land
> enough. . . . I tell you, we will give him Oregon for his
> summer shade, and the region of Texas as his winter
> pasture. [Applause.] Like all his race he wants salt, too.

> Well, he shall have the use of the two oceans—the mighty Pacific and the turbulent Atlantic shall be his. . . . He shall not stop his career until he slakes his thirst in the frozen ocean. [Cheers.]

Continental expansion was regarded as part of God's plan for the American Republic. The New York *Morning News* confessed: "Our own idea is that the American idea or impulse, is fit and just, in harmony with the fair and bountiful orders of nature and with the manifest designs of the Creator." Economic motives, however, were more obvious and important stimulants to expansion. Businessmen and politicians regarded the West as a market for the growing industries of the East, as a rich source of raw materials, and as a base from which to extend American commerce across the Pacific to the teeming markets of the Far East.

American continental expansion inevitably brought her into conflict with Great Britain. Yet the possession of a common language and culture and Britain's desire not to lose the splendid opportunity of investing in the United States proved stronger than the legacy of suspicion from the American Revolution and the War of 1812. Thus, despite the crisis that emerged in the 1840's it was in this period that Anglo-American friendship began, as both countries made great efforts to settle their differences amicably.

The first problem to be resolved concerned the border between New Brunswick and Maine. The boundary had not been clearly established after the American Revolution, and in 1839, rival lumbermen clashed over disputed timber rights in the Aroostook Valley. A truce was arranged, but a final settlement of the boundary was urgently needed. In 1841 Lord Ashburton was sent to the United States to negotiate a settlement with Daniel Webster, the Secretary of State. Lord Ashburton was a member of the Baring family which controlled a large British financial house, with very substantial sums invested both in the United States and in British North America, and war did not appeal to him as a method of settlement. Eventually, the Webster-Ashburton Treaty of 1842 granted the United States most of its boundary claims.

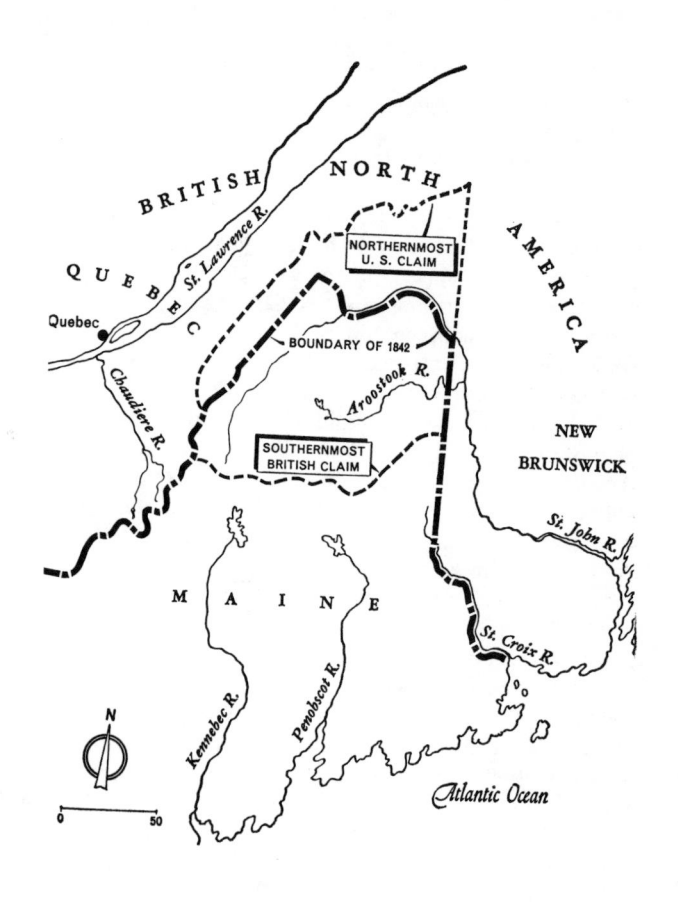

THE MAINE-NEW BRUNSWICK BORDER DISPUTE

Britain's concession was clearly dictated by Imperial interests rather than by those of the British North American colonies. Yet the Treaty was widely criticized in the United States, and many expansionist Democrats felt that Webster had been bought by an Anglo-American "money interest" and a smooth-talking British diplomat.

Far more troublesome and important than the Maine-New Brunswick boundary was the problem of Texas. The United States had renounced its claim to Texas in the treaty of 1819 but during the 1820's twenty thousand settlers with two thousand slaves from the Southern United States moved into Texas, with the approval of the Mexican government. The Mexicans, however, soon realized that the new population of Texas would encourage American annexationism. In 1836 when General Santa Anna's government attempted to curb further immigration and to enforce Mexican tariff and anti-slavery laws, the Americans in Texas revolted. Led by experienced Indian fighters from the southern frontier, the Americans fought desperately against the Mexican forces led by Santa Anna. The most famous battle was at the Alamo Mission in San Antonio where one hundred and eighty-five Americans were killed, including such folk-heroes as Davy Crockett and James Bowie. After several further battles, Americans under General Sam Houston captured Santa Anna in a surprise attack and forced from him a treaty conceding the independence of Texas. In 1837, just before he left office, Andrew Jackson issued diplomatic recognition to Texas as an independent republic.

Recognition was the first step necessary to securing entry into the American Union. The great majority of Texans favoured annexation to the Union but in the United States many people had doubts. Anti-slavery elements were strongly opposed, because they feared that the South wanted Texas admitted so that it could create several new slave states and thus control the Senate. The mood of the country, however, was so clearly expansionist that the outcome was predictable. After her brief career as the Lone Star Republic, Texas entered the Union in December 1845. Annexation, however, had been complicated by demands from the North for the outright acquisition of Oregon, whose ownership had been left undetermined by the Convention of 1818, to balance the annexation of Texas. The problems of both Texas and Oregon were central to the Presidential election campaign of 1844.

The Whigs nominated, as their candidate for President, Henry Clay who sought to remove the Texas issue from politics, while the Democrats nominated James K. Polk, an uninhibited expansionist. In a hard-fought election, Polk and the Democrats argued vigorously for expansion and the campaign gave rise to the cry "fifty-four forty or fight," implying that if Britain did not concede all of the Oregon country up to the southern border of Alaska to the United States there would be war. To appease Northern opponents of Texas annexation, the Polk Democrats successfully associated it with general expansion to the Pacific, calling for "the reoccupation of Oregon and the reannexation of Texas." Polk won the election by a slim margin. A colourless Tennessee politician of little imagination, Polk was nevertheless tenacious and hard-working, and after his election he pressed his expansionist plans with no little skill.

The extreme expansionists thought they saw, in Polk's inaugural address, evidence that he intended to insist on all of Oregon up to 54° 40′. Others, however, began to suspect that he was entertaining the thought of compromise. The British ambassador, within a few weeks of Polk's inauguration, reported the latter impression to London, adding:

> Fortunately for the country, the party in the Senate who think with the extremists is so insignificant . . . that Mr. Polk need have no fear that he will not be supported amply, both in and out of the Senate, if he should wisely determine to adopt a moderate and pacific course of policy. . . .

Recognizing the dangers of openly breaking with Britain at the same time as he courted war with Mexico, Polk decided to settle the Oregon question first.

107

Before 1830, Oregon had been of interest mainly to fur-traders, but in the following two decades, hundreds of settlers had made their way to it by wagon-train thereby blazing the Oregon Trail. Despite the American claims of effective occupation, British historical claims to the country, as well as the presence of the Hudson's Bay Company in it, gave England the stronger case. Thus, in the negotiations to end the joint British-American occupation, Polk was willing to compromise. However, in abandoning his outrageous claim to the whole of Oregon, he gave up much less than did the British who were anxious for peace between Britain and the United States. The treaty of 1846 extended the boundary between British North America and the United States westward from the Rockies along the forty-ninth parallel to Puget Sound, and thence through the Straits of Juan de Fuca to the ocean. Although disappointed Northern Democrats protested vehemently, most Americans seemed happy in the knowledge that they had peacefully gained the richest part of the Columbia valley and valuable Pacific coast harbours.

While the Oregon settlement was being arranged, Polk prepared to acquire the southwestern empire of Texas, New Mexico and California. In November 1845 he sent a special envoy, John Slidell, to Mexico, with an offer to purchase New Mexico and California for thirty million dollars if Mexico would recognize the American annexation of Texas. When Slidell was not even received by the Mexican government, Polk ordered General Zachary Taylor to occupy the territory between the Nueces and Rio Grande rivers, claiming that the Rio Grande was the southern boundary of Texas. The Mexicans defended the territory, and President Polk sent a message to Congress declaring that "war exists, and, notwithstanding all our efforts to avoid it, exists by the act of Mexico herself." Congress accepted this diplomatic double-talk and immediately declared war on Mexico in May 1846. The Mexican War was popular with everyone except the Northeast and anti-slavery people who saw it as another manœuvre of the Southern slaveholders to extend their territory and increase their power. Whigs such as a

Congressman named Abraham Lincoln declared that Taylor was not on American soil when the first "incident" occurred, and voted against the declaration of war.

The chief results of the widely scattered warfare were the defeat of Mexico, the Treaty of Guadeloupe-Hidalgo, 1848, and the enhancement of General Taylor's reputation as a military hero. Mexico gave up her claims to Texas and ceded the whole of New Mexico and California to the United States for fifteen million dollars. Five hundred thousand square miles were thus added to the enormous continental domain of the United States. This western empire not only contributed immense wealth and excellent commercial ports on the Pacific; it intensified the mounting suspicion between North and South.

2. EXPANSION AND SLAVERY

The election of 1848 revealed the concern felt by the major parties about the relationship of westward expansion and the slavery question. Despite their previous opposition to the war, the Whigs, hoping to capitalize on expansionist sentiment, nominated the hero of the Mexican War, General Taylor, as their candidate for President. The Democrats nominated Lewis Cass, a Michigan Senator, who ran on a platform which purposely evaded all issues. A group of disaffected Democrats put forward a third candidate, former President Van Buren. The latter group received support from many former Whigs and Democrats who called themselves Free Soilers and who believed that slavery should be kept out of the West so that the land could be taken up by free farmers. The division in Democratic ranks ensured the election of General Taylor.

The pace of events sharpened the mounting political crisis. In 1849 gold was discovered in the Sacramento Valley of California. The gold rush of '49 gave California a population of eighty thousand by the end of that year. From all over the United States, from Europe and from Latin America adventurers raced to the new Eldorado. Overland across the plains and the Rockies, through the steaming jungle of Panama or by the long, dangerous voyage around Cape Horn, came thousands in search of "easy" wealth. The Forty-Niners who poured into California in the thousands found a ramshackle capital in San Francisco. A city even then, with more than a little glamour, it also teemed with lawless adventurers from the East. These conditions produced many songs such as this:

> *Oh what was your name in the States?*
> *Was it Thompson or Johnson or Bates?*
> *Did you murder your wife,*
> *And fly for your life?*
> *Say, what was your name in the States?*

Gambling, drinking and fighting in a lawless society, the Forty-Niners nevertheless managed to produce a constitution for the territory which prohibited slavery and authorized the government, elected under its authority, to seek the admission of California to the Union.

In the face of Southern opposition to California's entry, Taylor endeavoured to emulate the vigorous executive role of Jackson. He invited California, New Mexico and Deseret (Utah), where a Mormon community had sprung up on the edge of the desert, to formulate constitutions for submission to Congress. Each of the constitutions forbade slavery. The South was furious as it saw the prospect of the free states outnumbering slave states. As Senators and Congressmen turned up in Washington armed with knives and revolvers, it became evident that only compromise could avoid civil war.

Attempts at compromise had, of course, to take account of past American experience and of changing attitudes. There had always been Americans who disapproved of slavery, but it was not until the 1820's that the abolitionist or anti-slavery forces began to gain prominence. By 1831, when William Lloyd Garrison founded an abolitionist newspaper, the abolitionist crusade began to assume major significance. Many Northerners became convinced that human bondage was an intolerable evil which denied all the principles upon which the United States had been founded. More moderate Northerners argued that Congress should at least use its authority to prohibit the expansion of slavery into the territories.

This "free soil" argument annoyed the Southerners not only because they were anxious to preserve their "peculiar institution." They were also convinced that they had to maintain power in the Senate to prevent the federal government from adopting such measures as a high tariff which would endanger their economic interests. Southern spokesmen answered Northern attacks on the slave system by arguing that it was essential to the cotton economy and denying that it was a moral evil. Such eloquent defenders of the slave system as John C. Calhoun passionately insisted that slavery was justified by scripture and by usage in history. "I hold that in the present state of civilization," he argued, "where two races of different origin, and distinguished by colour, and other physical differences, as well as intellectual, are brought together, the relation now existing in the slaveholding states between the two is, instead of an evil, a good — a positive good."

According to Southerners, moreover, slavery was an essential foundation for a democratic society and they pointed to ancient Athens to support their case. By having the menial economic and domestic tasks performed by slave labour the more intelligent, white classes were allowed the leisure to develop strong political and cultural traditions. Slavery became in these terms, a prerequisite of freedom and democracy. Finally, Southern politicians argued, Congress could not regulate slavery in the territories since the federal government was only the agent of the states in administering the territories ; in addition the Constitution actually guaranteed property and recognized slaves as property. Thus, they argued, only a *state* government could prohibit slavery. Bitterness mounted rapidly as the abolitionist campaign

111

gained impetus, flooded the South with propaganda and pressed Congress for action.

The argument reached a critical juncture in 1849 when California applied for admission as a state. A further complication was added when some Westerners, like Senator Stephen A. Douglas of Illinois, suggested that in the territories to be established in the land ceded by Mexico the inhabitants should be allowed to choose whether or not to prohibit slavery. This idea was called "popular sovereignty" or "squatter sovereignty." Southerners remained very suspicious of this proposal and suggested instead the extension of the Missouri Compromise line, 36° 30′, to the Pacific.

By late 1849 this critical issue demanded solution. Henry Clay, the seventy-three-year-old author of the Missouri Compromise and the 1833 Tariff Compromise, was now given a final opportunity to play a great role in mediating between the sections. In January 1850 he presented a series of compromise resolutions to Congress, which provided that: California was to be admitted to the Union as a free state; territorial governments of Utah and New Mexico were to be established in the rest of the Mexican cession, which could determine the status of slavery themselves; the slave trade, but not slavery, was to be abolished in the District of Columbia; Congress was to enact a stringent fugitive slave law; the Texan public debt was to be assumed by the United States to compensate Texas for giving up claims to part of New Mexico.

Debate on these proposals was bitter and prolonged. Southern extremists wanted definite congressional support of slavery in the new territories. Northern extremists, like Senators William H. Seward of New York and Charles Sumner of Massachusetts, declaring that slavery was a sin in the eyes of God, said it should be prohibited in all the territories. Despite the revulsion of even moderate Free Soilers at the proposal to tighten up the fugitive slave laws, Daniel Webster persuaded many to support the Clay formula. So ill that he had to be helped up the Capitol steps on February 5,

1850, Henry Clay delivered one of the most significant speeches of American history. Supporting the various resolutions of the 1850 Compromise, the physically exhausted statesman spoke for three hours and on the following day spoke nearly as long again. His theme was clear and to it he returned repeatedly: "Mr. President, it is passion, passion; party, party; and intemperance—that is all I dread in the adjustment of the great questions which unhappily at this time divide our distracted country." A Southern convention at Nashville, Tennessee, failed to support a proposal that the Southern states should secede from the Union, and in the end national unity was temporarily preserved.

The Compromise of 1850 saved the Union for ten years. But Calhoun's last speech in the Senate revealed how difficult those ten years would be. Dying, and unable to speak because of his perpetual coughing, Calhoun had his speech read for him to a crowded Senate. His central point was that the "great and primary cause" of the controversy was "that the equilibrium between the two sections has been destroyed." Arguing that the South was virtually denied access to the new territories, he declared that the ties that bound the states together were slowly but surely breaking. Northern opposition to slavery was splitting even the churches and political parties. Only a complete guarantee to the South of security for her institutions and of a low tariff could prevent dissolution of the Union.

3. THE FAILURE OF COMPROMISE

While the 1850 Compromise "worked," it silenced none of the forces that were opposed to it. Already, the temper of the North in its contest with the South was beginning to harden. This was seen particularly in the passage by many Northern state legislatures of the Wilmot Proviso, which was originally an amendment to a congressional act of 1846. President Polk described it in his diary:

Late in the evening of Saturday, the 8th [of August

1846], I learned that after an exciting debate in the house a bill passed that body, but with a mischievous and foolish amendment to the effect that no territory which might be acquired by treaty from Mexico should ever be a slaveholding country. What connection slavery had with making peace with Mexico is difficult to conceive.

The amendment was defeated in the Senate, but its effect remained. David Wilmot, the Pennsylvania Democrat who moved the amendment, had seen the connection between slavery and peace with Mexico, and by 1852 his "Proviso" had virtually become a political platform for Northern opponents of slavery. However, the Democratic candidate for President, Franklin Pierce, won the election of 1852 on a platform which endorsed the 1850 settlement. By that time many Whigs had left their party, either to join the Free Soil party or the Southern wing of the Democratic party, and the Whig party was close to its death.

Not all the provisions of the 1850 Compromise were honoured. In the North, mass meetings of abolitionists and Free Soilers agreed to ignore the new Fugitive Slave Law, and Northern legislatures passed "personal liberty laws" which forbade the holding of fugitive Negroes in state jails. The publication of Harriet Beecher Stowe's *Uncle Tom's Cabin* added fuel to the spreading fire of Northern anti-slavery sentiment. When Harriet Beecher Stowe was introduced to Lincoln in 1862 the President observed: "So you're the little woman who wrote the book that made this great war." Considering the book's impact upon both North and South, Lincoln's exaggeration was pardonable.

As abolitionist pressure mounted, the South became more aggressive in its own defence. With the silent approval of the New Yorker, William L. Marcy, who was Secretary of State, Southerners concocted a plan to purchase or seize Cuba as an outlet for Southern expansion. When the plan became too well known it had to be repudiated by Marcy because of the furious Northern opposition to it. Such opposition was the more outspoken because of the previous passage in 1854 of the extremely controversial Kansas-Nebraska Act.

That Act was designed to give territorial government to the vast area between the Missouri River and the Rocky Mountains. In its final form it drew a line across the region at the fortieth parallel of latitude, naming the northern section Nebraska and the southern Kansas. The provisions of the Act repudiated the 1850 Compromise by specifically repealing the Missouri Compromise of 1820. The assumption behind the Act seemed to be that Nebraska would eventually become a free state and Kansas a slave state. The principle of "popular sovereignty," introduced first in the 1850 Compromise, was employed again in the provision of the Kansas-Nebraska Act that settlers in the new territories were to be "perfectly free to form and regulate their domestic institutions in their own way."

The chief author of the Act was Stephen A. Douglas, the Little Giant of Illinois, a diminutive but powerful politician who represented expansionist railway and real estate interests of the North. A transcontinental railway supported by federal land grants was planned which would pass through Nebraska. The Southerners wanted to have a southern route, the Northerners a northern route, with Chicago as terminus. The proposed southern route from New Orleans to the Pacific had the advantage of passing through territory which was already largely settled. The Northerners were anxious to overcome this advantage by hastening settlement on the northern plains. To surmount Southern opposition to voting for a northern route, Douglas had to offer a substantial inducement, namely, repeal of the Missouri Compromise and the consequent opening of the plains to slavery. To Northerners he argued that this was only a nominal concession since, "in that climate, with its production, it is worse than folly to think of its being a slaveholding country." More important, thought Douglas, repeal of the Compromise would solve the Kansas-Nebraska problem, retain the unity of the Democratic party, and possibly hoist Douglas himself into the Presidency. But Douglas badly miscalculated the effect of the Act which was finally passed on May 25,

115

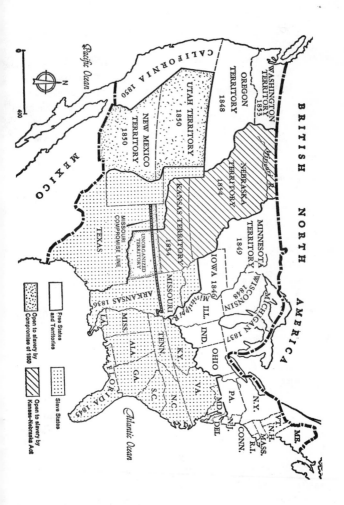

1854. The North suspected him of selling out to the slave interests and imperilling the agrarian future of the plains. The South began to suspect him of double dealing when they heard him say slavery could not survive in the new territory.

The vote in Congress on the Kansas-Nebraska Act split both the Whig and Democratic parties. In the summer of 1854, largely at the instigation of the Free Soil leaders, local conventions were held throughout the Northwest to establish a new Republican party, which held its first national convention in 1856. The Republican party expressed both Northern ambitions to control the West and the mounting Northern resentment against Southern attempts to dominate the Senate and Cabinet. Many Republicans were morally outraged by slavery and many others felt that, while the "peculiar institution" might be tolerated in the South, its advance into the West would block off that great region from settlement by free Northern farmers. A majority of Northerners believed that a strong new party was necessary in order to obtain congressional action to maintain or increase tariff protection, to keep slavery out of the West and to subsidize transcontinental railways and other internal improvements. Thus, although the Republicans were strictly a sectional party, they appealed to very many Northern Democrats who disapproved of the Kansas-Nebraska Act, most Conscience Whigs (the name given to those opposed to slavery), and all the Free Soilers.

Meanwhile, events in Kansas moved the Union closer to disintegration. Pro-slavery and anti-slavery migrants streamed into Kansas. Missourians, described as border ruffians by Northerners, poured across the border on the first election day and succeeded in fraudulently electing a pro-slavery territorial legislature. In January 1856 Free Soilers elected their own legislature and governor. Open violence soon erupted. Rifles supplied to free-state supporters through the efforts of a Brooklyn abolitionist preacher, Henry Ward Beecher, were known as "Beecher's Bibles." The *Squatter Sovereign*, a pro-slavery newspaper, said Southerners would "lynch and hang, tar, feather and drown, every white-livered

117

abolitionist who dares to pollute our soil." The attacks and counter-attacks took over two hundred lives. The area was termed Bleeding Kansas in the national press and the struggle was not finally settled until 1861, in the first year of the Civil War, when Kansas was admitted to the Union as a free state. In these same years Northern abolitionists, with some Southern sympathizers, organized the Underground Railroad to assist escaping slaves. Over 100,000 slaves valued at some $30,000,000 are supposed to have escaped to the North and to Canada. One valiant Negress, Harriet Tubman, went back many times to the South and led more than three hundred slaves to freedom along the intricate network of the "Railroad."

With Kansas a burning issue in 1856, the Democrats nominated James Buchanan of Pennsylvania rather than Stephen Douglas as their candidate for President. Although he won the election, Buchanan was too cautious, too anxious to evade rather than settle issues, to be a successful leader in a time of crisis. The deepening crisis, moreover, was emphasized when the Republican candidate took thirty-three per cent of the popular vote, all of it from states north of the Mason-Dixon line, the traditional dividing line between North and South.

Within a week of Buchanan's inauguration sectional fevers were heightened by the Supreme Court decision in the Dred Scott case. Dred Scott was a Negro slave in Missouri who had previously travelled with his owner in the free state of Illinois and in Louisiana Purchase territory which had been declared free by the Missouri Compromise. He was persuaded to sue for his liberty on the grounds that he gained his freedom by living in a free state and in a free territory. The majority decision, written by the Southerner, Chief Justice Roger B. Taney, stated that no Negro could be a citizen of the United States. In addition, Taney wrote that by the Fifth Amendment the Constitution required the federal government to protect property in all the territories. Therefore, he concluded, the Missouri Compromise was unconstitutional since it deprived masters of their property in slaves. The implication of this decision was that slavery could not be prohibited by territorial legislatures, and that it could therefore be extended indefinitely in the territories. To Northerners, this meant that Douglas' "popular sovereignty" doctrine was a sham which could not prevent the spread of slavery.

A serious financial crisis in 1857 further aroused the North. As prosperity continued to decline in 1858-59 there was serious unemployment and distress in the North. This had two significant political results. Since Southerners escaped the worst effects of the depression, they clung more stubbornly to their faith in their agricultural economy, particularly in cotton, which boomed through these years. In the North the Republican party responded to the depression by pressing for a higher protective tariff and free homesteads in the West. This platform helped to consolidate Republican strength in many Northern areas.

At this time there began to emerge from relative obscurity the towering and tragic figure of the man upon whom would be laid the responsibility for the ultimate "solution" of the sectional strife. Abraham Lincoln wrote of himself in 1858: "It may be said I am, in height, six feet four inches, nearly; lean in flesh, weighing on an average one hundred and eighty pounds; dark complexion, with coarse black hair and gray eyes." He might have added that his face was gaunt, his nose prominent, his eyes unusually deep-set, all of which suggested his somber, brooding character. He educated himself by reading the Bible, biographies, and books on history and law. As a young lawyer in Illinois, Lincoln became a Whig, with distinctly conservative attitudes to politics and society. On its formation, he became associated with the Republican party. He was elected four times to the Illinois state legislature, and served for one term in the House of Representatives at Washington. While generally popular in his own district, "Honest Abe" leapt to no one's mind as Presidential material. He liked and often told amusing stories but his most marked characteristics were those of melancholy and quietness. Beneath all this, however, lay a cool accuracy in the assessment of political problems, a chess-like approach which sometimes seemed to lack scruple.

Lincoln never believed that the Negro was equal in capacity to the white man, although he did believe that he should, by gradual emancipation from slavery, be given equal *rights*. As he saw the nation falling apart, with the slavery issue aggravating all the other points of difference, Lincoln came to believe that the fundamental issue was nothing less than maintenance of the Union itself. In 1858 he made this clear in a speech to a Republican Convention:

> In my opinion, the agitation against slavery will not cease until a crisis shall have been reached and passed. "A house divided against itself cannot stand." I believe this government cannot endure permanently half slave and half free. I do not expect the Union to be dissolved; I do not expect the house to fall; but I do expect it will cease to be divided.

At that convention the Illinois Republicans nominated Lincoln to contest the Senate seat held by the famous Democratic orator, Stephen A. Douglas. Douglas accepted Lincoln's challenge to a series of public debates. He read Lincoln's past speeches carefully and decided to pillory his opponent as the advocate of a "war of extermination." Lincoln replied that he did not propose war, but advocated constitutional means of excluding slavery from those territories where it did not already exist. During one debate at Freeport, Illinois, Lincoln asked Douglas, in the light of the Dred Scott decision: "Can the people of a United States territory, in any lawful way, against the wish of any citizen of the United States, exclude slavery from its limits prior to the formation of a state constitution?" Lincoln hoped to trap Douglas into either abandoning his popular sovereignty doctrine or repudiating the Dred Scott decision. Douglas replied with a statement that quickly became known as the Freeport Doctrine: "The people have the lawful means to exclude it or include it as they please, for the reason that slavery cannot exist a day or an hour anywhere, unless it is supported by local police regulations." The declaration gratified Democratic supporters of popular sovereignty, but it also showed Southern Democrats that Douglas did not believe that the territories were really open to slavery. Thus, while Douglas won the Senate election, he was to lose the support of more than half his party when he was nominated for President in 1860.

The Lincoln-Douglas debates boosted Lincoln's political reputation, but they did little to calm sectional feelings. The crisis deepened in October 1859 when a band of fiercely evangelical abolitionists, led by a fiery fanatic named John Brown, seized a federal arsenal at Harper's Ferry. They intended to seize weapons, retire to the Virginia mountains and from there conduct other raids to free the slaves. Undoubtedly, Brown planned to spread his operations throughout the South and free all the slaves, possibly by mass insurrection. His coup failed; he was captured, tried, and convicted of treason in a Virginia court, and hanged. Extremists in both sections seized upon the event to advance their cause. Southern "fires eaters" said Brown's raid was the product of a widespread plot in the North. Northern writers practically deified Brown: Emerson called him "the rarest of heroes, a pure idealist," while Thoreau declared ominously after the execution that Brown had become "more alive than ever he was." This idea was popularized in the song "John Brown's Body," which later became the marching song of Northern troops during the Civil War.

By the summer of 1860, with relations between North and South at low ebb, it was clear that the Democratic party was mortally divided. Its national convention which met at Charleston, South Carolina, to nominate a Presidential candidate rejected a plank endorsing slavery and its territorial extension. On this the delegates from eight Southern states withdrew from the convention, thus depriving Stephen Douglas of the two-thirds majority necessary for nomination as the party's candidate. A second convention at Baltimore nominated Douglas, but only after the Southerners had again departed. The Southern Democrats then nominated a separate candidate, John C. Breckenridge of Kentucky, on a defence-of-slavery platform. Since most of the Protestant churches and many other institutions had already broken into two sections over the issue of slavery, the disruption of national parties severed the last intersectional bond in the country.

Unlike the Democrats, the Republicans were in basic agreement as they met in Chicago to nominate their candidate and write his platform. The main planks of the platform included federal aid for a transcontinental railroad, no extension of slavery in the territories, a protective tariff and free homestead grants in the West. Each of the last three planks was a direct challenge to the Democrats. In 1857, under Southern leadership, a Democratic Congress had enacted the lowest tariff since 1816, and the same forces had blocked successive bills to provide free grants of territorial land to farmer-settlers.

Because some of the best known Republicans were either too radical in their abolitionism or too obviously the representatives of special interests, the delegates passed them by in choosing a Presidential candidate. On the third ballot the careful planning of Lincoln's convention managers paid off, and Lincoln won the nomination as the compromise candidate most acceptable to Eastern and Western Republicans. A reporter at the crucial convention observed: "There was a moment's silence . . . and as deep breaths of relief were taken there was a noise . . . like the rush of a great wind, in the van of a storm—and in another breath, the storm was there. There were thousands cheering with the energy of insanity."

The Chicago Lincoln-boosters were right in their predictions of sectional voting strength. The Republicans won every Northern state, including California and Oregon. Breckenridge won the Deep South plus Maryland and Delaware, while Douglas, with nearly as many popular votes as Lincoln, carried only Missouri. Only twenty-six thousand votes were cast for Lincoln in the entire South. The sectional cleavage appeared to be complete; Lincoln was elected President by the North and with a minority of the total votes cast.

What followed was the most disastrous "lame duck" period in American history, the period between the election of a President in November and his inauguration in March. For four months Buchanan remained President but he was unwilling to take strong action, while Lincoln did not have power until March and refused till then even to give clear recommendations to the Republicans in Congress. In these circumstances, no one exercised leadership and the nation drifted into war by what appeared on the surface to be inevitable steps.

With the announcement of Lincoln's election, Southern extremists at once declared that the South must secede from the Union. It could not, they declared, remain safe under a "Black Republican" President. Distorting the facts, these leaders vigorously spread the idea that the Republicans wished to abolish slavery everywhere in the Union and to crush the South economically. Since the Republicans controlled neither the House of Representatives nor the Senate, and possibly never would have gained such control if the South had not pursued the course it did, the logic of the Southern extremists was obscure. But this did not prevent it from being effective. Many Southerners were unable to discern the real facts, as they read and heard daily the most terrifying predictions, and saw the President-elect cartooned as a coarse baboon with the abolitionist William Lloyd Garrison coiled about his body like a serpent. They were told that the South was a nation in its own right and was economically healthier than the North which depended upon the "white slave labour" of the factory system bolstered by a tariff which strangled Southern commerce. Southerners also conjured up a vision of a Southern nation, expanding into Cuba, Mexico and even further.

As in 1832, radical Southern opinion was led by South Carolina, where a convention on December 17, 1860 unanimously passed an Ordinance of Secession from the Union. Although moderate spokesmen in the South opposed South Carolina's action, the extremists prevailed, and by February 1, 1861, Florida, Georgia, Mississippi, Alabama,

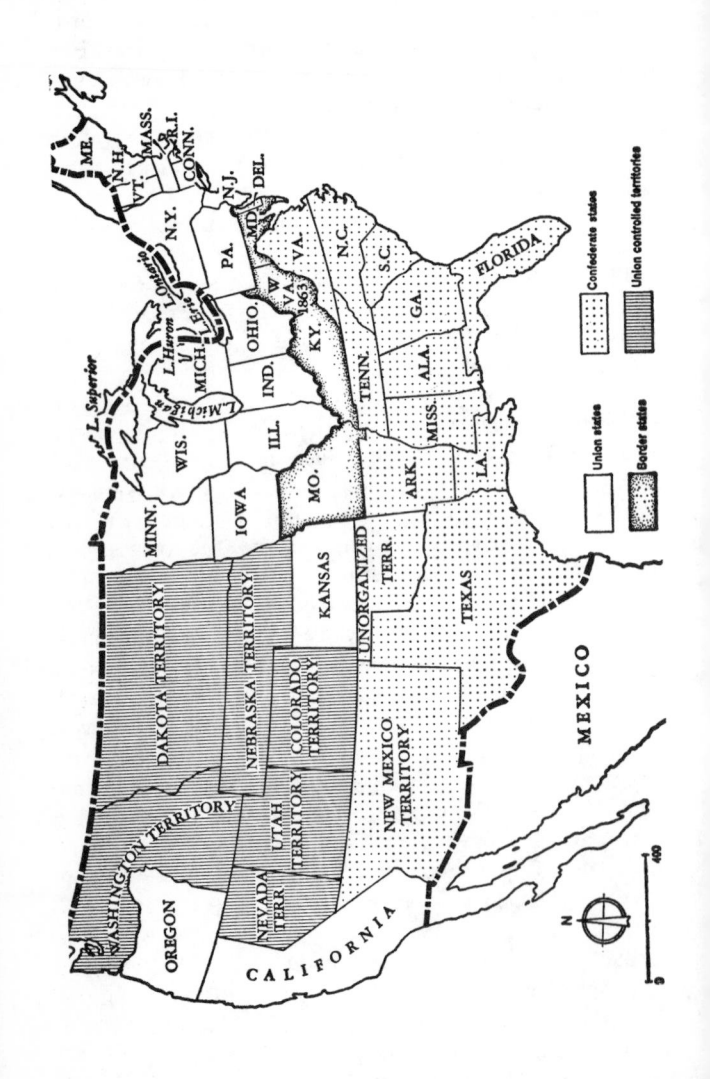

THE ALIGNMENT OF THE STATES IN 1861

Louisiana and Texas had all joined South Carolina to form the Confederate States of America. Confronted by the accomplished fact, many moderates then gave up their opposition. Jefferson Davis, Senator from Mississippi and former Secretary of War, was chosen President, and Alexander H. Stephens of Georgia, Vice-President of the Confederacy. By March 4, 1861, when Lincoln was inaugurated, a strong Southern government already existed. Many Southerners had been persuaded that secession could be accomplished peacefully, and emissaries were sent to Washington to arrange for the division of federal property in the South. Nevertheless, a substantial army was also being recruited.

In his inaugural address Lincoln was both conciliatory and firm. He promised to enforce all United States laws and to retain possession of all Union property. Hoping to influence anti-secessionist opinion in the South, he declared: "In your hands, my dissatisfied fellow-countrymen, and not in mine, is the momentous issue of civil war. The government will not assail you. You can have no conflict without being yourselves the aggressors." His opinion was not shared by all Northerners.

Many businessmen of New York and New England, particularly textile manufacturers, bankers and shippers, whose prosperity was closely connected with the cotton industry and with financing the Southern economy, believed that if the South really wanted to leave the Union it should be allowed to do so in peace. At the same time there were a number of serious attempts at compromise. The most significant was a set of resolutions proposed in the Senate by John J. Crittenden of Kentucky. These were in the form of proposed amendments to the Constitution which would ban slavery in the territories north of 36° 30′, but would establish it by law south of that line; whenever Northerners frustrated the Fugitive Slave Law, the slave owner was to be compensated; and there should be a special denial of the right of Congress ever to prohibit slavery within a state. Extremists in both sections opposed the Crittenden proposals.

While refusing to give official advice to Republicans in Congress, since he had not yet been inaugurated, Lincoln wrote to one Congressman: "Entertain no proposition for a compromise in regard to the extension of slavery. The instant you do they have us under again: all our labour is lost, and sooner or later must be done over." Here Lincoln was explaining his fundamental position: if slavery were permitted to move into the territories the Republican party would fall apart. The agreement to oppose the extension of slavery lay at the very centre of Free Soil-Republican political organization. In Lincoln's view, political unity in the North, on a platform that *should* appeal to moderate opinion in the South, was the only hope of holding the American Union together. His most basic political belief was in the sanctity of that Union: a Union which he was convinced was organic and antedated the Constitution itself. This philosophy he made clear at his inauguration when he declared:

> No State upon its own volition can lawfully get out of the Union; that resolves and ordinances to that effect are legally void; and that acts of violence, within any State or States, against the authority of the United States, are insurrectionary or revolutionary, according to circumstance.

The circumstance occured almost at once. During Buchanan's last weeks in office the Confederacy had seized most federal property in their states. Intent upon acquiring Fort Sumter in Charleston harbour, the chief remaining federal military post in South Carolina, the Confederate government ordered General Beauregard to demand the surrender of the fort. The fort's commander, Major Anderson, refused to surrender and the Confederate batteries opened fire on the fort at 4:30 a.m. on April 12, 1861, half an hour after the deadline set by Beauregard. After thirty-four hours of steady bombardment, and with his fort a flaming pile of rubble, Anderson lowered the Union flag, to the intense excitement of the society of Charleston which had been watching from their grandstand seats on the harbour front. The warning of Robert Toombs, Confederate Secretary of State, who had advised against attacking the fort, was about to be realized: "The firing upon that fort will inaugurate a civil war greater than any the world has yet seen."

7

Civil War

THE AMERICAN Civil War illustrated two major forces in the mid-nineteenth-century western world: nationalism and democracy. Nationalism was most perfectly expressed in Lincoln's belief that maintenance of the Union was the highest principle for Americans to follow. In this sense the war was for the reunification of the American nation-state, just as Bismarck's wars and the Italian wars of reunification, fought at about the same time, were for the establishment of comprehensive national states. The war also hammered home, by the ultimate appeal to force, the doctrine of majority rule, which underlies all forms of democracy. But the action of the North in rejecting the right of the South to secede, even after popular conventions in the Southern states had elected that course, confirmed the fears expressed by a French visitor, de Tocqueville, early in the century, that majority rule must ultimately weaken American liberalism and the respect for minority rights.

1. ISSUES AND DIVISIONS

Perhaps the principal irony of the Civil War was that the slaveholding South, denying liberty to millions of human beings within its borders, fought for the liberty of its white population to refuse dictation from the Northern majority. It was on issues of this sort, more than on the apparently uppermost question of slavery, that families were divided and the nation torn asunder. And behind all of the great moral-political questions lay a multitude of economic ambitions.

128

Southern cotton planters sought unlimited expansion of their agrarian-commercial society based on slavery; Northern manufacturers, railway promoters and land speculators wanted to integrate the West into a huge business complex, not only to provide markets for Eastern manufacturers and a field for investment, but to counterbalance Southern votes in Congress in order to assure the maintenance of a protective tariff and other legislation favourable to Northern business. The economic ambitions of the North increased as the demands of war revealed the strength of the Northern economy, and approaching military victory made political and economic domination of the entire nation by the North possible.

Following the bombardment of Fort Sumter, Lincoln waited to see what course the uncommited border states, like Virginia, which formed a buffer between the Confederacy and the North, would take. After a few days of futile negotiations between the Union government and representatives of the border states, however, he called up seventy-five thousand men from the state militias. As a result, Virginia decided to join the Confederacy rather than contribute troops for the invasion of the South. Not all the people of Virginia favoured secession, however. The people in the northwestern part broke away from the state and drew up a constitution; and in 1863 the district was admitted to the Union as the state of West Virginia. Despite sharp divisions of opinion among the people, Arkansas, Tennessee and North Carolina followed Virginia out of the Union almost immediately. Division of loyalties was deep also in the slave states of Missouri, Kentucky, Maryland and Delaware, which, after considerable debate, decided to stay inside the Union.

Equally tragic were the personal decisions which had to be made. In North and South, families divided as brother fought brother, and son fought father. The Lincoln family had close relatives in the Confederate armies, while the family of Jefferson Davis, President of the Confederate States, had relatives fighting for the North. A civil war is always the most bitter kind of conflict and the scars of the American Civil War have yet to heal completely. In an effort to smooth over some of the legacy of hard feeling, modern historians have renamed the struggle "The War Between the States," or "The War for Southern Independence." Whatever it is called, it remains one of history's most tragic conflicts, involving greater numbers of casualties than either Napoleon's long campaigns, or those of Bismark to unify the German Empire.

2. THE MILITARY CAMPAIGNS

At the outset, most European observers believed that the Confederacy would win its independence. While the twenty-three Union states had a population of twenty-two million and the Confederacy only nine million (of whom nearly four million were Negro slaves) the South had the advantage of interior lines of communication and supply, and a much higher morale. Hundreds of thousands of people living in the "loyal" border states, as well as in the southern districts of Indiana, Ohio and Illinois, were pro-Southern. Moreover, the training of Southern soldiers and the ability of Southern commanders were far superior to that of their Northern counterparts. But, in spite of these positive advantages, the only real hope of the South lay in achieving an early victory.

Northern armies outnumbered the Southern by three to two at the beginning of the war; by the end of the fighting the proportion was two to one. Virtually all of the textile, iron, steel and munition factories were in the North, as were the major banking institutions. Moreover, the North produced much more foodstuffs and provisions than the South. Since most of the merchant marine and navy were in Union hands, a Northern blockade of Southern ports went into operation at once and became increasingly effective as the war progressed, despite the daring exploits of the Southern blockade runners.

For two years a quick Southern victory appeared possible. To break the Confederacy, the blue-clad Northern armies were forced to take the offensive. Their strategy was to move directly against Richmond, Virginia, the Confederate capital, only a hundred miles from Washington, and simultaneously secure command of the Mississippi River in order to encircle and strangle the South. At Bull Run in the summer of 1861 the first attempt on Richmond ended in the rout of General McDowell's Union Army. By the spring of 1862, the Union General, George B. McClellan, had reorganized the Army of the Potomac and prepared again to move on Richmond. Taking the peninsular route between the York and James rivers, McClellan reached Fair Oaks from which he could see Richmond. A too cautious man, he waited for reinforcements and when General Robert E. Lee, the Confederate commander, launched a counter-attack, McClellan retired. Lee was perhaps the most brilliant soldier on either side and he was surrounded by able commanders. A few months after Fair Oaks he routed the Northern forces at the second Battle of Bull Run. What had started as a Union drive on Richmond was turning into a Southern invasion of the North, with Washington in continuous danger. McClellan and Lee met at Antietam in mid-September, 1862. The Confederate army was forced to retreat, but McClellan did not pursue his advantage. Following victories at Fredericksburg in December and Chancellorsville in May 1863, Lee once more invaded the North through Maryland and Pennsylvania, again threatening the cities of Washington, Baltimore and Philadelphia.

To stop the Southern advance Lincoln placed General George C. Meade in command of the Northern forces. On July 1 Meade's ninety thousand men met Lee's seventy thousand grey-clad Confederate soldiers at Gettysburg, a small Pennsylvania town. For three blood-stained days the battle raged in the valleys, on the ridges and across the town. On the third day Lee ordered General G. E. Pickett with fifteen thousand of the best Confederate troops to make a desperate attempt on the key Northern position at Cemetery

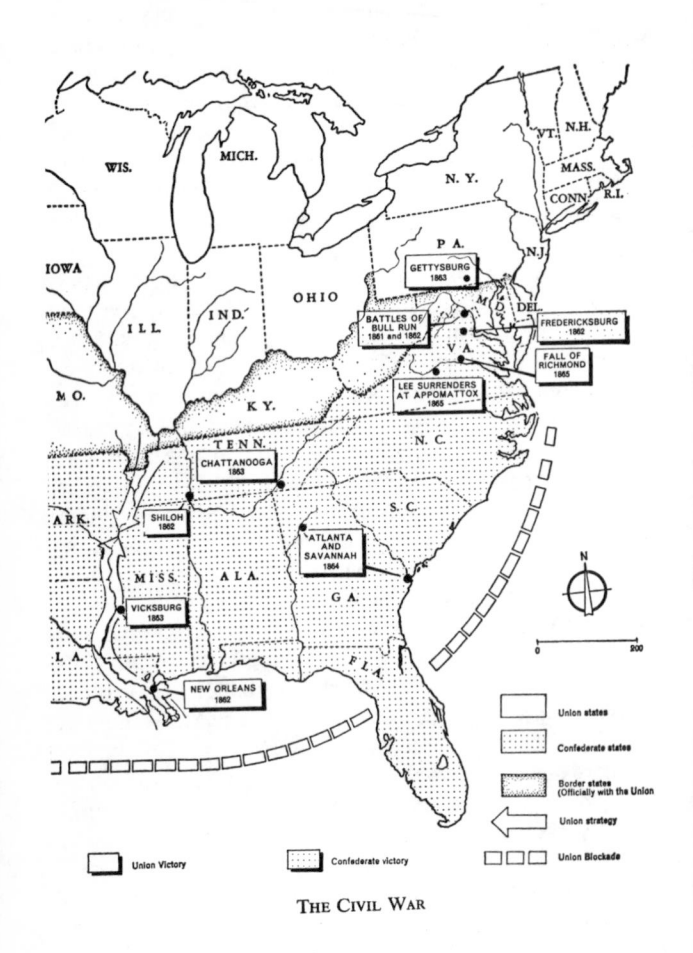

THE CIVIL WAR

Ridge. The assault was made and a few men actually gained the ridge, but the main body had been slaughtered by murderous Union artillery and rifle fire. The following day Lee withdrew across the Potomac. Once more a Union General, this time Meade, was slow in pursuit, and allowed Lee to escape. President Lincoln was frustrated by the Union's constant inept generalship. "We had them within our grasp; we had only to stretch forth our hands and they were ours," he wrote. "Still, I am very grateful to Meade for the great service he did at Gettysburg," he added. Gratitude was in order, for Gettysburg was perhaps the most decisive battle of the war.

Meanwhile, the steady tightening of the naval blockade was slowly but inexorably smothering the South. In a desperate effort to break the blockade, the South invented a novel device. Naval engineers covered the hull of an old frigate, the *Merrimac*, with iron plate and sent her into Hampton Roads where she easily demolished three wooden blockade ships. The North had prepared for such a vessel, however, and when the *Merrimac* returned on the following day she encountered the *Monitor*, a heavily-armoured pill-box with powerful cannon mounted on a hollow raft. The two iron-clads fought to a draw, neither being able to sink the other. The effort to break the blockade failed, but a new era in naval warfare had begun.

The first sign of a Northern victory appeared in the West, where a brilliant American general had been serving his apprenticeship. General Ulysses S. Grant was one of the Northern graduates of West Point who had failed to obtain preferment in the army before the war, due partly to Southern domination of the War Department and the higher military offices. He had resigned his commission and in private life had failed both in farming and business. Re-entering the army at the beginning of the war he was assigned to the western campaign under General Halleck. Here he distinguished himself by cracking the Confederate defences in Kentucky and Tennessee and withstanding an all-out counter-attack at Shiloh. By July 4, 1863, with the capture of Vicksburg, Northern forces controlled the Mississippi and had thus cut off Louisiana, Arkansas, Mississippi and Texas from the rest of the Confederacy.

In March 1864 Lincoln placed Grant in command of all Union armies and the new commander prepared the final strategy of the war. General Meade was to continue pressing Lee back upon Richmond; a land and sea attack was to be made on Mobile, Alabama; and the western armies were to move eastward as rapidly as possible. Grant himself moved to the Richmond front, while Generals Sheridan and Sherman wreaked havoc in Virginia's Shenandoah Valley and in Georgia. Grant ordered Sheridan: "In pushing up the Shenandoah Valley it is desirable that nothing should be left to invite the enemy to return. Take all provisions, forage and stock wanted for the use of your command. . . . Do all the damage to railroads and crops you can. Carry off stock of all descriptions and Negroes, so as to prevent further planting. If the war is to last another year we want the Shenandoah Valley to remain a barren waste." The orders were carried out faithfully. Sherman was even more thorough. He captured and burned Atlanta, Georgia in September 1864, and from there cut a swathe of total devastation across Georgia to the sea, where he arrived at Savannah in December. His exploit is commemorated in the song "Marching through Georgia."

The stage was now set for the final pincer movement of the war. Sherman moved north through the Carolinas, laying waste everything in his path including the important cities of Columbia and Charleston. On April 25, 1865, his Southern opponent, General Johnston, surrendered outside Durham, North Carolina. Meanwhile, Grant had pushed southward on the road to Richmond. In the spring of 1864, he had started moving through the Wilderness, a massive marshy forest, where he was stoutly opposed by Lee. Already criticized in the North for his willingness to lose large numbers of men in costly, if victorious manoeuvres, Grant declared: "We have now ended the sixth day of very heavy fighting. . . . I propose to fight it out on this line if it takes all summer."

Fifty-five thousand Northern soldiers died in the Wilderness campaign. The battles which followed were equally wasteful of life, but the war of attrition succeeded and Richmond fell early in April 1865. Lee tried desperately to escape southward but, cut off from supplies and blocked by Union forces moving north, he finally met Grant at Appomattox Court House on April 9, 1865, to seek terms of surrender. For the South it was unconditional surrender, relieved only by the personal military generosity of Grant. Grant undertook to provide rations for twenty-five thousand Southern troops; officers and men of the Confederate army were paroled; officers were allowed to keep their side arms; and all were permitted to keep their own horses, since these would be necessary to work the farms to which most of the Confederate soldiers would now return.

3. THE WAR ON THE HOME FRONT

The greater resources of the North had turned the tide in the final year of the war, but not before many serious crises had been weathered. Both sides had resorted to conscription and to bounties for enlistment. The North provided that exemption from military service could be purchased for three hundred dollars. Opposition to this concept of "a rich man's war and a poor man's fight" led to several riots, the worst of which lasted three days in New York in the summer of 1863. The South found its power to meet the immense financial needs of war severely restricted and tried to solve its problems by printing vast amounts of paper money. The North resorted to the printing of paper money also, but had superior resources to back it. In the North, an income tax, levied for the first time, and tariff increases, which reached an average rate of forty-seven per cent, provided increased revenue to finance the war. Despite this, most of the cost of the war was raised by huge loans, government war bonds which were sold by private firms on a commission basis. The chief bond salesman was Jay Cooke of New York, who became the richest banker in the country. To encourage the sale of bonds the National Banking Act of 1863 permitted any group of businessmen who had certain specified resources to secure a charter for a "National Bank," provided their bank then subscribed at least one-third of its capital to government bonds. This borrowing provided about four-fifths of the Northern war costs and the bonds became a handsome business investment by the end of the war. It was a Hamiltonian process which tended to increase business interest in the operations of the federal government.

The war made possible the realization of several planks in the Republican platform. In 1862 the Homestead Act provided one hundred and sixty acres of land in the public domain free to any *bona fide* settler, a measure which had long been blocked by Southern planters in Congress. In 1864 an Immigration Act permitted businessmen to import industrial labourers. Furthermore, in 1862 Congress had chartered a railway system to be paid for largely out of public resources to connect Chicago with San Francisco. These various measures, passed during the course of the war, represented the achievement of a generation of Whig-Republican demands. Another demand, however, became particularly crucial as the war progressed: emancipation of the slaves. Lincoln had never regarded emancipation of the slaves as the major issue in the war. Indeed, he wrote in August 1862:

> My paramount object in this struggle is to save the Union, and is not either to save or destroy slavery. If I could save the Union without freeing any slave, I would do it; and if I could save it by freeing all the slaves I would do it; and if I could do it by freeing some and leaving others alone I would also do that.

But as the war dragged on, more and more Northerners agreed with the abolitionist wing of the party that the war could be justified only if it resulted in freedom for the Negro slaves. To this body of opinion was added that of many businessmen who had at first been either lukewarm or opposed to the war. They now foresaw the economic opportunities that could be opened for themselves by destroying the political and economic power of the Southern planters. The representatives of this group within the Republican party became known as the Radicals. In the spring of 1862 Congress emancipated the slaves in the District of Columbia and in the territories. But led by Thaddeus Stevens in the House and by Charles Sumner in the Senate the Radicals demanded total and immediate emancipation of all slaves as well as a tough post-war policy to prevent the resurrection of a Southern-dominated Democratic party.

In addition to mounting pressure within his own party, Lincoln faced serious difficulties which might be solved by emancipation. Britian and France both favoured the South, and English policy was of crucial importance. The English textile manufacturers depended on Southern cotton, and the upper class sympathized with the more aristocratic Southerners. Relations between England and the North worsened rapidly, and war nearly broke out late in 1861 when a Union cruiser stopped a British mail steamer, the *Trent*, on the high seas and removed from it two Confederate diplomats who were travelling to England and France. The British government protested vigorously, sent nine thousand troops to Canada in preparation for a possible war, and alerted the Atlantic naval squadrons. Lincoln disavowed the action and released Mason and Slidell, the two diplomats. While this avoided an open break, the Northern blockade continued to create critical difficulties between the two countries. Cotton shipments were reduced which annoyed the British; and the British government winked at the building of Southern commerce raiders in British ports which angered the North. These raiders, of which the best known was the *Alabama*, did great damage to Northern shipping and led to further diplomatic friction between Britain and the United States.

Lincoln decided in the summer of 1862 that he must weaken his Radical critics and also allay anti-Northern opinion in England, particularly since the war was then going very badly for the North. Under the authority of his wartime powers as Commander-in-Chief he issued an Emancipation Proclamation on January 1, 1863. The President noted that emancipation had become "a military necessity absolutely essential for the salvation of the Union." Since this was its purpose, the Proclamation "freed" only those slaves in any state which was then in arms against the Union, leaving slaves in the loyal border states untouched. Many people in the North thought this hypocritical and while the Proclamation weakened abolitionist attacks, it also strengthened the political opposition of Northern anti-war Democrats. However, the Proclamation was useful as a symbol. English anti-slavery opinion was impressed by it. Richard Cobden wrote: "The great rush of the public to all the public meetings called on the subject shows how wide and deep the sympathy for personal freedom still is in the hearts of our people." Moreover, English businessmen began to feel that Northern grain to make bread for the textile workers was as important as Southern cotton with which to feed the machines, particularly as alternative sources of cotton were developed. In short, the danger that Britain might give aid to the Confederacy was avoided and time was given for the superior strength of the North to have its effect.

Scepticism in the North about ever defeating the South helped to prolong the war. In 1862, a year of dismal military reverses, Democrats gained seats in the House of Representatives; and before the Presidential elections of 1864 even Lincoln believed that he would be defeated by the Democratic nominee, General McClellan. However, the Democratic claim that the war was a failure and that peace should be negotiated was disproved by Union victories in the autumn. Lincoln was re-elected, with Andrew Johnson, an ex-Democrat from Tennessee, as Vice-President.

Much of the oppostion to Lincoln stemmed from dislike of his heavy-handed methods on the domestic front. He tolerated no open opposition to the Union war effort, enforced conscription as rigidly as was possible, imprisoned opponents and set up military courts in border states to suppress opposition. Personally concerned about the extent to which he was using the executive power, Lincoln was anxious to have constitutional authority for the final emancipation of the slaves. Thus an amendment to the Constitution was put before Congress early in 1864. It required almost a year and a good deal of sharp political pressure to get the necessary two-thirds vote in each House, but by December 1865, Congress had passed the measure and the necessary three-quarters of the states had ratified the Thirteenth Amendment which declared:

> Neither slavery nor involuntary servitude, except as a punishment for a crime whereof the party shall have been duly convicted, shall exist within the United States, or any place subject to their jurisdiction.

Economically, the North prospered in the final two years of the war. Capital was actually accumulated faster than it was consumed. On the farms and in the factories new machinery was extensively introduced, production of coal, metals and timber soared, and the railway systems were extended and improved. These developments, together with the financial, tariff and land legislation mentioned earlier, laid the basis on which Northern business organizations could become completely national in extent. The boom also meant high prices, profiteering in war production, and low wages. The fortunes which grew out of the war catapulted a group of Northern businessmen into positions from which they could control the nation's post-war economic life.

The war thus laid the basis for reunification, but it was an expensive basis by any measurement. Six hundred thousand men had died and an equal number had been wounded. Huge areas of the South lay devastated and on the verge of famine. Over five billion dollars had been spent, and the costs of recovery and pensions doubled that amount. But the great question was on what basis a conquered South would resume its place within the Union. The Radical Republicans urged exclusion from government of all former Confederate leaders until such time as the Republican party was organized throughout the South and in a position of permanent control. Others saw the inhumanity of such a policy of vengeance. The leader of the moderates was the President himself. Tempered by the burden of wartime responsibility, Lincoln was acutely aware of the extent of the tragedy through which his nation had passed. As he told his Cabinet he hoped that "there would be no persecution, no bloody work, after the war was over. None need expect [he would] take any part in hanging or killing these men, even the worst of them. . . . Enough lives have been sacrificed. We must extinguish our resentments if we expect harmony and union." To the end he clung to his purpose of maintaining the Union. The end came too soon.

On April 14, 1865, eleven days after the fall of Richmond, and while Washington was still in a state of jubilant celebration, Lincoln attended a stage performance at Ford's Theatre in the capital. As he sat in his box he was shot and killed by a demented actor, John Wilkes Booth, as part of a plot to avenge the South. The murder of the President removed the principal force that might have restrained the Radical demand for recriminatory policies against the South. Herman Melville, one of the country's greatest writers, summed up the meaning of the President's death:

> *He lieth in his blood—*
> *The father in his face;*
> *They have killed him, the Forgiver—*
> *The Avenger takes his place.*

8

Radical Peace and Bourbon Triumph

IN THE spring of 1865 the South lay in ruins. The economic, social, political and moral destruction of the area can hardly be exaggerated. Most of its railway system had been torn up and the rolling stock burned. In wide regions nearly all livestock had been slaughtered or driven away, houses looted, towns and cities burned to the ground. Scarcely a factory was left standing. With so many men in the army, the plantation structure had crumbled. The organization of churches, schools and universities had, in many districts, withered away. With all available funds, private and public, absorbed by the war, relief agencies established by the Confederacy disappeared. In the near absence of a transportation system the few available stocks of food and other supplies could not be properly distributed. Famine stalked the Southern land, turning thousands of recently wealthy planters' families into hungry beggars and visiting death by starvation upon thousands of liberated slaves. Whitelaw Reid, a New York journalist, described in detail the pauperization of the South which made even less bearable the military devastation:

> Window glass has given way to thin boards in railway coaches and in the cities. . . . A complete set of crockery is never seen, and in very few families is there enough to set a table. . . . At the tables of those who were once esteemed luxurious providers you will find neither tea, coffee, sugar, nor spices of any kind. Even candles, in some cases, have been replaced by a cup of grease in which a piece of cloth is plunged for a wick.

141

Faced with the results of such deliberate annihilation and wartime pressures, the spirit of Southern white leaders was not likely to be conciliatory. That spirit, which was to govern white politics in the South for generations after the war, is best seen in the revised will of a ruined planter, written in 1866:

> I give and bequeath to my . . . descendants throughout all generations, that bitter hatred and everlasting malignity of my heart and soul against all the people north of Mason and Dixon's line, and I do hereby exhort and entreat my children and grandchildren . . . to instill in the hearts of . . . all their future descendants from their childhood, this bitter hatred and these malignant feelings. . . .

Faced with the problem of reconstructing their crumbled society, Southern white political leaders thought of restoring a plantation economy as similar as possible to what had existed before the war. This purpose was frustrated by two powerful factors: Northern insistence on completely subjugating the South, and the Thirteenth Amendment to the Constitution which gave immediate legal freedom to four million slaves. The problem of what to do with the "freedmen" was extremely pressing. The South had deliberately kept the Negroes illiterate and they had no appreciation of political questions. They naïvely believed that emancipation meant a permanent holiday. Furthermore, unlike most peasants of Europe, when they were freed from serfdom, the American freedmen received no land. They became a vast wandering and propertyless population. Such a situation was an open invitation to chaos, riot and chronic lawlessness. Moreover, abolition of slavery meant that planters were deprived of their labour and if not quickly solved, the lack of labour would prevent even the beginnings of Southern economic recovery. These, then, were some of the problems with which white Southerners had somehow to grapple and with which Washington had to deal legislatively.

1. RADICAL RECONSTRUCTION

In the midst of the war, Lincoln had prepared his answer to the problem of reconstructing the post-war Union. He declared that since secession was not legally possible the Confederate states had never been outside the Union. At the end of 1863, using his executive power of pardon, Lincoln granted pardon to any Southerners who swore allegiance to the Union, excluding only the leaders of the Southern army and governments. He proclaimed that when ten per cent of the 1860 voters of any Confederate state had sworn to support the Constitution and emancipation, they could re-establish a normal state government. By the spring of 1865 Arkansas, Louisiana and Tennessee had reconstructed state governments on this basis. The Radicals in Congress, however, refused to accept the conciliatory policy of Lincoln. They argued that the Confederate states *had* left the Union, had waged war upon the United States, and were thus "conquered provinces" at the end of the war. Moreover, they declared, the power of admitting such "new" states to the Union was vested by the Constitution in Congress and not in the executive. By this argument, Congress, not the President, had the exclusive power to plan "reconstruction."

This claim led to the passage through Congress of the Wade-Davis Bill in 1864, which asserted congressional control of the South, and provided that a *majority* of voting citizens must swear allegiance before a Confederate state could be readmitted to the Union. Lincoln refused to sign the Bill and it died because the session ended before Congress could again pass it. Such was the situation at the time of Lincoln's assassination.

As Vice-President, Andrew Johnson automatically became chief executive on Lincoln's death. Johnson was a "poor white" Tennessee farmer who had been a Jacksonian Democrat before the war. Without any formal education he had risen through politics to become a Senator and had served as military governor of Tennessee after Union troops occupied the state. He was a sincere man of considerable

143

ability, but possessed little tact or diplomatic skill. Like most poor whites of the South, he had an abiding dislike of big planters. He was, therefore, expected to side with the Radicals in their policy of destroying the political and economic power of the Bourbons, as the conservative Democrats of the Southern states were sometimes called by their opponents because of their autocratic ways. After his first few weeks in office, however, he adopted Lincoln's conciliatory policy. In doing so, he invited an open struggle with the Radicals in Congress.

By the autumn of 1865 all of the seceded states except Texas had accepted the Presidential conditions for reconstruction and had functioning state governments. To deal with the problem of economic recovery and of the freedmen, the new Southern governments passed black codes, which required freedmen to accept work, to live in designated districts, and to become "apprentices" if they were children. Negroes were also excluded from trades in which they might compete with white workers. In other ways, too, the black codes severely limited the civil rights of Negroes, and none of the codes gave Negroes the right to vote. A great many freedmen, lacking skills or property, had little alternative but to return to their former owners, either as servants or as sharecroppers, where they could farm small plots owned by a planter and receive a small share of the resulting crops. Usually the local storekeeper charged more for the goods the Negroes bought than the Negroes were able to pay for from their share of the crops, and the latter were soon sunk in perpetual debt and disabled from ever owning land of their own. These conditions, which were to endure in the South for many years, led to severe racial friction. Race riots and lynchings scarred the South, especially in Mississippi in 1866, and produced a growing conviction in the North that the Democrats were trying to re-establish slavery under different names. Conversely, as Southern planters and merchants, lacking capital of their own, went deeply into debt to Northern commercial houses, they felt that they were being mercilessly exploited by avaricious Northern businessmen and their political henchmen. The Freedmen's Bureau, established in March 1865 as an agency of the War Department to assist freed Negroes, mediated between white people and Negroes in relation to work contracts, reported cruelty and injustice to the Northern military commanders, and helped establish Negro schools. Despite President Johnson's opposition to the good work of the Bureau, Congress extended its authority in 1866. Ex-Confederates loathed the Bureau and were additionally incensed when it actively assisted the Republican party to secure Negro votes.

In the congressional elections of 1866, Northern suspicion of Southern anti-Negro feelings, President Johnson's refusal to compromise with the Radicals, and the determination of Northern businessmen to exploit the South gave the Radicals a majority in both Houses of Congress. As a result they were in a position to override Johnson's veto of their legislation. They refused to seat Southern Congressmen and Senators who had been elected under the Presidential reconstruction terms and instead established their own conditions on which the ex-Confederate states might again enter the Union. These conditions were defined in the Reconstruction Act of 1867 which placed the South under Union military rule. Only when a seceded state adopted a new constitution, which disfranchised a large proportion of white political leaders, enfranchised adult male Negroes, and ratified the Fourteenth Amendment could it re-enter the Union. Speaking for the Radicals, Thaddeus Stevens declared: "We hold it to be the duty of the Government to inflict condign punishment on the rebel belligerents, and so weaken their hands that they can never again endanger the Union." Southern whites resented bitterly their "subjection" to Northern reconstruction policy.

The Fourteenth Amendment provided full citizenship to the freedmen and sought to protect their civil rights by declaring that no state might enact "any law which shall abridge the privileges or immunities of citizens of the United States," or which shall "deprive any person of life, liberty or property, without due process of law," or which would "deny to any person within its jurisdiction the equal protection of the laws." The Amendment declared that "all persons born or naturalized in the United States, and subject to the jurisdiction thereof, are citizens of the United States and of the State wherein they reside," thus denying the contention of Chief Justice Roger Taney in the Dred Scott case that Negroes were not citizens. Finally, it debarred from public office any Confederate leader who had not been specifically pardoned by Congress and refused to honour debts contracted by the Southern states during the period of Confederacy.

Under the congressional reconstruction policy, state governments were established throughout the South, based upon Negro suffrage and restricted white suffrage. As a result the new legislatures were composed of illiterate freedmen, scalawags and carpetbaggers. Carpetbaggers were Northern opportunists who invaded the South looking for commercial opportunities and who organized branches of the Republican party, while scalawags were opportunistic white Southerners who threw in their lot with the Republicans. Although these legislatures passed some constructive legislation, particularly in educational matters, many of them suffered from a large degree of corruption. Furthermore, because of their composition and the military supervision under which they were established, they also stimulated mounting racial friction.

In Washington, the Radicals sensed complete victory. When Johnson tried to block their attempt to destroy permanently white Southern political influence, the Radicals passed the Tenure of Office Act and the Command of the Army Act. The first prohibited the President from removing any member of the Cabinet without the consent of two-thirds of the Senate, thus depriving him of control of the Cabinet. The second transferred control of the army from the President to Congress. When Johnson dismissed Edward Stanton, his Secretary of War, because Stanton betrayed Cabinet information to Radical congressional leaders, the House of Representatives voted to impeach Johnson. On trumped-up charges the House alleged that the President had committed "high crimes and misdemeanours" in trying to block the Radical policy. At the impeachement trial in the Senate, the House prosecutors failed by one vote to convict the President on the charges. It was a very close call for the doctrine of separation of powers. Had the Radicals succeeded, a precedent would have been established which, if repeated, might have destroyed the independence of the Presidency.

2. THE GRANT ADMINISTRATION

By the time of the Presidential election of 1868 the Southern states had ratified the Fourteenth Amendment and had been readmitted to the Union. As their candidate for President, the Republicans nominated the Civil War hero, General Ulysses Grant. Waving "the bloody shirt" (which meant playing up the Civil War and Northern losses) and crying "Vote the Way You Shot" the Republicans sought approval of the Radical reconstruction policy. The Democrats tried to make the issue "cheap money" and appealed to the debt-ridden farmers by proposing to re-issue greenbacks, or paper money, which the government had been withdrawing from circulation under business pressure. The real issue, however, remained that of the Radical reconstruction policy.

While Grant won by two hundred and fourteen to eighty votes in the electoral college, in the popular vote of 5,700,000 his majority was a mere 300,000. Without the Negro vote the Democratic candidate would undoubtedly have been elected. The election not only testified to the growing disenchantment with the Radical Republicans but confirmed the Radicals in their view that the Negro vote was essential to their hold on power. The Radicals immediately proposed and obtained ratification of the Fifteenth Amendment to the Constitution in 1870 which guaranteed more specifically than had the Fourteenth the freedman's right to vote.

White political leaders in the South also realized that it was the Negro vote which deprived them of their accustomed role of dominance. They decided that the only means of retaliation left open to them was intimidation and violence. They formed secret societies with such mysterious names as Knights of the White Camellia and Ku Klux Klan. Hooded in white sheets, the Ku Klux Klan members rode forth at night issuing spectral warnings against voting to the defenceless Negroes. By day the Klansmen visited their wrath upon carpetbaggers, scalawags and Negroes, shooting, flogging, burning and generally terrorizing all who disregarded their warnings. Against this kind of secret organization neither the Radical Congress nor carpetbag governors prevailed. Attempts to enforce the reconstruction legislation were ineffective and under the sway of the "Redeemers" of Southern white power one state after another returned to the Democratic political fold in state and federal politics. Meanwhile, Northern businessmen had begun to doubt the wisdom of the Radical policy. By the Amnesty Act of 1872 Congress removed the political limitations of the Fourteenth Amendment for all but five hundred Southerners. At the same time, the Freedmen's Bureau, established by Congress in 1865 to protect Negro rights, was allowed to die.

Meanwhile, in the North, corruption was as widespread under the Grant administration as it was under the Southern reconstruction governments. Honest but dull, Grant stood as the symbol of official Republican respectability, behind which financial speculators and railway promoters like Jay Gould and "Jubilee Jim" Fisk manipulated prices and took huge profits from publicly protected or subsidized enterprises. Grant, who supported the most extreme Radical policy in the South, was an expansionist in foreign policy. He was barely restrained by his able Secretary of State, Hamilton Fish, from helping rebels to throw the Spaniards out of Cuba, and he supported an abortive plan to annex Santo Domingo. Grant was also cool toward attempts to lower the tariff or to reform the civil service, which was a chief centre of governmental corruption. In short, he seemed to represent the worst spirit of acquisitive materialism in the victorious North, just as he had represented the high human costs of winning the war.

Nevertheless, Grant and the Republicans won the election of 1872. In his second term Grant softened his policy toward the South, but this merely had the effect of hastening the return of white supremacy. Even scalawags were returning to the Democratic party, and by 1876 only three Southern states remained uncertainly in Republican hands. Meanwhile, other events weakened the Republican party elsewhere in the nation. Late in 1872 the Credit Mobilier scandal burst upon the nation. Credit Mobilier was a construction company organized by promoters of the Union Pacific Railway. The construction company was given building contracts at huge profit rates by Union Pacific directors and then the same men, as controllers of Credit Mobilier, pocketed the proceeds. In order to fend off legislative interference with this process, considerable sums were spent in bribing both Congressmen and state legislators, including many leading Republicans. Then, early in 1873, a fierce depression which was to last for five years hit the nation. Despite popular cries that more paper money should be issued to restore the sources of credit, the Republicans stuck to the conservative policy of withdrawing paper money, and making payments in specie or coin, a policy which only helped to lengthen and deepen the depression.

3. THE END OF RECONSTRUCTION

While businessmen supported the general tariff, monetary and railway policies of the Republicans, many of them began to think the cost of corruption too high. The cost was symbolized not only in the Credit Mobilier scandal but also in the activities of such men as Senator Roscoe Conkling. This enterprising lawyer was the Republican political boss of New York State and had complete control of the patronage connected with the Customs House at the Port of New York. Millions of dollars were extracted annually by Conkling and his Customs appointees from importers and other merchants for facilitating their business at the Customs House. The money was then distributed in such a way as to support

Republican political power and enrich insiders like Conkling himself.

Facing the election of 1876, Republicans sought to avoid the taint of corruption by refusing to nominate for President James G. Blaine of Maine, who was closely associated with legislative bribery, and by nominating instead Rutherford B. Hayes, an honest and undistinguished politician from Ohio. After sixteen years out of office, the Democrats were more than anxious to return. Although they were divided on some matters like the tariff, they were united in support of their candidate, Samuel J. Tilden, a wealthy corporation lawyer and Governor of New York. Tilden was widely known for having dealt a heavy blow to the notorious Democratic machine of Tammany Hall by sending its boss, William Marcy Tweed, to the penitentiary for his long record of municipal graft.

The nomination of Tilden revealed that the parties were becoming more and more similar. Each was now a great intersectional alliance endeavouring to appeal to all the chief interest groups in the country, and each was increasingly dominated by Eastern business. The pattern of politics for the ensuing two decades was becoming clearly established.

The election itself was very close. When the popular vote was counted, Tilden appeared to be the victor, with a plurality of 250,000. However, there were conflicting returns from three Southern states which were still under military supervision, and from Oregon which had entered the Union in 1859. The task of selecting the victor was given to a special congressional commission whose members, voting on party lines, gave all the disputed states to Hayes. Although the Democrats knew that they could hold up the decision by strong opposition in the House, they suddenly ended their opposition and Hayes was declared President.

The Democratic capitulation was due to extremely important behind-scenes bargaining. Business interests with both Northern and Southern connections persuaded Democratic leaders in the South to accept Hayes as President in return for an unwritten promise by Hayes and the Republicans to withdraw troops from the South, appoint Southerners to the Cabinet and, not least important, grant subsidies for Southern railways. This alliance of Southern Democrats with Northern Republican businessmen brought about the formal end of Radical reconstruction in the South. Despite passing frictions, it has also continued to be the most consistently powerful political alliance in the United States. Because the South voted almost solidly Democratic until 1928, and has voted predominantly so ever since then, the Democrats have enjoyed an unbroken influence in the congressional committees which possess an almost life-or-death power over proposed legislation. The chairmanship of Senate and House committees is decided by seniority, and the Southern Democrats have thus held disproportionate power in Congress. They have usually voted with conservative Republicans to block "progressive" legislation.

The end of reconstruction also opened the door to the triumph of "Jim Crow" or segregationist legislation throughout the South. By the end of the 1880's terrorism as a means of eliminating Negro political activity gave way to special laws. These laws provided that no one could vote unless he had paid a poll tax or, in some cases, unless he could pass special literacy tests. Since many white people could fail both of these tests, some states enacted "grandfather clauses" which allowed any adult male to vote if his father or grandfather had been enfranchised on January 1, 1867, a date prior to the First Reconstruction Act and the Fourteenth Amendment. Other laws prohibited Negroes from using the same railway cars as white people and segregated the races completely in schools and other public places. These laws were clearly a violation of the Fourteenth Amendment, but for the time being at least the Supreme Court concurred in the return of white supremacy in the South.

It is not difficult to condemn the use of force to compel the South to remain in the Union; the use of force to carry through total and immediate emancipation of four million slaves, without at the same time accepting responsibility for establishing them in freedom; and the failure to curb corrupt exploitation of the Northern victory. Much of subsequent American history has been deeply and often adversely affected by the aftermath of the Civil War and reconstruction.

9

The Businessman's Revolution

AT THE end of the Civil War the United States was still principally a farming country. While capital was being accumulated with which to finance large scale industry, most business firms were relatively small and most of their business was carried on locally. But, by 1900 business organization was nation-wide and controlled by giant industrial and financial companies. Governments underwrote the privileges of wealth, and helped to promote the rapid growth of class differences, with tariff legislation, distribution of natural resources either free or at a fraction of their real worth, by clearing western Indians off the most valuable western land, and by using force to suppress labour unrest. As early as 1873 Mark Twain helped to write a book entitled *The Gilded Age* which described contemporary life. So effective was his description of the way in which men were making and spending money at that period that historians have borrowed his title to designate the years from the end of the Civil War to 1900. Another writer called the period "The Great Barbecue" because during those years it was so easy for political camp-followers to get a share of the public wealth in lands, timber-rights, mineral deposits, or franchises to operate public utilities.

1. REVOLUTION ON THE RAILWAYS

United States economic growth was stimulated by the completion of the western railway network. In 1873 there were about 70,000 miles of railroad in the country. Twenty years later there were 170,000 miles. This railway network made possible the economic integration of West and East. Railway-building also employed hundreds of thousands of labourers and attracted millions of dollars of investment from European and American financiers. Along each of the western lines dozens of towns sprang up, each expecting to be a great mercantile or industrial centre, each attracting land speculators, small businessmen and farmers, and each requiring heavy financial credit from Eastern sources at high rates of interest.

The resource used to finance railways was public land. From 1862 to 1871 Congress granted to railroads, either directly or through state legislatures, one hundred and sixty million acres of public land whose value was in excess of four hundred million dollars. The pattern was set in 1862 by legislation chartering the Central Pacific and Union Pacific railways, the former to build eastward from Sacramento and the latter to build westward from Omaha. Each was given free right of way and, along the right of way, ten square miles of land, in alternate sections, for each mile of track constructed. In addition, the roads could import steel rails free of duty and could obtain interest-free government loans ranging from $16,000 for each mile built in level country to $48,000 per mile in the mountains. Thus the company which laid the most track received the largest measure of public support. In the race to reap these rewards, the Central Pacific Railway imported ten thousand Chinese labourers while the Union Pacific employed similar numbers of Irish immigrants. The construction camps of both companies were scenes of violence as the labourers drank, gambled and fought. In addition, much time was spent fighting off the desperate assaults of Cheyenne, Shawnee and Arapaho Indians who realized that the railways spelled an end to their way of life. Nevertheless, in May 1869, the two lines met at Promontory Point, Utah, and a golden spike was driven to symbolize the wealth that would flow from the immense achievement.

So huge were the fortunes to be made as an insider of

"The Great Barbecue" from the distribution of public resources, that the men who shared in the spoils soon wielded great economic and political power. Outstanding among the "Robber Barons," as such men have been called, was Jay Gould who rose to eminence through railway and associated financial operations. Gould's financial transactions are instructive. He sold his holdings in the Erie Railroad at a huge profit just before a financial crash in 1873, and then began to purchase the shares of the Union Pacific whose value had been depreciated by the depression. By 1878 he controlled the Union Pacific and was buying stock in other western railways. As soon as he had gained control of the Kansas Pacific he was in a position to threaten ruinous competition with the Union Pacific which he also controlled. To avoid this the Union Pacific was compelled to buy his Kansas Pacific shares at nine times what he had originally paid for them. Transactions of this kind weakened the financial condition of Union Pacific. When Gould saw the shaky condition of Union Pacific he secretly sold all his stock in the company, but not before he had had the railway issue ten million dollars in new stock to raise money for the construction of branch lines. Much of this money went to a contracting company which Gould largely owned. Gould played a similar game with the Southern Pacific Railway. By gaining control of competing roads in Texas, Gould forced Southern Pacific into joint manipulation of rates and traffic.

Similar financial battles occurred among the men who controlled other large railways systems, battles in which the banking houses of New York became more and more involved as the total investment in railroads increased rapidly. Since all economic activity was ultimately linked with banking and transportation, the railroad financiers became increasingly important on the national scene. Men like Gould, Collis P. Huntington, Leland Stanford, J. J. Hill, Commodore Cornelius Venderbilt or Edward J. Harriman emerged from the financial battles richer than the medieval barons or oriental potentates of history. While they stand as symbols of "self-made" men and the principle of competition, their wealth really came from public resources. Their goal was the elimination of competition by forming ever larger rail networks under unified control or by "sharing" arrangements between competitors. By the end of the century six men owned or controlled 100,000 miles of American railways, and these six were closely associated with either the House of Morgan, or Kuhn, Loeb and Company, two gigantic banking firms in New York.

2. THE REVOLUTION IN BUSINESS ORGANIZATION

Technological changes, such as the Bessemer process in steel making, and the development of labour-saving machinery offered unlimited opportunities of expansion in industry. But they also encouraged the growth of large corporations because amounts of capital larger than were usually available through individual ownership or simple partnership were required if the opportunities for development were to be seized. Thus the corporation, which had taken some root before the Civil War, came into full flower after 1865. In the post-war period of cut-throat competition the well-financed corporation was in a position of great advantage. It could survive price-wars and buy out its smaller competitors; it could spread branches across the country, organize "pools" with others to share the markets and maintain high prices; and it could, on occasion, even bargain with the railroads for favourable rates.

However, American law provided penalties for "conspiracies in restraint of trade," that is, for practices whereby competitors secretly agreed to fix prices and lessen competition. To get around the law, groups of investors combined their resources to purchase controlling blocks of stock in a number of companies. They then formed a board of trustees, or a trust, which could manage all the companies they controlled as a single organization. By this trust method, competition was cut down or eliminated entirely in a wide range of manufacturing industries and in transportation, communications and utilities. The goal of business organization became the establishment of a monopoly, which is the exclusive right to operate in a certain field. Defenders of the system argued that monopolies were the most efficient and cheapest form of business enterprise. They pointed out that the monopoly, or trust, controlled the raw materials, had lower administrative costs, used modern and expensive mechanical inventions, and eliminated competitive production and distribution. However, the undoubted savings of the monopolies or trusts were seldom passed on to the consumer in the form of lower prices, while the costs of labour-saving machinery were frequently met by increasing the employees' hours of work or reducing wages. As the national economy grew more wealthy in these years the actual number of firms decreased; at the same time the operations of the beef trust, the sugar trust, whisky trust, the oil trust and others, grew in volume.

The growth and nature of the trusts is well illustrated by the career of Andrew Carnegie and the growth of the steel industry. The son of Scottish immigrants, Carnegie had started work as bobbin boy in a cotton factory at a dollar twenty a week. At thirty, he was able to quit his job as a district superintendent for a railroad and start his own construction business which specialized in building iron bridges. This led him to investigate the problems of iron and steel production. After a trip to England he decided that the new Bessemer process of steel manufacture was the key to the future. Forming the firm of Carnegie, McCandless and Company he built a huge steel mill near Pittsburgh. His connection with railway operators brought him a steady flow of large orders, and by 1879 Carnegie's factory was producing most of the nation's steel.

In 1882, Carnegie combined his operations with those of Henry C. Frick who controlled most of the coking industry. This was a first big step in the creation of a "vertical" monopoly in steel, that is, a trust controlling all the stages and materials that enter into the production of steel. He went on to buy vast areas of the great Mesabi iron range of Minnesota, extensive coal fields in Pennsylvania, limestone quarries, a fleet of iron ore ships and scores of railway cars. By the end of the century, when he had bought out many competitors and established a virtual empire of steel production, profits on his undertakings amounted to forty million dollars each year. In 1901 he decided to retire. So great were his assets that it required the largest investment banking house in the country, J. P. Morgan and Company, to arrange a whole new trust, the United States Steel Corporation, to acquire the Carnegie interests. United States Steel was capitalized at $1,400,000,000 and controlled more than half of all American steel production. By that time the total steel production in the United States was more than that of England and Germany combined.

Carnegie himself was part of the spirit of his times. He was ruthless in eliminating his competitors, hired private armies to suppress workers who organized strikes in his mills, and used his full financial power to influence government and courts in his favour. Unlike many of his brother financiers he professed no religious faith, unless it was a gospel of wealth and competition. As he wrote:

> The contrast between the palace of the millionaire and the cottage of the labourer with us today measures the change which has come with civilization. This change, however, is not to be deplored, but welcomed as highly beneficial. It is well, nay essential, for the progress of the race, that the houses of some should be homes for all that is highest and best in literature and the arts, and for all the refinements of civilization, rather than that none should be so. . . . We might as well urge the destruction of the highest existing type of man because he failed to reach our ideal as to favour the destruction of individualism, Private Property, the Law of Accumulation of Wealth, and the Law of Competition; for these are the highest results of human experience.

In retirement he spent a portion of his fortune endowing public libraries and art galleries.

John D. Rockefeller was to oil what Carnegie was to steel. Starting with nothing Rockefeller worked his way up in the wholesale produce business and through incredible thrift saved enough to establish an oil-refining firm. Having made his original profits from Civil War demands for produce, Rockefeller went ahead rapidly after 1865. His methods of forcing companies to sell out to or join with him were utterly ruthless and included disruption of competitors' operations by strong-arm squads as well as continuous threats of economic destruction. By the end of the century, his company, Standard Oil, was one of the most notorious monopoly trusts. Nevertheless, it was able to survive all attempts by judges and legislators to break it up. Rockefeller gave a slightly different view of the process of industrial combination than did Carnegie:

> This movement was the origin of the whole system of modern economic administration. It has revolutionized the way of doing business all over the world. The time was ripe for it. It had to come, though all we saw at the moment was the need to save ourselves from wasteful conditions of competition. . . . The day of combination is here to stay. Individualism has gone, never to return.

The pattern of combinations, monopolies and trusts spread to all sections of the United States economy and constituted a second industrial revolution which affected every aspect of American life. It vastly increased the national wealth and made the owners of big business the most influential men in the country. As more and more Americans went to work in industry, cities and towns grew in size and began to challenge the farm regions in political importance. Most of American political and social history in the years 1865 to 1917 is a record of attempts to adjust the forms of American life to the facts of the industrial age. The concluding stages of western settlement, the conduct and goals of foreign policy, the nature of the party system, and social policy were all affected by the businessman's revolution.

3. THE LAST FRONTIER

The last American land frontier in the Far West was different in many ways from the pre-war frontiers east of the Mississippi. Railways, telegraphs and business organization caught up quickly with the frontiers of the post-Civil War years. In 1860, the only state organized in the Great Plains was Texas. But by 1890, on the basis of population density figures, the census bureau declared that there was no longer a frontier settlement.

The western mining frontier was also fast-moving. Everywhere in the mining communities the lure of sudden wealth, combined with the absence of federal law and order, produced conditions of anarchy in which murder, gambling and prostitution were glorified as "freedom," suspicion of the police was rampant, and the most widely accepted faith was in the six-shooter. To remedy these conditions, temporary governing committees, often, at least to begin with, vigilante committees, were formed. Eventually territorial status was granted to the area and with it came federal marshals to maintain law and order. Territorial status was followed by the territory's admission to the Union as a state. This policy was repeated again and again in the West, bringing into existence the states of Nevada, Colorado, Wyoming, Arizona, Idaho, Montana and North and South Dakota.

As territorial government was established, and as mining gave way to farming and ranching, the Plains Indians knew that their original fear of railways had been well justified. In 1860 the Indian population of the plains and mountains numbered about 250,000, about 75,000 more than the number of white men in the same region. Their way of life was simple. They lived off the huge herds of buffalo estimated as high as twelve million head in the early 1860's. Tough buffalo-hunting tribes such as the Apaches, Navajos and Sioux captured and trained wild horses both for hunting and warfare. Superbly skilled as cavalry, the warriors of the plains could ride slung beside or under the bellies of their horses at a full gallop, and at the same time deliver a stream of deadly arrows. A single skilled bowman could have as many as eight arrows in the air at one time.

As the westward thrust of population pushed the eastern Indians past the Mississippi, Indian wars became more frequent and more vicious, and the defending plainsmen became more deadly as warriors. Gradually, railways were driven into the area, and wagon trains brought miners and settlers. Pony Express riders established communications and army posts were established to police the country. A long war of attrition was begun with the grim aim of eliminating the last Indian barrier to settlement.

The first stage of the war was the decimation of the buffalo population by rifles. The most famous of the buffalo-hunting white men was Buffalo Bill Cody who is reputed to have shot more than four thousand buffaloes in a year and a half, for sale as meat to the construction camps of the Kansas Pacific Railway. Other hunters, organized by Eastern businessmen, slaughtered millions of the prairie herds for the Eastern market in hides and fur. Thus by the end of the 1880's there were only a few hundred buffaloes left in the entire West. Since the Plains Indians had depended upon the herds for everything from shields and clothing to teepees and food, the destruction of the buffalo helped to destroy their way of life. It remained only to subdue, in a series of bloody and often merciless battles, the last fierce show of Indian spirit.

The policy of the federal government was to force the Indians into tribal reservations, usually in the regions of the country thought to be least valuable. Indians fought this policy the more bitterly since the Bureau of the Interior, which was responsible for Indian affairs, and its Western agencies, were riddled with corruption. Agents cheated the Indian even when he did enter a reservation by depriving him of what good land had been within the reservation's boundaries, over-charging him for goods, and demoralizing him with liquor. The most valiant of the last Indian rebellions were fought by the Sioux under such famous chiefs as Crazy

161

Horse, Little Crow and Red Cloud. The region reserved for the Sioux had been penetrated by the Northern Pacific Railway and then violated by white miners after a gold strike had been made there. In 1876 the federal government sent a large military force to subdue the Sioux. The force was commanded by General George Custer, a famous Civil War leader. When Custer's force and the Sioux met in the Little Big Horn River region in the Dakota badlands, the Indians under Sitting Bull wiped out Custer's cavalry detachment. But such victories could not prevent the steady, irresistible flow of white settlement and the remorseless imposition of the white man's rule.

Following protests against the brutality of the federal government's Indian policy, Congress passed the Dawes Act in 1887. This legislation broke up the tribal reservations and granted small sections of land to each family. This policy, however, was not successful. The Indians found the transition from nomadic life to farming in a permanent settlement extremely difficult. Moreover, under the terms of the Homestead Act white men frequently got the best land. Some Indians did leave their local communities and succeeded in the white world, but their success was the exception that proved the rule. By 1934, although all Indians had been granted citizenship ten years earlier, the steady decline and pauperization of the Indian population prompted a reversal of policy. The Wheeler-Howard Act established tribal landholding on reservations, and endeavoured to encourage self-government within reservations as well as preservation of Indian crafts and customs.

With the elimination of the Indian barrier, the way was opened for the establishment on the plains of the Cattle Kingdom, whose origins lie in the Texas of the 1820's. American immigrants in the Mexican province rounded up herds of wild cattle and wandering horses and branded them. They adopted the range equipment developed by Mexican cowherds—lasso, chaps, "five-gallon hats," and specially adapted saddles, spurs and bits. Until the end of the Civil War, Texan longhorn cattle were sold mainly for their

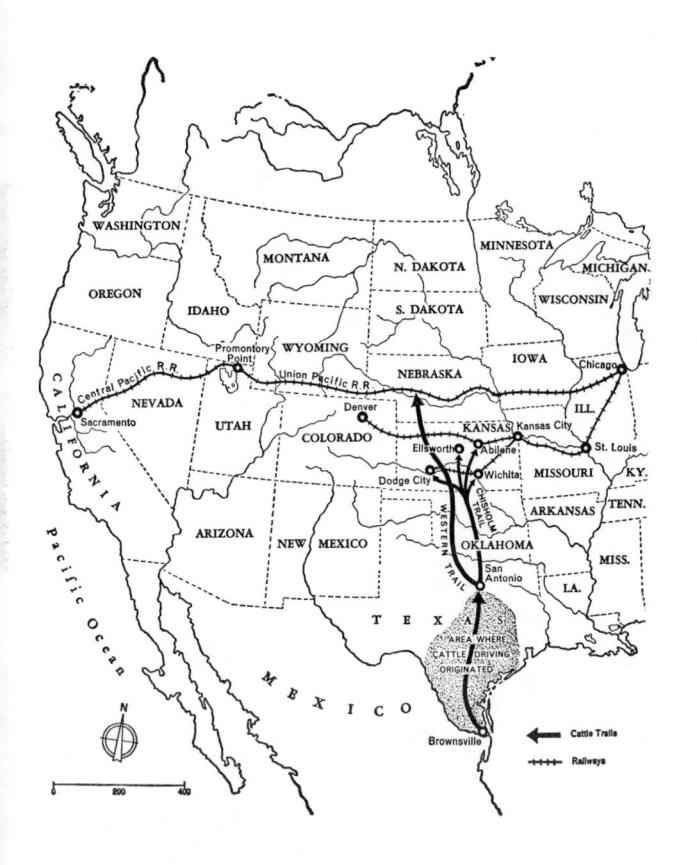

CATTLE TRAILS AND RAILROADS

hides. After 1865, however, with the completion of the railway network, Eastern demands for beef could be met from the West, and the Cattle Kingdom entered its golden age. A steer which could be bought in Texas for three dollars was worth as much as forty dollars in an Eastern market. The problem was to move the cattle from the range to the railhead. This was solved by the cattle drive which was made possible by the existence of the huge stretch of unfenced grassy plains reaching from Texas to Canada and from the farms of the midwest to the Rockies.

Each spring marketable cattle were rounded up and under a cattle boss and a team of cowboys were driven slowly north across the plains, fattening on the lush grasses as they went. The direction taken by these long annual drives was determined by water and grass supplies along the way, but eventually they ended at a railroad. A typical railhead was one developed by Joseph McCoy, a Chicago meat wholesaler, who arranged with the Kansas Pacific Railroad for special freight rates on cattle shipments. At Abilene, Kansas, McCoy built huge stabling and loading facilities, and constructed a hotel where the cattle bosses could do business with the agents of Eastern abattoirs. Abilene, the first of a series of "cow-towns," handled seventy-five thousand head of cattle in 1868, and at its peak activity in 1871, seven hundred thousand longhorns were herded through the town's pens.

Other railroads were quick to follow the lead of the Kansas Pacific. Along the prairie lines there sprang up a whole series of cow-towns similar in their violent character to the mining towns. In Dodge City, for example, twenty-five men were murdered in the town's first year, and the inhabitants are credited with converting the word "stiff" into a noun. Social chaos stemmed partly from the relatively slow growth of local institutions of law and order and partly from the intense boredom, as well as constant danger, of the cowboy's life. Nor did the cowboy, unless lucky at gambling, have the prospect of an easy fortune that lured the miner. His pay was usually between twenty and forty dollars a month, and all of it could be lost in one night at the gaming tables of

Wichita or Sedalia. The money in the Cattle Kingdom was made by the big herd-owners, the service towns and railways, and the meat-packing industry. As profits grew, more and more Eastern money and even European money, was invested in the herds of the open range.

The cattle industry, too, was transformed by inventions. The refrigerated railway car made it possible for the meat-packing industry to move closer to the range, and Kansas City and Chicago became the chief centres. Refrigeration on ocean ships extended the markets for American meat to Europe. These developments led to the growth of huge trusts which dominated the meat-packing industry.

The Cattle Kingdom's period of prosperity was brief, lasting little more than the twenty years between 1865 and 1885. In 1862, the Homestead Act gave one hundred and sixty acres of free public land to any settler who would pay a small recording fee, live on the land and cultivate it for five years. Settlement of the forbidding plains under the Homestead Act was slow, for the plains were generally believed to be a region of desert, while the tough prairie grass, the absence of water, and the threat of roving cattle and horses constituted other problems. The invention of the steel plough provided an implement to deal with the tough prairies sod, and in the 1850's a simple framework windmill was devised which, mass-produced by the Fairbanks-Morse company, by the late 1860's, solved the water problem. Factory production of barbed-wire fencing in the 1870's enabled farmers on the treeless plains to build effective fences. By 1880 this bane of the cattlemen was being sold at the rate of eighty million pounds a year. Five years later the open range was nearly at an end as overstocking, criss-crossing by the fences of wheat and sheep farmers, and quarantine laws limiting regional movement of cattle all led the heavily financed cattle industry to adopt fenced-in ranches. The cowboy of the open range became the much less romantic ranch-hand.

The West was hostile to the first farmers. In the early period of settlement thousands of them lived in sod houses and faced the rigours of sub-zero blizzards with a bare minimum of protection. Always they faced the enmity of cattle barons and their henchmen, who fought the farmers' advance every inch of the way. Nevertheless, by 1900 eighty million acres had been granted to settlers under the Homestead Act. The rapid growth of western settlement owed much to the railroads, which spent millions of dollars advertising their lands in the eastern states and in Europe. To Minnesota, Wisconsin and the Dakotas came hundreds of thousands of Germans and Scandinavians and to the rest of the Western states went a mixed but unbroken stream of ambitious Easterners and Europeans. Occupied farming land in the United States more than doubled between 1860 and 1900, rising to 841,000,000 acres in the latter year. With this inflow of population, the last territorial governments disappeared. In 1912 the admission of Arizona and New Mexico brought the number of states to forty-eight where it remained until the admission of Alaska and Hawaii in 1959. Led by Frederick Jackson Turner, many American historians have declared that the westward movement of the frontier is the most important theme in American history and explains the development of American character and institutions. In 1893, just as the frontier was coming to an end, Turner wrote:

> To the frontier the American intellect owes its striking characteristics. That coarseness and strength combined with acuteness and inquisitiveness; that practical, inventive turn of mind, quick to find expedients; that masterful grasp of material things, lacking in the artistic but powerful to effect great ends; that restless nervous energy; that dominant individualism, working for good and evil, and withal that buoyancy and exuberance which comes with freedom—these are the traits of the frontier, or traits called out elsewhere because of the existence of the frontier.

4. ECONOMIC AND SOCIAL TENSION

Economically, the new West restored agricultural production to its former place in the balance of total American production. The wheat farms of the prairies, using the steadily improved farm machinery turned out by the Mc-Cormick and other Eastern implement factories, quadrupled American grain production between 1860 and 1900. But western farmers had mortgaged their land to Eastern banks and trust companies in order to buy improved machinery and more land. Toward the end of the 1880's the price of wheat began to fall with the entry of Australia into the world market and the revival of wheat production in Russia and even Germany. At the same time, a period of continuous good rainfall ended on the plains, and in 1893 a sharp depression hit the country. All of this brought the farmers lowered incomes and mortgage foreclosures. These troubles brought about the formation of a number of farmers' protest organizations.

Trouble was also brewing in the booming East where workers had failed to share in the business prosperity and were the first to feel the economies introduced during a depression. In the growing industrial cities the contrast between abject poverty and unprecedented riches, which fascinated so many contemporary writers and cartoonists, was difficult to exaggerate. In 1893 government census bureau figures indicated that over seventy per cent of the national wealth was owned by less than nine per cent of American families. The wealth of the new millionaires was conspicuously consumed. Their immense houses were the setting for opulent entertainments attended by platoons of servants. Luxury hotels were the scenes of dinners and balls at which guests were offered favours such as cigarettes rolled in one hundred dollar bills. At one party the financier, August Belmont, appeared in a suit of armour inlaid with gold; at another, given by Randolph Guggenheim, at a cost of two hundred and fifty dollars a place, the meal was eaten to the accompaniment of the singing of nightingales perched in transplanted rose trees. The Guggenheim evening was topped off by gifts to guests of jewelled match-box souvenirs. In New York and other industrial cities, the wealthy filled their mansions indiscriminately with statuary and paintings gath-

167

ered on European tours. Each summer they made pilgrimages to famous seaside towns, like Newport, Rhode Island, where the Vanderbilt marble house cost more than $9,000,-000 to build. The social Four Hundred of New York entertained senatorial political bosses at glittering restaurants such as Delmonico's, and deftly ensured, by financing the major party campaigns, that legislative, executive and judicial policy would interfere with their interests as little as possible. Such extravagant display by the "Robber Barons" aroused a mixture of envy and hatred in those who witnessed but did not share in it.

By the end of the century it was apparent that the process of consolidating the control of capital through trusts and interlocking membership on boards of directors had resulted in virtual control of American economic life by the great financial houses. As one candid member of the moneyed class put it:

> We own America; we got it, God knows how, but we intend to keep it if we can by throwing all the tremendous weight of our support, our influence, our money, our political influence, our political connections, our purchased senators, our hungry congressmen, and our public-speaking demagogues into the scale against any legislation, any political platform, any Presidential campaign, that threatens the integrity of our estate.

Complicating the structure of American society was a sharp increase in immigration and a more rapid growth of urban as compared to rural population. Between 1860 and 1890 more than nine million people came to the United States from Europe, particularly from the British Isles and Germany. The Scandinavian countries also sent many immigrants in the 1870's and 1880's, who settled mainly in the midwest and northern prairies. Late in the 1890's a fresh influx came from southern and eastern Europe, Italy, Russia, the Balkans and Poland. This was the last big surge of immigration to the United States, and it reached its peak in the first decade of this century when nearly nine million

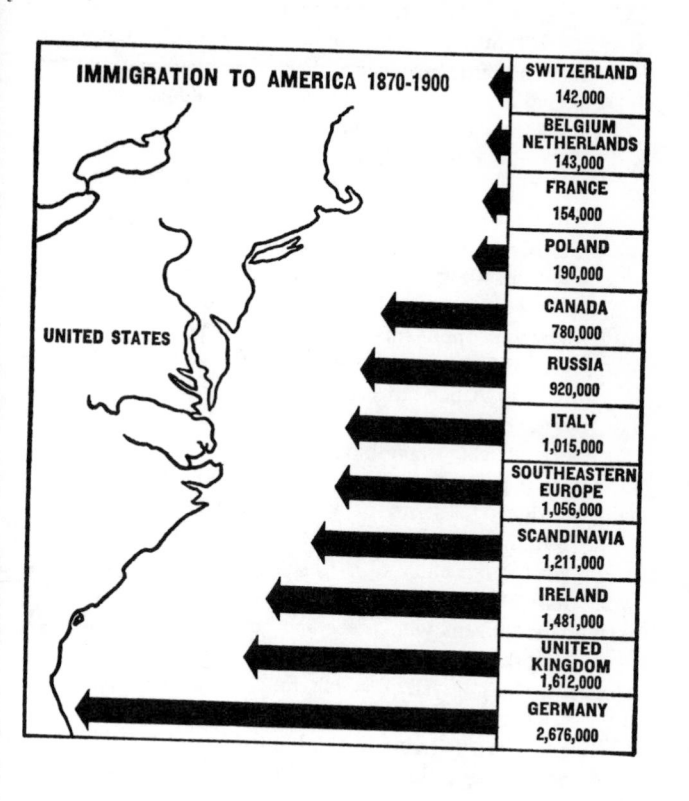

IMMIGRATION TO AMERICA 1870-1900

UNITED STATES

SWITZERLAND	142,000
BELGIUM NETHERLANDS	143,000
FRANCE	154,000
POLAND	190,000
CANADA	780,000
RUSSIA	920,000
ITALY	1,015,000
SOUTHEASTERN EUROPE	1,056,000
SCANDINAVIA	1,211,000
IRELAND	1,481,000
UNITED KINGDOM	1,612,000
GERMANY	2,676,000

people moved through the reception station at Ellis Island in New York Harbour. While many of the German and Scandinavian immigrants went west, most of the later immigrants settled in the cities.

Once again "nativism" assumed dangerous proportions, as native-born Americans irrationally blamed the new arrivals for depressions and anything else of which they disapproved. Even industrial leaders, who generally favoured an increase in the supply of labour, because it made lower

169

Manifest Destiny

wages possible, supported the mounting demand for restrictions on immigration. Some of the new Americans
brought with them European radical ideas, from anarchism
to socialism, and since this was a time of intense industrial
strife, it was an easy step to blame all unrest on "foreign agi-
tators." As the railroad lawyer, Chauncey M. Depew, remarked: "The ranks of anarchy and riots number no Americans. The leaders boldly proclaim that they come here not to
enjoy the blessings of our liberty and to sustain our institutions but to destroy our government, cut our throats,
and divide our property." The labour unions became the
most vociferous opponents of immigration not only because
it was very difficult to organize immigrants who were un-
accustomed to American problems and habits, but because
the newly arrived were often willing to accept lower wages
and poorer working conditions than those accepted by the
native-born. Pressure for restriction of immigration eventually produced a series of very effective laws. In 1882
Chinese immigration was prohibited; in the 1890's regulations prohibited entry of diseased persons; in 1907, by a
"gentleman's agreement," Japan undertook to refuse pass-
ports to its citizens who wished to go to the United States
to seek work; between 1921 and 1924 the United States
adopted a quota system which limited immigration from
any European country to two per cent of the number of that
country's nationals living in the United States in 1890. Despite special legislation after 1945 favouring persons displaced by war and revolution, immigration since 1921 has
remained slight.

However, immigration greatly stimulated industry and
population growth. Western and midwestern farm areas
grew so rapidly that the centre-point of population moved
from Ohio in 1860 to Columbus, Indiana by 1890. At the
same time, urban population grew much more quickly than
rural, and Eastern farm regions actually declined in population as people moved to industrial jobs in towns or to fertile
lands farther west. Many new midwestern towns and cities,
whose industry was based on iron and steel, or on the pro-

cessing of agricultural commodities, grew fantastically. By 1880 Chicago, with a population of nearly a million, had replaced Philadelphia as the country's second largest city.

In both Eastern and Western industrial cities, sprawling tenements and slums stood in marked contrast to the great mansions of the wealthy. Almost without property, urban industrial workers depended entirely on wages which were usually at bare subsistence level. While the total "national wealth" was growing at unprecedented rates, and the cities boasted such new amenities as gaslight, sewer systems and in the 1880's even electric arc-lamps and tram lines, the great majority of urban dwellers lived in conditions that rivalled the filth of medieval towns and bred both vice and violence.

Amidst the teeming growth and unrest of these years there were substantial advances in education and literature. One of the most startling developments was the appearance of mass-circulation daily newspapers. Newspapers such as Joseph Pulitzer's St. Louis *Post Despatch* and the New York *World* introduced the use of cheap wood-pulp paper, typewriters and linotype machines. Publishers like William Randolph Hearst and E. W. Scripps, seeking new ways to increase production, improved their news services, introduced coloured comics, and printed sensational exposés of corruption in politics. Circulation rose from three million in 1870 to twenty-four million in 1899, and with mounting revenue from advertising, newspapers became big business. Popular magazines recorded similar circulation increases. "Crusades" to reform municipal politicial machinery were mixed indiscriminately with jingoistic condemnation of foreign nations and demands for assertion of American rights and power. Such journalism stimulated the outburst of expansionism of the late 1890's and a widespread reform sentiment in the early twentieth century.

As businesses mainly concerned with profit and loss, the newspapers seldom challenged the basic assumptions of middle-class American society. They constantly elaborated the theme of "rags to riches" and seldom missed an oppor-

171

tunity to explain that failure was the result of sloth and lack of initiative. The stories of Horatio Alger, with their reiteration of the success which invariably attended honest endeavour in an America of limitless opportunity, became symbols of the age. Thousands of aspiring middle-class Americans took up the cult of "self-improvement" of which the outstanding expression was the Chautauqua lectures given by travelling speakers who brought "culture" to ordinary men and women throughout the nation.

More serious efforts to improve the cultural level of the nation resulted in rapid expansion of all levels of public education. By 1900 most states had compulsory school attendance laws for primary grades, and between 1880 and 1900 high school enrollment rose from 100,000 to 500,000. State governments founded universities to supplement the facilities of the older private universities. Under the Morrill Act of 1862 the federal government granted land to the states for the purpose of improving agriculture and scientific education. In the older universities, graduate studies began to develop and to reflect the influence of research scholars trained in British and European, particularly German, universities.

Thus, despite the uneven growth and the increasing class distinctions, the early years of the "businessman's revolution" were a time of very real opportunity. The excitement of a nation on its way to world power, the adventurous avenues that led to the West or to mastery in business, the insistent urge in sensitive minds to portray in literature the nature and meaning of America—to become a Mark Twain, a Stephen Crane, a Henry James—all of this was a part of the post-Civil War years. When some of the avenues were closed by spreading monopoly or by economic depression many Americans turned their energies to fighting for rights and opportunities in a land of natural plenty.

10

Parties and Protests

THE YEARS following 1865 saw revolutionary social and economic changes in American society but these were not reflected in the nation's major political parties. On the contrary, the parties remained the instruments by which the privileged and wealthy controlled American life. In 1888 the party system in the United States was closely examined by an astute British diplomat, Lord James Bryce, in a notable book, *The American Commonwealth*. Bryce wrote:

> Neither party [Republican or Democratic] has any clear-cut principles, any distinctive tenets. Both have certainly war cries, organizations, interests, enlisted in their support. But those interests are in the main the interests of getting or keeping the patronage of the government. Tenets and policies, points of political doctrine and points of political practice, have all but vanished.

1. PARTY POLITICS 1876-1896

By the end of the 1870's the Republicans had fulfilled the purposes for which the party had been founded. They had eliminated "the slavery threat" to western expansion, gained free land in the West, and encouraged industrial development with a high tariff and federally endowed railways. During the same period the Democrats had defended as best they could the rights of the white South. In 1876-77 the political compromise between Southern Democrats and Northern Republican businessmen had brought about a new alignment of forces and with it a disappearance of party

173

principles. The result was a long seesaw battle in which the voting strength of the major parties was remarkably even. The Democrats did not win the Presidency from 1860 to 1912, except for Grover Cleveland's two terms (1885-89; 1893-97), but they enjoyed majorities in Congress more often than the Republicans. On the other hand, in the elections of 1876 and 1888 a Republican President won in the electoral college, though he had only a minority of the popular vote.

The real debates on policy took place within rather than between the parties. Both the Democratic and Republican parties were controlled by conservatives who accepted, broadly, a poltical philosophy to which the name "Social Darwinism" has been given. Briefly, this philosophy applied the ideas developed in Charles Darwin's *The Origin of Species* (1859) to the problems of social and economic policy. Darwin believed the species had evolved over a period of millions of years through a process of "natural selection," in which the weaker members died off and the stronger survived. The corollary of this doctrine of the "survival of the fittest" was that one should not interfere with the supposed natural law governing the process. As expounded by the English writer, Herbert Spencer, Social Darwinism held that millionaires were the fittest to survive because they had obviously adapted best to the natural laws of economics. Conversely, slum-dwellers were the least fit. Attempts to overcome social inequality by such means as unemployment relief, regulations governing wages, hours of work and other economic activity, or even by providing free education, were harmful because they interfered with "natural processes" of survival and progress.

Spencer's books were read by millions of Americans, and he had many outspoken disciples among writers, scholars, judges, politicians, editors, clergymen and businessmen. As used in general discussion, Social Darwinism was simply an argument for keeping government out of business and social relationships. Yet the very people who used the argument to oppose government regulation of business saw nothing incongruous in demanding that government should maintain a high protective tariff, assist businessmen by grants of natural resources, or by suppressing strikers. The doctrine of Social Darwinism was also convenient for those who were extending Jim Crow laws in the Southern states or endeavouring to preserve a privileged status for native-born Americans. In order to defend white supremacy in the South, nativism in the North, and later, overseas expansion, the argument was put forward that the "Anglo-Saxon race," by its dominant position in the world, was obviously the fittest to survive.

R. B. Hayes, who had become President as a result of the compromise of 1876-77, fulfilled the bargain by which his election had been secured in Congress. The government withdrew troops from the South, appointed a Southern conservative to the Cabinet and secured minor measures of reform in the civil service. Congressmen gave Hayes little support for that kind of honest reform, but they applauded his tough handling of the bitter railway strikes of 1877, which resulted from heavy wage cuts. When rioting occurred in Pittsburgh and West Virginia Hayes sent federal troops to suppress the strikers.

In 1880 the Republican General James A. Garfield of Ohio was elected President. Garfield had been a compromise between General Grant, who sought to return to the Presidency, and the openly corrupt J. G. Blaine. Chester A. Arthur, who had been Customs Collector of the Port of New York under the régime of the corrupt Roscoe Conkling, the political boss of the city, became Vice-President as a concession to the party stalwarts. The depth of political corruption in the period was illustrated when Garfield was shot four months after his inauguration by a disappointed office-seeker. To the surprise of the Conkling gang, Arthur, who as Vice-President succeeded Garfield, showed signs of independence, and sympathy for reform. He supported the Pendleton Act of 1883, which prohibited party assessment of civil servants for political contributions and which proposed the practice of appointing civil servants on the basis of competitive examinations. The later growth of the Pendleton system was spasmodic and, although the Civil Service Commission now administers appointments to most positions, the majority of the really important posts still remain outside its jurisdiction. One unforeseen result of the Pendleton Act was that the party bosses turned increasingly to big business for contributions to political funds.

As the federal elections of 1884 approached, the Republicans were badly split. The old guard, who disliked Arthur for his sympathy to reform, succeeded in denying him a second term, and nominated Blaine as their candidate for the Presidency. As a result, many Republicans supported the Democratic nominee, Grover Cleveland. Cleveland was Governor of New York State and had been Mayor of Buffalo. In both offices he had earned a reputation for honesty and independence. Cleveland was elected President, but Republicans retained control of the Senate and effectively blocked much of the administration's legislative programme.

Cleveland stood for upright if unimaginative administration. He made himself unpopular with Democratic party leaders by vetoing many private bills for increased Civil War pensions. He also took back over eighty million acres of land from railroads that had not fulfilled the conditions of their grants. More and more strongly he supported lowering the tariff on the ground that it was unjust taxation, often due to political pressure from certain powerful manufacturers. As the belief began to spread in the West and among Eastern reformers that the tariff was the "father of trusts," in that it gave unreasonable protection against British competition, Cleveland openly supported tariff reduction in 1887.

His tariff proposals were defeated in the Senate, and in the 1888 elections the Republicans elected their candidate Benjamin Harrison on a platform that included an unequivocal protectionist plank. Harrison believed in high tariffs, hard money, and in general, in the right of business to control government. He was content to have his Cabinet selected by Republican party leaders. Under the leadership of William McKinley, a Senator from Ohio, the Republicans framed a new tariff law. Enacted in 1890, the McKinley tariff satisfied even the most extreme protectionists. Higher tariffs, however, meant a higher cost of living, and this, in turn, brought political discontent. In an attempt to stem this discontent in the agrarian West and South, the government passed the Sherman Silver Purchase Act in 1890, providing for government purchase of the estimated output of the western silver mines. The silver was to be used as specie against which the government could issue more banknotes, thereby putting more money into circulation and aiding debt-ridden farmers. Unfortunately, too little silver was purchased and too little paper money was issued for the Act to be really effective.

Serious labour unrest from 1890 to 1892 added to the disenchantment with the Republicans. The labour discontent culminated in a strike in 1892 against the Carnegie Steel Company in Homestead, Pennsylvania. A vicious industrial war followed. Although Harrison supported the employers, the party managers realized that a combination of Western farm resentment and Eastern labour unrest could be fatal at election time, and Andrew Carnegie was asked to make concessions to labour. But Carnegie was determined to defeat the union at all costs, and refused. As Henry Frick, his partner and manager of the steel company, wrote to Carnegie: "I feel sorry for President Harrison, but I cannot see that our interests are going to be affected one way or another by the change in administration." In the desperate strike the Company imported bands of armed Pinkerton detectives. Amidst flowing blood these men crushed the strike. Grover Cleveland, no radical himself, commented on "the tender mercy the workingman receives from those made selfish and sordid by unjust governmental favouritism."

Many business leaders put their faith in Cleveland in 1892 and their support won him the Democratic nomination for President. They knew that he was "sound" on gold, that is, opposed to the issue of paper money and consequent inflation, and that his attitude to the tariff had been much modified during the four years he spent in New York business circles after his defeat in 1888. The Republicans nervously put forward Harrison for re-election. In a comparatively quiet election the Democrats won by a very narrow margin.

Cleveland's second administration was marked by depression, industrial warfare and social upheaval. Even before inauguration day, 1893, a panic on the New York stock market had set the stage for a depression which lasted until 1896. Cleveland employed his full powers as chief executive to use military force and the courts in suppressing strikes. He resisted attempts to increase credit for hard-pressed Western farmers, and refused to veto the act which imposed the very high tariff of 1894. By 1896, although incapacitated much of the time by attacks of gout, Cleveland had managed to offend every major group in the nation, save the most powerful businessmen. Just before the nominating convention of that year, a prominent Southern Democratic newspaper observed: "Grover Cleveland will go out under a greater burden of popular contempt than has ever been excited by a public man since the formation of the government."

The people's dissatisfaction with Cleveland as President, and with their inability under the existing party system to share in the choice of candidates for government office, was reflected in growing demands for reform.

2. THE DEMAND FOR REFORM

In the 1880's and 1890's not all Americans accepted the ideas of Social Darwinism. Men of letters constantly criticized the materialism of the age. Mark Twain's *The Gilded Age* was only one of many books which reflected deep discontent with social injustice and merely material progess. Perhaps the most widely read book of the period was Edward Bellamy's *Looking Backward*. Bellamy pictured the United States as it would be in the year 2,000 when the problems of the 1880's had been solved. He forecast that during the twentieth century, the American people would recognize the efficiency of the monopolistic system in industry but, to eliminate social injustice, would place all big business under government ownership. Bellamy wrote that under this new "nationalist" ownership, the more rational application of scientific methods would enable men to move constantly towards a "nobler, happier plane of existence." In cities all over the United States "nationalist" clubs and magazines sprang up to promote various aspects of Bellamy's version of socialism. Americans increasingly discussed the merits of public ownership of utilities and railways, telegraphs, banks, and more extensive aid to education.

Other writers analyzed American industrial society and often deplored the control exercised by private corporations over the nation's destiny. In his moving book *The Bitter Cry of the Children,* the socialist muckraker, John Spargo, describes the plight of children working in the coal mines:

> Work in the coal breakers is exceedingly hard and dangerous. Crouched over the chutes, the boys sit hour after hour, picking out the pieces of slate and other refuse from the coal as it rushes past to the washers. From the cramped position they have to assume, most of them become more or less deformed and bent-backed like old men. . . . The coal is hard, and accidents to the hands, such as cut, broken, or crushed fingers, are common among the boys, Sometimes there is a worse accident: a terrified shriek is heard, and a boy is mangled and torn in the machinery, or disappears in the chute to be picked out later smothered and dead.

Henry Demarest Lloyd led a group of writers who presented carefully documented studies of the actual operation of particular monopolies. His major book, *Wealth Against Commonwealth* (1894), was a detailed history of Rockefeller's Standard Oil trust, and an indictment of the "Robber Barons."

Our barbarians come from above. Our great money-makers have sprung in one generation into seats of power kings do not know. . . . Without restraints of culture, experience, the pride, or even the inherited caution of class or rank, these men, intoxicated, think they are the wave instead of the float, and that they have created the business which has created them. . . . They claim a power without control, exercised through forms which make it secret, anonymous, and perpetual.

Other social scientists in the 1880's and 1890's rejected the idea that uncontrolled private enterprise produced the best kind of life and maintained that "the doctrine of *laisser-faire* is unsafe in politics and unsound in morals." Some Protestant clergymen pointed out that the Christian gospel had a social message as well as an individual one, and that the state should regulate business to ensure everyone equality of opportunity. The Social Gospel Movement declared that love and co-operation were better Christian principles than competition and "survival of the fittest."

This movement in the Protestant churches, and the concern of the Roman Catholic church, led to an increase in charitable work. Some individuals founded "settlement houses," which, like Jane Addams' Hull House in Chicago, were attempts to help the poor by providing day nurseries, discussion clubs and gymnasiums. From the workers in private charities and the settlement houses, came a growing pressure for reform which forced reluctant city governments to provide playgrounds, parks and kindergartens for the poor. Some reformers went further and demanded the elimination of corruption at city hall, strict regulation of housing standards, and public ownership of municipal utilities.

Associated with the mounting reform spirit in the 1890's was a movement for equal rights for women which gained momentum as more and more women entered colleges and business. The movement finally culminated in 1919 in ratification of the Nineteenth Amendment by which women won the right to vote.

From the ranks of labour came further stimulus to the

spirit of reform. After the Civil War, labour tried to improve its position by extending and broadening its basis of organization. If labour were to bargin effectively with the nation-wide organization of capital, it too would have to organize on a national basis. It would have to represent not just the "aristocracy" of skilled workers but also the great masses of unskilled and semi-skilled labourers. It was to be a long, hard fight, however, before such an organization would be achieved. Ranged against labour were not only the powerful industrial leaders, but usually the state and national governments, the press and the courts as well. Moreover, there were divisions within the ranks of the labour movement itself.

The first attempt to establish a national union of all workers ended in failure when the National Labour Union, founded in 1866, collapsed in the depression of 1873. A second union, the Noble Order of the Knights of Labour, was organized in 1869 and enjoyed much greater success. The Knights' immediate goals were the traditional ones of most unions: "to secure to the toilers a proper share of the wealth that they create," an eight-hour day, prohibition of child labour, equal pay for both sexes and legislation to safeguard the workers' safety and health. Their long-term aims were more radical, for the Knights sought to reform the whole industrial structure by establishing a kind of guild socialism in which all industry would be co-operatively owned and run. They actually launched thirty co-operative undertakings, but most of these failed because of business hostility and inexperienced management.

In 1885 the Knights of Labour reached its peak of influence, when it staged a successful strike against the mighty railway empire of Jay Gould. In the following year its membership increased seven-fold to 700,000 and its success seemed assured. But in that very year disaster struck the movement. On May 1, the Knights led a widespread strike in support of the eight-hour day. During one of the great outdoor meetings, in Haymarket Square, Chicago, someone threw a bomb which killed one policeman and injured

181

several others. The guilty person was never found, but business and government leaders used the occasion to attack the successful national union. Eight anarchists were falsely accused of murder, and seven were sentenced to death.

Some definite conclusions were drawn from these events by a cigar-maker named Sam Gompers. Gompers' family had come to New York as immigrants in 1863 and Sam had gone to work at the age of ten in a cigar-making factory. Gompers' observations persuaded him that labour should fight for limited aims only and that it should use economic weapons exclusively. In 1886 Gompers became one of the founders of the American Federation of Labour, and was to be A.F. of L. President from then until his death in 1924.

The A.F. of L. was a federation of craft unions, each of which retained a large degree of autonomy. A craft union was one in which members of the same trade, printers, railwaymen etc., were grouped together. Since many of these unions had branches in Canada, they become "internationals." A.F. of L. unions, and the Federation itself, had little interest in organizing any but skilled workers. Believing in "business unionism" they concentrated on making industry bargain with A.F. of L. unions. They also worked to ensure that industry should hire only union members, improve wages, hours and working conditions, and enter into contracts with labour on all such matters. They decided to avoid partisan politics and to gain their ends by bringing pressure to bear on individual legislators and executives. As Gompers said, he was "partisan for a policy rather than for a party." By the early 1890's the A.F. of L. unions had a membership of 250,000 skilled workers. But strikes in 1892 and 1894 further increased middle-class hostility to unionism of any kind, and growth was very slow for another decade. By 1900 the A.F. of L. had achieved a membership of 500,000.

Except in railways, mines and the lumbering industry, unskilled and semi-skilled workers remained largely unorganized until the 1930's. This meant that labour did not, until that period, achieve a degree of strength that could even begin to match that of capital. For this failure "Gomperism" was the principal reason; nevertheless, for skilled workers, the A.F. of L. secured many gains. But while Gompers' policy remained dominant, there also developed a body of opinion in American labour which favoured direct political action for socialist goals, and organization on an industrial rather than a craft basis. An industrial union is one which includes all workers in a single industry, such as steel production or mining, rather than a single craft such as carpentering or plumbing.

Eugene V. Debs was the most influential advocate of combining socialist political action with industrial unionism. In 1893 before he was converted to socialism he had organized the American Railway Union which, unlike the major Railroad "Brotherhoods," was open to all railway workers regardless of trade or skill. Within a year the A.R.U. had 150,000 members. In 1894 Debs demonstrated the principle of labour unity by giving support to workers who had gone on strike against the Pullman Palace Car Company in a suburb of Chicago.

Following the financial depression of 1893, George Pullman, the great railway car manufacturer, had discharged a third of his workers and lowered wages for the remainder by forty per cent. In the company-owned town of Pullman, store prices and rents were kept at their previous levels. When the Pullman workers struck, Debs gave the strikers help from A.R.U. funds, while A.R.U. members boycotted all trains carrying Pullman cars. Fearful that the strike might succeed and industrial unionism spread, the railroads asked the federal government to support them with federal troops. President Cleveland and Attorney-General Olney responded quickly, despite the constitutional provision that federal troops should be used internally only at the request of the state governor or legislature. When Governor Altgeld of Illinois argued that there was no necessity for the intervention, the President evaded the Constitution by ordering the troops to protect the mails, a federal responsibility. At the same time Attorney-General Olney obtained from a Chicago federal court an injunction, or court order, to prohibit the strike. Troops were used to break the strike, despite Altgeld's protests to Cleveland, while Debs and other strike leaders were arrested and jailed for violating the court injunction.

The Pullman strike had significant results. The violence which accompanied it strengthened middle-class hostility towards trade unionism and the successful use of the court injunction showed employers how to break future strikes. The authority for issuing the injunction was the Sherman Anti-Trust Act which had been passed in 1890, ostensibly for the purpose of preventing "conspiracies in restraint of trade," that is, business monopolies and trusts. Its use as a weapon against labour disillusioned many working-class people.

Debs' experiences converted him to socialism and he was Presidential candidate for the newly-formed Socialist party in elections from 1900 to 1920. But despite deplorable social conditions and inequalities, American workers did not give majority support to parties or unions which advocated anything more radical than minor modifications of the capitalist system. Although radical movements like the Industrial Workers of the World (disrespectfully known as the "Wobblies") gained considerable strength in the Western forest and mining industries in the first two decades of the twentieth century, the conservative A.F. of L. remained the dominant voice of labour.

3. THE FARMERS' PROTEST

The history of farmers' organizations and labour unions is similar in many ways, but the farmers faced several problems peculiar to agriculture. On the great plains of Nebraska, western Kansas and the Dakotas, drought and locusts often left a trail of complete desolation and doomed whole communities to chronic indebtedness. Moreover, farmers had no control over prices on the world agricultural market. A large wheat crop would bring prosperity to a Western farm only if the market price of wheat were high; bumper crops in the

Ukraine or Argentina might cause wheat prices to tumble. Moreover, wheat prices were at the mercy of speculators who bought and sold on the commodity exchanges in Chicago and New York. United States farmers protested vigorously against high tariffs and trust control of railways and bank credit. They argued that such policies kept farm costs so high that it was often cheaper for a Western farmer to burn his corn or wheat than to pay the cost of marketing it. Although Southern farmers did not need as much expensive farm machinery as the Westerners, they, too, often paid more for necessary equipment and fertilizer than they received from the sale of their crops.

As prices fell, more and more farmers were forced to take out new mortgages or increase old ones. When prices failed to revive and costs remained high, farmers could not meet their high interest payments and many lost their farms. By 1900, more than one-third of all American farm families did not own their farms.

Western and Southern farmers determined to band together to exert more influence on government and business policies. The first major farmers' organization was the Patrons of Husbandry, organized in 1866. Known also as the Grange, the Patrons—more commonly called Grangers—soon had local Granges in all "farm states" and by 1875 boasted of 800,000 members. The Grangers sought to overcome the loneliness of isolated Western farm life by organizing social and educational activities. They also established co-operatives for buying farm machinery and other equipment, in order to get wholesale prices. Many of these co-operatives, like those established by the Knights of Labour, were deliberately undersold by merchants and bankers who foresaw a serious loss of profit if the co-operative movement succeeded. The Grange also brought pressure to bear on local legislatures and Congress for such measures as currency inflation to ease the repayment of debts, tariff reductions and railway rate regulation. In the depression year of 1873 the protesting Grangers issued a "Farmers' Declaration

185

of Independence" couched in terms which suggested a sense of historical precedent:

> When in the course of human events, it becomes necessary for a class of people, suffering from long continued systems of oppression and abuse, to rouse themselves from an apathetic indifference to their own interests, which has become habitual; to assume among their fellow citizens that equal station, and demand from the government they support, those equal rights to which the laws of nature, and of nature's God entitle them; a decent respect for the opinions of mankind requires that they should declare the causes that impel them to a course so necessary to their own protection.

One of their main complaints was against the railway companies:

> The history of the present railway monopoly is a history of repeated injuries and oppressions, all having in direct object the establishment of an absolute tyranny over the people of these states unequalled in any monarchy of the Old World, and having its only parallel in the history of the Medieval Ages, when the strong hand was the only law, and the highways of commerce were taxed by the Feudal Barons, who from their strongholds, surrounded by their armies of vassals, could levy such tribute upon the traveller as their own wills alone should dictate.

In the early 1870's, beginning in Illinois, the Grangers succeeded in getting state laws to regulate railway and warehouse rates.

Railroads and other businesses reacted violently to rate regulation, afraid that if it were to succeed government control might be further extended to business methods and profits. Thus railway lawyers challenged the "Granger Laws" in the courts. But in 1877 the Supreme Court decided that state governments did possess the right to regulate many kinds of business. Chief Justice Waite gave his opinion that "When private property is devoted to public use, it is subject to public regulation." Despite this victory, the Grangers failed to influence monetary or tariff policy or to promote government regulation of the trusts. By the 1880's the Grangers had become a purely social organization and their political activity was taken over by Farmers' Alliances and independent political parties in many states.

One factor which had stimulated the farmers to take political action and, as one of the Western Alliance women said, "to raise less corn and more Hell," was a Supreme Court decision in 1886. A Supreme Court Judge, Mr. Justice Field, gave it as his opinion that to limit profit was, in effect, to deprive the business owner of some of his property: "All that is beneficial in property arises from its use, and the fruits of that use," he wrote, "and whatever deprives a person of them deprives him of all that is desirable or valuable in the title and possession." Now, the Fourteenth Amendment, originally passed to help the freedmen after the Civil War, declared that no state shall "deprive any person of life, liberty, or *property*, without due process of law," and the Fifth Amendment placed a like restriction upon Congress; the implications of Field's decision, then, were that government could not regulate business. Specifically, however, Field's decision declared that state regulation of railways was unconstitutional because it infringed upon the congressional power to regulate "interstate commerce." Since practically all railways were parts of systems which crossed state lines, Field's decision seriously undermined any attempts at state regulation.

As protests against the monopolies and the trusts, and demands for their regulation continued to mount, some measure of reform was gained. Congress gave in to the demand from farmers and some businessmen who objected to discriminatory freight rates, and passed the Interstate Commerce Act. This Act attempted to establish a federal commission to regulate freight rates. Conservative business interests, however, challenged the legislation and the Supreme Court acted quickly. In 1890, and again in 1897, it ruled that fixing railway rates by government action meant depriving the railways of "property" without "due process of law," that is, court action. The implication of these and other court decisions was that a corporation was a "person" in the eyes of the law, and thus was entitled to all the protections of personal rights provided in federal and state constitutions.

The other main result of political protests against monopolies had been the Sherman Anti-Trust Act passed in 1890. After a congressional investigating commission had revealed details of trust operations, the Act was passed through both Houses with only one opposing vote. The Sherman Act made illegal "every contract, combination in the form of trust or otherwise, or conspiracy in restraint of trade or commerce among the several states or with foreign nations." It empowered the government to prosecute violators of the Act. But since many of its terms were not clearly defined, the Sherman Act was not very effective.

The failure of most attempts to bring the giant trusts under public control left many doubts about the success of the democratic process, and promoted another round of efforts to achieve political reform. For such a political reform movement there were many precedents reaching back to the days of Jefferson and Jackson. One of the most recent had occurred in the 1870's and was known as the Greenback movement, "greenback" being the popular name for government-printed currency. The Greenback party advocated the printing of more paper money as a means of easing financial credit for farmers. A ringing declaration in the platform revealed its basic attitude:

> We demand a government of the people, by the people and for the people, instead of a government of the bondholders, by the bondholders and for the bondholders.

Greenbackers elected fourteen Congressmen in 1878 and enjoyed considerable electoral success in the 1880's. At the same time farmers throughout the West and South formed Farmers' Alliances to press state and federal legislatures to pass laws favourable to agriculture. By 1890 the Southern

Alliance had three million white members while the Coloured Farmers' Alliance had another 700,000. Combined Alliance membership in the West was about 650,000.

By 1889 a united farmers' party seemed possible. In a convention at St. Louis the leaders of the various Farmers' Alliances found many points of agreement for what might be a national "farmers' platform": government control of railways and public utilities; tariff reform; easier farm credit; monetary inflation; and government warehouses for farm produce. But there were also points of disagreement. Northerners resisted the Southern Alliance's refusal to admit Negroes to its membership, which meant that the Coloured Alliance had to remain a separate organization. Southerners, on the other hand, were reluctant to undertake the formation of a separate national political party. They were accustomed to working inside the Democratic party, which was the only effective party in the South, and they did not want to form a third party, because it might weaken the anti-Negro Democrats in the South and lead to increased Negro rights.

Most Southern farm leaders, however, set their third party doubts aside temporarily to help in establishing the National People's party. The new organization was generally known as the Populist party and its platform included all of the essential Alliance planks: a flexible national currency issued solely by the central government; unlimited minting of silver coins; a graduated income tax to replace revenue lost by lowering the tariff; a government sub-treasury which would pay farmers eighty per cent of the value of crops stored for sale in government-operated warehouses; public ownership and operation of telegraph and telephone systems as well as of all railways; and elimination of corporate land speculation in the West. The general point of view of the Populists was clearly shown in a few bitter sentences:

> Corruption dominates the ballot-box, the Legislatures, the Congress, and touches even the ermine of the bench. The people are demoralized. . . . The newspapers are largely subsidized or muzzled, public opinion silenced, business prostrated, homes covered with mortgages,

labour impoverished, and the land concentrated in the hands of capitalists. . . . The fruits of the toil of millions are boldly stolen to build up colossal fortunes for a few, unprecedented in the history of mankind; and the possessors of these, in turn, despise the republic and endanger liberty.

In the 1892 Presidential election the Populist candidate, James B. Weaver, won more than eight per cent of the popular vote. The Populists also elected seven Senators and a considerable group of Representatives as well as several state governors and numerous state legislators. No third party had done as well since the birth of the Republican party in the 1850's, and Populist hopes ran high. But the Populist vote was very weak in the older agricultural states such as Iowa, Illinois and Wisconsin and negligible in the populous Eastern states. Moreover, white Southern Populists remained sceptical of the third-party idea and continued to devote most of their energy to capturing state branches of the Democratic party. Even in the West, the idea of capturing the Democratic party and using it to achieve Populist reforms was spreading.

4. THE ELECTION OF 1896

By 1896, some Populist leaders were ready to return to the Democratic party in an effort to capture the federal Democratic convention. They were aided in this plan by President Cleveland's extreme unpopularity and the continuance of the depression which inclined many Democrats to be sympathetic towards reform ideas. Some Democratic leaders felt that the central Populist idea of inflation and "free silver" would be a very popular election issue. The Democrats, therefore, decided to "steal the Populists' thunder," and the chief proponent of this strategy was William Jennings Bryan of Nebraska.

The 1896 Democratic convention was divided sharply on the issue of a gold standard versus a silver standard (or hard money versus inflation) but it was clear that the supporters of gold, who would have nominated Cleveland, were in a minority. The Democratic platform repudiated all of Cleveland's policies, from the gold standard and hard money to anti-labour measures. Although Bryan was supported by wealthy Western silver interests, he persuaded the delegates he was a reformer and carried the convention with one of the most famous speeches in American history:

> If they ask us why it is that we say more on the money question than we say upon the tariff question, I reply that, if protection has slain its thousands the gold standard has slain its tens of thousands . . . when we have restored the money of the Constitution, all other reforms will be possible. . . .
>
> You come to us and tell us that the great cities are in favour of the gold standard; we reply that the great cities rest upon our broad and fertile prairies. Burn down your cities and leave our farms, and your cities will spring up again as if by magic; but destroy our farms and the grass will grow in the streets of every city in the country. . . . Having behind us the producing masses of this nation and the world, supported by the commercial interests, the labouring interests and the toilers everywhere, we will answer their demand for a gold standard by saying to them: you shall not press down upon the brow of labour this crown of thorns, you shall not crucify mankind upon a cross of gold.

Bryan's silver tongue brought the convention to its feet in a frenzy of emotion. But although he repeated his "cross of gold" speech in various forms across the country and the Populist party endorsed his candidacy, he did not win the election. The Democrats in urban centres refused to support him, and this more than offset the support he gained from the Populists. More important, Bryan's campaign for inflation had little appeal for the worker who, with more-or-less fixed wages, did not see how he could benefit from inflation. Divisions within the Democratic party proved disastrous. Very astute Republican tactics and an increase in the price of wheat two months before the election together proved disastrous to Democratic hopes and the Populist movement.

The Republican party in 1896 was largely managed by Marcus A. Hanna, a wealthy businessman from Cleveland, Ohio. Hanna had groomed William McKinley, a Senator from Ohio, for the Presidency, as a man of no ideas who would do what he was told. Billing McKinley as "the advance agent of prosperity" and author of the 1890 high tariff, Hanna easily secured for him the Republican nomination. During the election McKinley delivered a few ghost-written and non-committal speeches from his verandah in Canton, Ohio, while Bryan covered 18,000 miles in an exhausting speaking tour. Businessmen contributed over $10,000,000 to the Republican war chest, while Democrats fought the campaign with $425,000. Farmers were threatened with foreclosure of mortgages, and factory hands with unemployment should Bryan be elected and "free silver" triumph. The election of 1896 came close to being a class struggle and was described by a "conservative" observer as:

> A rising of miserable bankrupt farmers, and day labourers who have made the greatest fight against organized capital of the world that has ever been made in this country—or perhaps ever. No money, no press, no leaders, no organization. Amidst abuse, ridicule, intimidation, bribery—against forces so powerful and so subtle that they reach the bravest and most honest men in the country.

Although McKinley won 271 electoral college votes to Bryan's 176, the Republican plurality was only 600,000. But in other ways it was a decisive election. The Populist party died with Bryan's defeat, killed by rising farm prices, and by the decision to co-operate with the Democratic party. Conservatism took on a new lease of life. The way was prepared for expansion overseas. The result also reflected basic changes in American society, particularly the steady progress of urbanization. Many reformers and liberals who were concerned about city and industrial problems were not enthu-

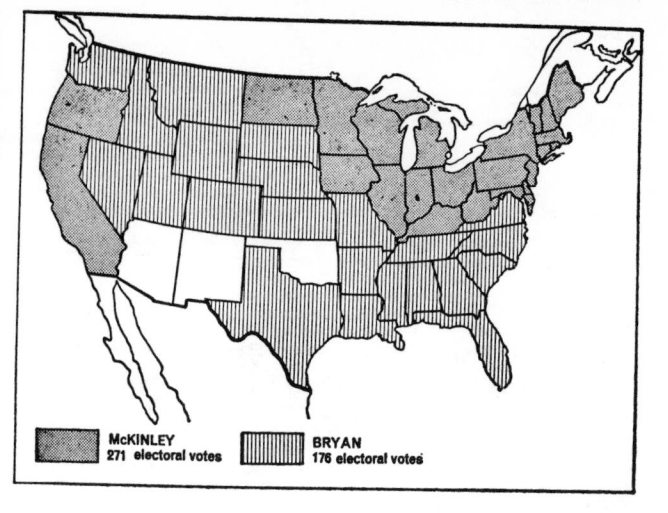

THE ELECTION OF 1896

siastic about Bryan with his stress on Western farm interests. To some extent the Bryan "crusade" was the last political explosion of agrarianism. While many reform planks from Western protest movements were to appear in later party programmes, after 1896 the initiative for reform was to come primarily from the cities and towns of the East and Midwest.

11

"A Splendid Little War"

THE AMERICAN spirit of "Manifest Destiny" which had remained unbroken since the founding of the Republic reached one of its periodic peaks of enthusiasm at the end of the nineteenth century. The years following the Civil War had seen a steady preparation for this. In 1867, for example, William H. Seward, Secretary of State under Lincoln and Johnson, was quite confident that his purchase of Alaska from Russia was a prelude to the peaceful annexation of Canada. His successors used the new American foothold in the north to declare that the Bering Sea was *mare clausum*, that is, a closed sea in which American authority was absolute. In other areas of the Pacific, as well as in Latin America, the growing assertiveness of the United States became more and more evident as the century drew to its close.

1. "MANIFEST DESTINY" ABROAD

One spectacular illustration of the American sense of destiny was occasioned by a border dispute which arose between Venezuela and the colony of British Guiana. The dispute was a long-standing one, but it came to a head when gold was discovered in the area. Britain repeatedly refused to submit the dispute to arbitration. In 1895 Secretary of State Olney wrote a note to the British Prime Minister in which he reasserted the Monroe Doctrine, and claimed that no European power had the right to interfere in "American" affairs. Olney denounced European imperialism, and proclaimed that the Americas lay within the United States

194

"sphere of influence." "Today," he wrote, "the United States is practically sovereign on this continent, and its fiat is law upon the subjects to which it confines its interposition."

To support Olney's position, President Cleveland obtained funds from Congress for a commission to determine the boundary between Venezuela and British Guiana. He declared that it was the duty of the United States to enforce the findings of this commission "by every means in its power," which meant war if Britain remained adamant. At this time, however, various alliances were being formed on the continent of Europe, all of which excluded Britain. As a result, Britain was most anxious to have the friendship of the United States and she therefore refrained from forcing the issue and using her vastly superior naval power. The boundary question was resolved when Britain agreed to accept the decision of an arbitration tribunal which in the end upheld the British case.

Another aspect of the "sphere of influence" interpretation of the Monroe Doctrine was revealed in 1889, when delegates from the Latin American republics met with representatives of the United States in the first of what was to be a regular series of conferences. The delegates established the International Bureau of American Republics which later became the Pan-American Union, with its headquarters in Washington. Although the Union set up many useful committees for the purpose of exchanging information, the Latin American nations regarded it as an instrument of American influence, or even domination. Their conviction that they were not equals with the United States in the Union was strengthened when the American government directly interfered with a revolution in Chile in 1891, and a trade dispute in Brazil in 1893. More and more, it became apparent that the main concern of the United States in Latin America was to exclude European influence and to support politicians there who were favourable to the expansion of American trade and investment.

In Chile, Peru, Costa Rica and other Latin countries, Americans invested heavily in railways, copper, silver and

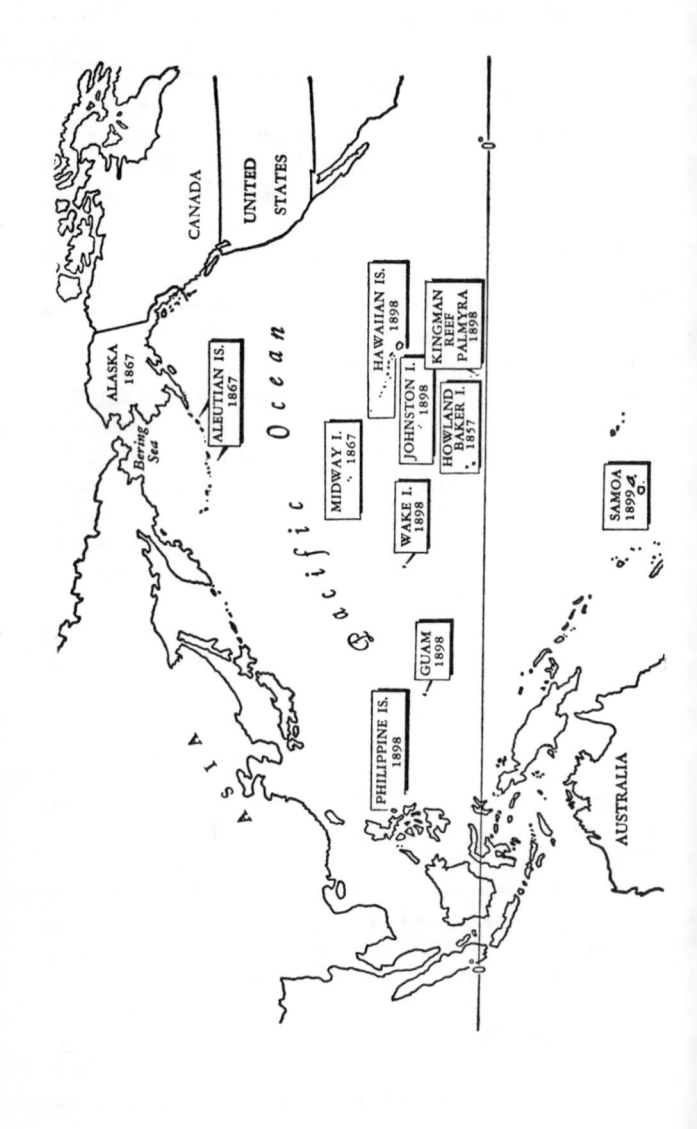

THE UNITED STATES IN THE PACIFIC

tin mines and grew increasingly influential in the politics of these countries. In 1899 the owners of American banana plantations formed the United Fruit Company, an American corporation which soon dominated the economic life of small states like Costa Rica, Nicaragua, Santo Domingo and Guatemala. The company, which also had large interests in Cuba and Colombia, came to exert great influence upon the policies of the American government towards the so-called "banana republics" in Latin America.

The expansion of the United States into the Pacific was also vigorous, if less firmly supported by public opinion. Ever since Commodore Matthew C. Perry opened Japan to American trade in 1853, American businessmen had taken an increasing interest in the commerce of the Pacific. Supported by farm-state representatives, Congress in 1856 passed a law enabling the President to annex any island which was rich in guano, a natural fertilizer. As a result, the United States acquired a considerable number of tiny islands in the Pacific. Other islands such as Samoa, with its fine harbour of Pago Pago, were desired as coaling stations for the United States Pacific trading ships. In 1878 a treaty with the ruling Samoan monarch gave the United States the harbour rights sought by American businessmen. But in 1889, the Germans, who also had economic interests in the islands, sought to undo this agreement by overthrowing the Samoan government. The matter was temporarily settled in that same year when Britain, Germany and the United States established a joint "protectorate" over Samoa. Ten years later a new agreement gave Pago Pago to the United States and the rest of Samoa to Germany.

Far more important to the United States in its expansionist mood was the acquisition of the Hawaiian Islands, first visited by American missionaries in the 1820's. Economic ties soon strengthened the religious connection. American immigrants produced sugar and pineapples there for the home market, and sailed their whalers into Hawaiian ports. Increasingly concerned about the dangers presented by imperialist rivalries in the Pacific, the Americans strengthened their naval power by securing from the Hawaiian government in 1887 the exclusive right to use Pearl Harbor. In the same year, seeking still greater control, American businessmen engineered the overthrow of the corrupt government of King Kalakaua of Hawaii and forced him to accept a new form of government—called the "Bayonet Constitution" by the Hawaiians—which gave white foreigners the vote and disfranchised the bulk of the native population. Six years later, when the Hawaiians under Queen Liliuokalani tried to regain power, the American community rose against them and set up a republic. Although the American minister in Hawaii supported the rising and authorized the use of American troops, the Cleveland administration in Washington was not enthusiastic about the means adopted and refused to annex the islands at that time.

2. THE NEW IMPERIALISM

By 1898 the United States, like the nations of Europe, was caught up in a wave of imperialism. During the nineteenth century, the United States had filled out her continental domain and reached tentatively into Latin America, Alaska and the Pacific. The new American imperialism of the twentieth century was a different matter, involving the annexation of far-flung islands in the Caribbean and the Pacific and the use of financial influence and naval power to secure control over the policies of other states.

Imperialism in the United States had roots similar to European imperialism. American capitalists sought new areas in which to invest their surplus money, new sources of raw materials to feed American industry, and new markets for industrial products. Since the achievement of these goals was felt to require the co-operation of government through appropriate foreign diplomatic policies and the use of armed forces, there developed an intimate relationship between business policy and American foreign policy. At the same time, as the economic depression lifted after 1896, a more confident national spirit began to assert itself in the

United States. Americans wished to turn away from the painful years of civil war, industrial strife and political bitterness, and to immerse themselves in some kind of unifying national achievement. Given these strong motives, other arguments for entry into the world of imperial competition fell quickly into place. The application of Social Darwinism to international relations led easily to the conclusion that the United States must increase in size and power in order to survive. The American dream required that the United States should use its new economic and military power to protect what the British poet Rudyard Kipling called "the lesser breeds without the law" and show them the road to republican democracy. Finally, it was confidently asserted that the United States must seize and safeguard the approaches to the New World or else its national security would be precarious in a world of grasping imperial powers and military alliances.

In the 1880's and 1890's many powerful advocates of imperialism appeared. The most literate imperialist was Captain A. T. Mahan of the United States navy. In his book *The Influence of Sea Power Upon History* and in many other articles and books, Mahan argued that British power had always depended upon her naval superiority which enabled her not only to act decisively in war, but to build the sinews of economic and military strength by controlling colonies, naval stations and even world commerce. As the proper inheritor of this British power, Mahan continued, the United States must act quickly to build a large navy and emulate earlier British imperial policies. It was therefore imperative that the United States control the Caribbean and construct a canal through the Central American isthmus. Mahan also expanded the current doctrine of Social Darwinism. The white Anglo-Saxons, he declared, had proved their exceptional power to survive in the evolutionary race and should face up to the challenge of the future, the principal feature of which would be an epic struggle between Eastern and Western civilizations.

A powerful group of young Republicans supported Mahan's arguments for a great navy and an imperialist foreign policy. Among the most prominent of these were Senators Henry Cabot Lodge of Massachusetts, Albert Beveridge of Indiana and William McKinley of Ohio. Theodore Roosevelt, who became Assistant Secretary of the Navy in 1897, and John Hay, who became Ambassador to London in 1897 and Secretary of State in 1898, were other prominent Republican imperialists. Their ranks were strengthened by the support of a number of Democrats outside Congress and several influential editors, clergymen and businessmen. One of the most voluble spokesmen of American imperialism was Josiah Strong, a minister who crusaded for reform in the cities but who also believed firmly in the superiority and "Manifest Destiny" of the American branch of the "Anglo-Saxon" people. In a widely read book, *Our Country*, he proclaimed that the "peculiarly aggressive traits" developed by Americans were calculated to spread reform, social justice and "spiritual Christianity" across the face of the earth.

Bowing to this imperialist persuasion, Congress passed a Naval Act in 1890, which appropriated money to construct ships of every class. By 1900 the United States navy, with an official policy of being "second to none," had become the world's third largest sea force. The navy was more than ready for the crisis that developed in 1898 in the affairs of Spanish Cuba.

3. THE SPANISH-AMERICAN WAR

American interest in Cuba was almost as old as the Republic itself. Before the Civil War, that interest had been mostly on the part of slaveholders who viewed Cuba as a possible new slave state. After the war, American investment in Cuban sugar plantations, processing plants and railways had grown steadily and by 1898 amounted to more than fifty million dollars. At the same time, the United States had become the major market for the sugar upon which the economy of Cuba rested. In 1894, however, the American duty on foreign sugar was increased, a move which brought economic ruin to Cuba. The Cubans, who with the Puerto Ricans were the last of Spain's subjects in the New World, were driven to desperation by this aggravation of their perennial poverty. Although the Cubans had been in chronic revolt against Spain since the 1860's, the fresh outbreak of rebellion in 1895 led some Americans to fear that success for the rebels might mean occupation of the island by another European power, possibly France which, through its project to build a Panama Canal, already had interests in that area.

Other factors combined to tempt American imperialists to think of intervening in the Cuban revolt. Cubans purposely damaged American property on the island, in the hope that the United States would intervene to protect its interests and ultimately help overthrow Spanish rule. Some American businessmen thought it would be well worth-while to impress the Latin American countries with the new power of the United States. The idea of acquiring Cuba, or a naval station there, also fitted admirably into the ideas of Mahan's followers. Finally, in attempting to put down the revolt the Spanish government resorted to a ruthless policy of repression. General "Butcher" Weyler and his 200,000 troops showed no mercy as they herded thousands of Cuban rebels into concentration camps. The sensational press in the United States covered the Cuban revolt in lurid detail, printing highly coloured stories and drawings of Spanish atrocities. The Spanish press replied in kind: "Scoundrels by nature, the American jingoes believe that all men are made like themselves . . . they are not even worth our contempt, or the saliva with which we might honour them in spitting at their faces." As newspaper circulation soared, an increasing number of Americans demanded that their government take action to liberate the Cuban people.

For a time there seemed some chance of a peaceful solution of Cuba's problems: the Spanish government in Madrid recalled Weyler and abandoned the concentration camp policy. Then, in February 1898, came a new crisis which made war with the United States almost inevitable. The great battleship, the U.S.S. *Maine*, pride of the new American fleet, blew up in Havana harbour. She had been sent there at the request of the American consul-general to "protect American lives and property." Although no one ever determined the cause of the explosion, the Hearst press and other sensationalist papers at once reported that the *Maine* had been blown up by "enemy" action. The big-navy men in the government, and the popular press clamoured for war with Spain. A flood of letters and personal appeals urged President McKinley to send a war message to Congress.

The President was reluctant to yield to this pressure, for the American ambassador in Madrid had just informed him that the Spanish government had agreed to meet every American demand, including an immediate armistice with the rebels. Spain was willing to accept independence, autonomy or American annexation as a future for Cuba. But the weak McKinley could not resist the popular clamour for war and finally accepted the arguments of close advisers like "Teddy" Roosevelt who maintained that the "blood of the murdered men of the *Maine* calls for the full measure of atonement." Roosevelt's real meaning was made clear in a hundred speeches and letters: the United States, he argued, needed a war to keep it from getting "flabby" and to advance its world mission. Other Republican leaders believed that a war would unite the nation, and reduce the mounting demand for political reform as well as the demand for government regulation of business that had been stimulated by the economic depression of the 1890's. On April 11, 1898, McKinley sent a message to Congress in which he said nothing of the latest reports of Spanish concessions and urged Congress to declare war against Spain.

The "splendid little war," as Secretary of State John Hay described the Spanish-American War, found the United States generally ill prepared. The navy, however, was ready.

Roosevelt, the Assistant Secretary of the Navy, had anticipated the war and had ordered Commodore George Dewey who was in charge of the Pacific fleet to stand ready to seize Manila, the capital of the Spanish colony of the Philippines. Aided by the benevolent neutrality of the British naval force in the area, Dewey succeeded in his mission. In Cuba American military success owed more to Spanish incompetence than to United States skill. The Secretary of War was a Michigan politician who had been more interested in patronage than in proper maintenance of the army. Thus American troops fought in heavy winter uniforms in the Cuban heat and far more died of disease than from enemy action. Nevertheless, several reputations were made in the Spanish-American War. The outstanding hero to emerge from the war was Teddy Roosevelt who organized a troop of cavalry, known as the Rough Riders, and was present at the principal battle of the war, the capture of San Juan Hill. In reality, the dangerous positions on the hill had been taken by American Negro troops before Roosevelt's famous charge was executed; but the charge caught the fancy of the people of the United States, and did much to aid Roosevelt's later political career.

The treaty with Spain, which ended the war in 1898, reflected the expansionist enthusiasm stimulated by the war itself. The United States took from Spain Puerto Rico in the Caribbean, and Guam and the Philippines in the Pacific. Cuba was given "independence" as an American protectorate. The United States paid twenty million dollars compensation to Spain for these acquisitions, and spent many more millions as well as hundreds of lives subduing a fierce three-year rebellion against American rule in the Philippines. An amendment to the congressional declaration of war had specified that Cuba should not be annexed, and it was not; but a measure passed in 1901 seriously limited Cuban sovereignty by leaving control of Cuban foreign and financial policy in United States hands.

The Spanish-American War had achieved much of the programme advocated by the imperialists, who immediately began to consolidate and expand their gains. One of the peace negotiators remarked that the acquisition of the Philippines made the Pacific an American lake, into which much commerce and investment was expected to flow. The success of the war, and general business prosperity, helped to bring about another Republican victory in 1900, in which McKinley was re-elected, with Theodore Roosevelt, the hero of the Rough Rider charge at San Juan Hill, as his Vice-President. Despite the founding of an Anti-Imperialist League, which gained the adherence of men in both parties, popular opinion supported the new aggressiveness of United States policy and, for good or ill, the United States was launched on an imperial course which would sweep her ever more surely into world politics.

4. THE COURSE OF IMPERIALISM

John Hay, McKinley's Secretary of State, followed up the new American gains in the Pacific by active intervention in Chinese affairs. In 1899, in diplomatic notes to Russia, England and Germany, he enunciated an "Open Door" policy to be followed by Western powers in their relations with the Chinese empire. Each of the three recipients of the notes already had territorial concessions and special trading rights in China. By these means they discriminated against other foreign traders and ignored the Chinese customs laws. The Chinese government was weak and corrupt and could not prevent the foreign powers from acting as they wished. In his note Hay declared that European powers active in China should give equal treatment to all nations, and should support the Chinese tariff collectors. This policy would be of advantage to the United States because the Chinese had already granted concessions on duties to American imports. The other powers accepted Hay's position in principle, especially since it did not involve any restriction on their acquisition of territory in China. In 1900 a rebellion, known as the Boxer Rebellion, broke out against foreign control of China. The United States participated with the other European powers and Japan in suppressing it and in forcing the payment of an indemnity by the Chinese government. The Americans agreed, however, that their share of the indemnity should be used to promote Chinese education.

In 1901 President McKinley was assassinated. Theodore Roosevelt became President and under him the imperial movement quickened. In 1904-05, Japan and Russia fought a war in which Japan was speedily victorious. Afraid that Japan might move to exclude the United States from the China Sea trade, Roosevelt accepted a Japanese request to mediate between the belligerents. Thus the treaty ending the Russo-Japanese War was concluded by negotiators meeting in Portsmouth, New Hampshire. The Treaty of Portsmouth seemed to symbolize America's advance into world politics. It also heralded the expansion of Japanese power in the Pacific. This ominous development induced Roosevelt to send the American navy on a "training cruise" around the world, as an exhibition of power. Nevertheless, the President arranged an agreement in 1908 in which Japan and the United States agreed to uphold the Open Door principle in China and recognize the integrity of China and each other's interests in the Pacific.

At home, Roosevelt moved quickly to consolidate United States control of the Caribbean and to construct a canal through the Isthmus of Panama. In 1901 Secretary of State John Hay turned to good use the growing willingness of Britain to co-operate with the United States by concluding a treaty by which Britain accepted the American plan to build and police a canal under United States authority. The route selected by the United States lay through the province of Panama, part of the Republic of Colombia.

Hay negotiated a treaty with Colombia by which that country granted to the United States a strip of land across the isthmus in return for ten million dollars and an annual payment of two hundred and fifty thousand dollars. The Colombian Senate, however, refused to ratify the treaty. Rather than be held up by this obstruction, Roosevelt gave clandestine support to several groups who wished to foment a

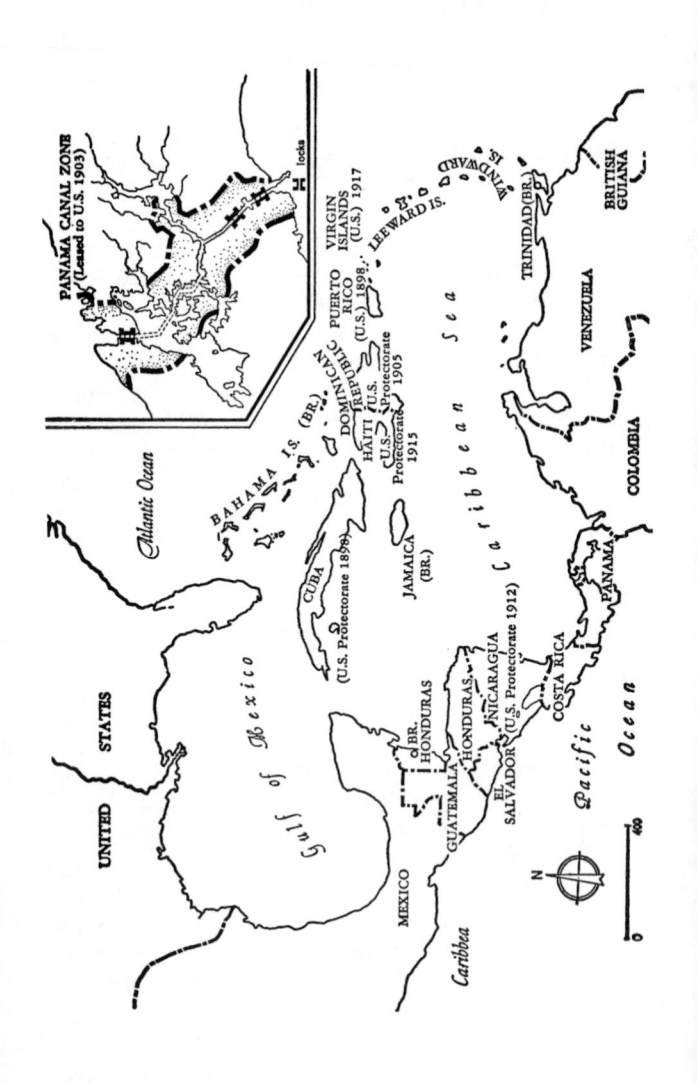

THE UNITED STATES IN THE CARIBBEAN

rebellion in Panama and to detach that province from Colombia. On November 3, 1903 the U.S.S. *Nashville* anchored off Panama and on the following day a "spontaneous" rebellion began. Other American ships joined the *Nashville* and prevented Colombia from suppressing the revolt. On November 6 the State Department recognized the rebel government and within a week Roosevelt received the chief organizer of the revolt as Ambassador of the new Republic of Panama. At once a treaty was arranged by which Panama granted the United States a permanent zone across the isthmus in return for the ten million dollars and two hundred and fifty thousand dollars annuity proposed to Colombia. In later years Roosevelt reminisced:

> If I had followed traditional conservative methods, I should have submitted a dignified state paper of probably two hundred pages to the Congress and the debate would be going on yet, but I took the Canal Zone and then left Congress—not to debate the canal, but to debate me, and while the debate goes on, the canal does also.

The Panama Canal, completed in 1914 after heroic engineering efforts, added greatly to the naval capability of the United States, and stimulated the economy of the entire west coast. But the method of its acquisition strained relations between the United States and Latin America for a long period of time. Although the United States made a compensatory payment of twenty-five million dollars to Colombia in 1921, the payment did little to soothe outraged Latin American opinion.

Roosevelt's motto was that in diplomacy one should "speak softly and carry a big stick." The "big stick" was again in evidence in a dispute with Canada over the Alaska boundary in 1903. By making it perfectly clear that failure by Britain to support the American claims would mean the use of force, Roosevelt made a mockery of the "impartial tribunal," set up to settle the boundary. The whole controversy produced tensions in Canadian-American relations similar to the effects produced in Latin America by the Panama adventure.

In 1905, asserting the right of the United States to intervene in the affairs of the Dominican Republic, Roosevelt proclaimed a corollary to the Monroe Doctrine. When the Latin republic defaulted in its foreign debt payments Roosevelt intervened in order to prevent a European creditor nation from employing forcible debt collecting. In cases of "chronic wrong-doing" by an American nation, said Roosevelt, the United States must itself act as policeman since, by the Monroe Doctrine it denied to European nations the right of intervention in the Americas. Following this doctrine under Roosevelt and the next two Presidents, Taft and Wilson, the United States intervened with her armed forces in the Dominican Republic, Haiti, Honduras, Nicaragua and other nations. Indeed, between 1900 and 1930, most of the Caribbean republics were little more than American protectorates. The period from 1909 to 1913 saw a particularly emphatic phase of imperialism, sometimes described by the term "dollar diplomacy." Philander Knox, President Taft's Secretary of State, induced American banking houses to extend their investments in Latin America and then to act as virtual government agencies. President Wilson professed aversion to "big stick" methods, but such procedures continued to be used after he became President in 1913. In Mexico, where American investment in railways, oil wells, mines and cattle had reached the impressive figure of over a billion dollars by 1913, Wilson intervened both indirectly and directly in support of the opponents of the "strong man" Huerta who was a threat to the stability required by United States investors. While Wilson insisted that his motives were liberal, the argument failed to impress Latin Americans.

By the time the First World War broke out in Europe, the United States had become a major world power. Its imperial interests reached across the Americas and to the Orient. Americans had even participated in the important European conferences at the Hague (1899) and Algeciras (1906). While many Americans were increasingly critical of imperialism and of any diplomatic connection with European powers, the involvement of the United States in world trade and politics was to make it more and more difficult for America to remain aloof from world affairs.

12

The Politics of Progressivism

THE YEARS after 1896 saw the collapse of the Populist programme and the triumph of imperialism in foreign policy,
but they also witnessed a surge of reform zeal which spread
from the cities to state and federal politics. The men and
women who urged a wide variety of reforms in these years
were called Progressives. Many of them had been inspired
by the Populist programme, while others were attracted by
the critical writings of men like Edward Bellamy and H. D.
Lloyd. Most of them were middle-class, professional people
and small businessmen who felt that the "businessman's
revolution" with its trusts and "kept politicians" had deprived them of their traditional status in American society.
Business decisions, they felt, were made at the board meetings of the great trusts, while political policy was made in
smoke-filled rooms presided over by powerful political
bosses. The Progressives asked the question: under such
conditions, where was the equality of opportunity supposedly
guaranteed by the American way of life?

1. THE DEMAND FOR REFORM

Like the Jacksonians of an earlier age, the Progressives
believed that most social ills could be cured by ensuring that
the control of government was at all times directly in the
hands of a majority of the people; and that monopoly or
special privileges of any kind were destructive of American
ideals. Many of them were alarmed by the growing inequality between classes in America, and felt that the powers

of government must be used to guarantee minimum standards of welfare and to prevent unlimited control of economic life by a few great trusts. Such beliefs plainly ran counter to the ideas of Social Darwinism, for they required government intervention in what Social Darwinists held was the "process of natural selection." Progressives argued that it was "natural" for men to seek social justice and to use a democratic government to achieve the desires of a majority of the people. Some Progressive writers pointed to examples of social economic legislation in Britain, Germany and France as worthy of imitation. They maintained that effective factory inspection laws, various forms of social insurance, workmen's compensation acts, and laws against child labour were necessary if democracy were to survive the triumph of large scale industrial organization and urbanization. In his inaugural address in 1913, President Woodrow Wilson summed up this aspect of Progressive thought:

> There can be no equality of opportunity, the first essential of justice in the body politic, if men and women and children be not shielded in their lives, their very vitality, from the consequences of great industrial and social processes which they cannot alter, or control, or singly cope with.

The demand for political and economic reform was reinforced by the spread of "social gospel" thought in the churches. Religious leaders argued that sin was encouraged by environment, and that Christians had a moral obligation to remove the social and economic evils in society. A host of journalists wrote articles for magazines exposing the facts about monopoly in banking, meat-packing, oil, steel and indeed every branch of industry and finance. These journalists, whose articles were based on the most careful research, probed all aspects of American life, from the appalling exploitation of children in industry to corruption in the Senate, from malpractice in municipal administration to the methods by which great wealth had been garnered by the few. Dozens of magazines devoted themselves to "muckraking," as this

211

kind of journalism came to be known. While some of the muckrakers became socialists and supported extensive public ownership and economic planning, the majority concluded that less drastic political, social and economic reforms could make the American system work satisfactorily.

Progressivism as a political movement originated in a multitude of demands for municipal reform. At the turn of the century, disgusted with the widespread graft of urban political governments, the people elected reform candidates to office in one city after another. Frequently the reformers met with violence and intimidation, but often, too, they were supported by substantial businessmen who disliked both the inefficiency and the dishonesty of rule by political bosses. In the 1890's New York's Tammany Hall machine was defeated and a reform mayor was elected in Chicago. In neither case was the change permanent, but the idea spread. In 1901 a prominent businessman, Tom Johnson, was elected mayor of Cleveland and held the post until 1910. Under Johnson the city's tax system was reformed and Cleveland became a model of good municipal government. Municipal reformers elsewhere developed the idea of "commission government," or civic government conducted by a commission of men without party affiliation. A number of cities carried this idea one step farther by having the elected commission appoint a single person as "city manager." Reform governments in many cities improved the quality of life by programmes of beautification, slum clearance and social welfare. Frequently, however, both the reform administrations and their reforms were short-lived, often because the ousted party politicians sought the help of their associates in the state government which had power to limit the activities of city governments. As a result, Progressives began to turn their attention to the reform of state politics.

Progressive movements appeared in most of the states during the first decade of the twentieth century, and affected the policies of both political parties. The outstanding Progressive state governor was Robert M. LaFollette of Wisconsin. First elected in 1900, LaFollette took over the

Republican organization and cleaned out its machine politicians. Using ideas produced by a "brains trust" of professors in the University of Wisconsin, the Governor launched a major reform programme. With the help of Progressive Republicans in the legislature he secured stricter regulation of railways and public utilities by the state government and a more equitable tax system. Progressives in many other states implemented similar if less extensive reforms.

In devising ways of ensuring popular control of governments at all levels, the Progressives borrowed ideas publicized earlier by Populists, and added several new ones of their own. As a means of preventing political parties or governments from being controlled by machines or corporations, the Progressives advocated "direct democracy," particularly the use of "initiative," "referendum," and "recall." Initiative allowed voters themselves to initiate legislation by providing that any bill which got the signature of a given percentage of the electorate (usually five to eight per cent) had to be introduced in the state legislature. If the legislature then turned such a bill down, it could be referred to the voters in a referendum. A referendum might also be requested for any bill which was before the legislature in the normal manner. Recall provided that any elected official could be removed from office before his term expired if twenty-five per cent of the electorate signed a petition for another election. In 1921 the Governor of North Dakota and some other administrative officers were removed from their positions by the use of recall. However, although many states adopted these procedures, none of them made any serious impact upon American democracy, and only in a few states are they still on the statute books.

Another Progressive plank was the "direct primary," which was first introduced by LaFollette in Wisconsin. By this procedure party candidates were to be selected not by caucuses or conventions but by "primary" elections in which all registered party members could vote. Designed to reduce the control of party bosses over candidates, it was adopted by all but three states by 1916, and soon applied to federal, state and even in some cases Presidential candidates. While the method permitted reform candidates to win party nominations over the opposition of party bosses it also increased the expenses of candidates by making two election campaigns necessary. Whether the direct primary actually made democracy more "direct" by increasing the voters' control of candidates and representatives is debatable. Some observers feel that it has merely made control of the major parties more complicated without making it more democratic. Similar doubts have been entertained about the direct election of federal Senators. Progressive agitation for this reform resulted in ratification of the Seventeenth Amendment to the Constitution in 1913, which provided that Senators were to be elected by the voters rather than by the state legislatures.

The political philosophy of the American Progressives exhibited a traditional aspect of American thought dating back to Tom Paine and Thomas Jefferson: the conviction that all government is suspect, in that it tends to breed vested interests and restrict individual liberty. Yet, the Progressive's suspicion of all government was continually in conflict with their other principal purpose of using government positively to ensure both equality of opportunity and social welfare. As a result, when the influence of the Progressives came to be felt in federal politics, there was lack of agreement on several basic ideas, and despite a widespread support for reform the outstanding Progressive Presidents, Theodore Roosevelt and Woodrow Wilson, were essentially conservative in temperament and policy.

2. THE ADMINISTRATIONS OF ROOSEVELT AND TAFT

Two curious political developments accounted for Theodore Roosevelt's accession to the Presidency. In 1900 Thomas Platt, the political boss of New York, had secured the Vice-Presidential nomination for Roosevelt, in order to "kick Teddy upstairs," because as Governor of New York Roosevelt had refused to co-operate with Platt's Republican machine. Not only had he opposed the appointment of Platt's nominees to public offices and the granting of legislative favours to Platt supporters, he had also indicated support of Progressive political ideas. Platt was not deterred from arranging the Vice-Presidential nomination by the warning of another party boss, Mark Hanna, who observed: "Don't any of you realize that there's only one life between this madman and the White House?" In Hanna's eyes Roosevelt as President would be a disaster because Roosevelt believed that the government should be as active in domestic affairs as it had been in foreign affairs. In September 1901 Hanna's worst fears were realized when President McKinley was assassinated by a half-crazed anarchist and Roosevelt became President. The party bosses received sceptically Roosevelt's assurance that as President he would "continue, absolutely unbroken, the policy of President McKinley."

Theodore Roosevelt was incapable of following anyone's policy unbroken. He became one of the most colourful of American Presidents. Born into a well-to-do middle-class family he had been a rancher in the West and advocated the "red-blooded" life for everybody. While he believed that large corporations were necessary to the continued economic growth of the country, he distrusted men of great wealth, particularly "vulgar" *nouveaux riches*, and thought that in the public interest trusts should be regulated by government. He also thought that the government should hold the balance between such contending interests in society as labour, farmers and industrialists.

In 1902 Roosevelt directed his Attorney-General to launch a suit under the Sherman Anti-Trust Act to dissolve a monster amalgamation of banking-railway interests known as the Northern Securities Company. This company held a controlling interest in several major railways. It had been formed after a battle in the New York Stock Exchange between two great finanical groups, each of which was striving for control of the railways involved. As the price of the railway shares fluctuated, many small investors were ruined, and in the end the prinicpal competitors came together to form the Northern Securities Company which would control all of the lines over which the battle had raged. In attacking this huge new trust Roosevelt knew that he was pursuing a popular Progressive line. Many Progressives believed that he was going to break up *all* the trusts and become a genuine "trust-buster." In fact, Roosevelt believed in using government power only to prevent glaring injustices resulting from the misuse of trust organizations. When the Supreme Court in the Northern Securities Case (1904) ordered the trust dissolved Roosevelt declared: "The most powerful men in this country were held to accountability before the law." Roosevelt's reputation for positive executive leadership had also been enhanced by his intervention in a coal strike in 1902. In this crisis he compelled the mine-owners to accept arbitration of the dispute by threatening to have the army take over operation of the mines.

By 1904 the President's popularity easily won him the Republican nomination. Disillusioned by two defeats under Bryan's leadership, the Democrats nominated as their candidate the conservative Judge Alton B. Parker of New York. Although many Progressive votes went to the Republican Roosevelt, he also retained the confidence of big business, which contributed heavily to his campaign in the belief that Roosevelt's brand of trust-busting was not a major threat to their interests. Winning every state outside the Democratic South, Roosevelt announced, after the election, with characteristic lack of caution: "Under no circumstances will I be a candidate for, or accept another nomination."

In his second term, Roosevelt continued to be Progessivism's best propagandist and supported a number of significant Progressive measures. Government regulation of railways was made more effective by the Hepburn Act in 1906, which increased the powers of the Interstate Commerce Commission and gave it some control over freight rates. "Muckraking" books on the dangers of patent medicines and meat-packing processes led to public demand for government action in these fields. As a result, Roosevelt supported congressional leaders in passing the Pure Food and Drugs Act of 1906 which outlawed some of the worst abuses in these industries. The President also led in the Progressive drive for conservation of natural resources, which were being savagely depleted by mining and lumber corporations. Roosevelt set aside nearly a hundred and fifty million acres of unsold timber land as forest reserves, and supported the appointment of Gifford Pinchot, a dedicated conservationist, to the Department of Agriculture, to supervise conservation. While the policy of conservation touched only the fringes of the problem, it was at least a long-delayed beginning.

Despite a financial panic in 1907, Roosevelt's popularity was at its peak when the Republican Convention met in 1908. The outgoing President used his influence to secure nomination of his close friend, William H. Taft. Although the Democrats turned again to W. J. Bryan, they failed to exploit effectively the Progressive mood of the country. Taft was elected and almost at once showed himself to be much less in sympathy with Progressive measures than Roosevelt had appeared to be. He failed to control the Republicans in the Senate and they took the party steadily toward conservatism. In 1909 Taft signed the Payne-Aldrich tariff bill, which favoured special interests and repudiated the Republicans' campaign plank of tariff reform. He also allowed the Roosevelt conservation policy to be jettisoned in favour of large corporations that wished to exploit reserved coal lands.

In 1911 Taft supported a movement to sign a reciprocity agreement with Canada. This alienated the Republican farm belt especially, while his apparent lack of interest in Progressivism offended many of Roosevelt's supporters. Led by G. W. Norris in the House, and Robert LaFollette and Albert Beveridge in the Senate, a group of Republicans organized the Progressive Republican League in 1911. The League endorsed LaFollette as its Presidential candidate. At this critical juncture Roosevelt returned from an African game-hunting holiday and explosively re-entered politics. Convinced that Taft had run the party on the shoals, and that he, Roosevelt, was the only one who could recapture Progressive voting strength, he announced that he was a candidate for the Republican nomination as President. This not only ruined LaFollette's chances but split the Progressive group, and in June 1912 the Republican Convention, under conservative control, renominated Taft.

Roosevelt's supporters withdrew to form the Progressive party with "T.R." as their candidate. The Progressive platform of 1912, described as the New Nationalism, included all the planks concerned with direct democracy and gave heavy emphasis to the need for closer regulation of big business, tariff reform and conservation. In addition, it specified a wide range of social reforms; minimum wage legislation, the eight-hour day, prohibition of child labour and "the protection of home life against the hazards of sickness, irregular employment and old age through the adoption of a system of social insurance adapted to American use." In a speech announcing his candidacy, Roosevelt had proclaimed that he felt just like a bull-moose entering the fray; the Progressive party was at once dubbed the Bull-Moose party.

3. WOODROW WILSON AND THE NEW FREEDOM

In 1912 Bryan's influence helped to swing the Democrats towards reform and win the nomination for Woodrow Wilson, who had gained a reputation as a reformer and honest politician when he was Governor of New Jersey. Before entering politics in 1910, the quiet and studious Wilson had been a professor of political science and, later, President of Princeton University. Of Virginia Presbyterian stock, Wilson possessed not only a stern piety, but also a distinctly conservative Southern outlook on such matters as the position of Negroes and women in society. He explained his ambition for power by arguing that power should be willingly accepted by men whose intelligence was matched by their sense of public responsibility. As a political scientist he had argued that the American congressional system, with its

218

sometimes paralyzing separation of powers, should be held together by strong and conscientious executive leadership. To many Americans, Wilson appeared as a cold and unbending figure; to others he embodied the triumph of idealism in politics.

The Democratic platform, termed the New Freedom, advocated more vigorous anti-trust action, lower tariffs, conservation, and banking and currency reform. The Democrats placed less emphasis on social reform, however, than did the Bull-Moosers. In actual practice, the differences between the New Freedom and the New Nationalism of the Progressives were slight. Louis D. Brandeis, a friend of Wilson's and one of the greatest American judges, said that Wilson was for regulated competition while Roosevelt was for regulated monopoly. Few people saw the distinction clearly if, indeed, there was much distinction. In practice, Roosevelt was more willing to accept as natural the increasing size of business units, as long as government remained strong too, while Wilson was more doubtful about the very

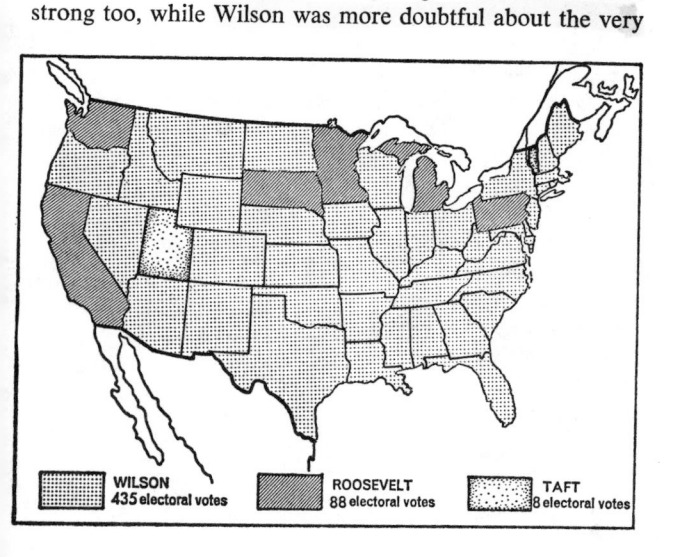

WILSON
435 electoral votes

ROOSEVELT
88 electoral votes

TAFT
8 electoral votes

THE ELECTION OF 1912

219

existence of trusts. In any event, the measures later supported by Wilson and passed by Congress from 1913 to 1916 were to add perceptibly to the positive role of government in the United States, while not lessening the tendency of economic power to be concentrated in fewer and fewer hands.

In the election of 1912 the deep split in the Republican ranks told heavily against them, while businessmen in the Democratic party did not feel that Wilson's brand of Progressivism was a real threat to them. The result reflected the Progressive mood of the nation. Wilson received 41.86 per cent of the popular vote; Roosevelt, 27.40 per cent; Taft, 23.18 per cent; and Debs, the Socialist candidate, 5.99 per cent. Since Wilson's majorities had been in the most populous Northern states, as well as in the South, his electoral college vote was a clear majority. The Democrats also won both Houses of Congress.

Like Roosevelt, Wilson used his executive powers with vigour. Calling a special session of Congress in 1913, he supported a tariff bill which cut the average duty from about thirty-eight per cent to twenty-nine per cent. When special interests lobbied strenuously against the bill the President openly denounced them, and intervened personally to secure its passage. The Sixteenth Amendment giving Congress specific power to levy income taxes was adopted in the same year. Indeed, the tariff of 1913 included such a tax, long demanded by Progressives, partly to provide revenue lost by the reduced duties, partly as a more equitable method of raising public money. In December 1913 Congress also passed banking legislation which went some way towards meeting the Populist-Progressive demands for an expandable currency and easier credit. The Federal Reserve Act established a Federal Reserve Board to supervise banking. In 1916 Congress also created a Federal Farm Loan Board which provided credit on favourable terms to farmers.

The Democrats implemented their anti-trust plank in 1914 by passing the Federal Trade Commission Act which forbade "unfair" business practices, without defining them, and by the Clayton Act, which attempted to define and outlaw the procedures by which giant trusts were formed and competition was lessened. Having received the support of the A.F. of L. and Sam Gompers in 1912, Wilson agreed to a clause in the Clayton Act excluding labour unions from prosecution as "combinations in restraint of trade." Gompers hailed this as a great victory but the Supreme Court later decided that such exclusion was impossible. On some occasions, however, Wilson showed decidedly conservative inclinations by failing to give his support to federal legislation against child labour until it became politically necessary to endorse the Keating-Owen Act of 1916, which attempted unsuccessfully to outlaw child labour in industry.

Much of the President's apparent purpose of regulating business was nullified by the appointment of anti-regulation businessmen to administrative positions, and the Clayton Act itself was suspended when war broke out in Europe in 1914. Deeply disillusioned, LaFollette observed that neither Roosevelt nor Wilson was a profoundly committed Progressive. Both Roosevelt and Wilson saw the necessity of catering to the Progressive mood, and both distrusted irresponsible economic power; but both also drew back before the prospect of a determined and sustained conflict with the nation's major economic leaders.

The Progressive period established precedents for positive government and placed on the statute books some salutary laws of a protective nature, but it did not seem to modify the basic direction of economic and political development. At the end of the period the Morgan and Rockefeller financial and industrial interests between them controlled corporations whose value was greater than the assessed worth of all property in all the states west of the Mississippi. The process of concentration of wealth was to be hastened by the First World War and by the conservative period that followed in the 1920's. On the other hand, Progressivism deepened the American faith that a democracy, given determined leadership, could control its own destiny. Thus, while many Progressives were disappointed by the relatively superficial reforms of the period, others were heartened by the evidence it provided of political vitality.

13

Wilson's Dilemma

WHEN WOODROW WILSON became President he had little interest in foreign affairs, yet they were to dominate the greater part of his public life. Although wedded to the ways of peace, he took his country into its first major overseas war and became deeply involved in the very European diplomacy which he decried.

1. THE BACKGROUND OF INTERVENTION

When, in 1914, war broke out in Europe between Britain, France and Russia on one side, and the empires of Germany and Austria on the other, Wilson issued a proclamation of neutrality in which he asked the American people to be "neutral in fact as well as in name." Strict neutrality, however, was not easy, for the majority of Americans, including the President, were sympathetic to Britain and France. At the same time there were large minorities who felt differently. In 1914 almost thirty-three million Americans were either naturalized citizens born outside the United States or were the children of such citizens. Of these, about eight million had a German background and over four million an Irish one. Unlike the native-born, the foreign-born were not swayed by the ties of language, custom and political tradition, or by Britain's pro-American diplomacy which had been the rule since the Civil War. The Irish, and many other foreign-born Americans, saw Britain as "perfidious." Some native-born Americans felt the European war was an imperialist conflict, just one more symptom of the sickness of

European diplomacy. Progressives felt that participation in such a war would destroy American liberal ideals. Faced with this kind of division in public opinion, the President decided the United States should remain neutral and should try to exercise a determining influence upon the post-war settlement, and perhaps even to mediate between the contenders in order to end the war more quickly. The events of the war and changing public opinion in the country, however, were to make this increasingly difficult.

A significant factor in changing public opinion was British control of the transatlantic cables. The heavily pro-Allied news that came by this route was supplemented by the skilful work of a Canadian writer, Sir Gilbert Parker, who became chief of British propaganda in the United States. Supplying speakers, information and editorial comment to newspapers, Parker effectively established the image of brutal and despotic Huns holding Belgian babies aloft on their bayonets and ready to crush all that was best in western civilization. For a while this process of opinion-forming was partly counterbalanced by American irritation with Britain's blockade of German ports, her supervision of all neutral shipping, and the long list of goods she declared contraband.

But Americans resented even more bitterly Germany's resort to submarine warfare. In February 1915 Germany declared that enemy merchant vessels in the seas around the British Isles would be sunk without warning and that neutral ships entering that zone would do so at their peril. In May 1915 a German submarine sank the Cunard liner *Lusitania* off the Irish coast, and a hundred Americans were drowned. The ship was carrying munitions and other contraband. Nevertheless, the sinking of the *Lusitania* made the agitation for American intervention in the war mount rapidly. Wilson sent extremely stiff notes to the German government, and Bryan, who was not in sympathy with this policy, resigned. (Bryan had tried to persuade Wilson to prohibit Americans from travel in the war zone.) He was replaced as Secretary of State by Robert Lansing, whose sympathies were strongly pro-British. In addition, the American ambassador in London, Walter Hines Page, and Wilson's personal friend and roving ambassador, Colonel Edward House, were urging the President to give more active support to the Allies.

For nine months after the *Lusitania* episode Germany refrained from extensive submarine attacks on merchant shipping, and even promised not to resume them. Meanwhile, through Colonel House, Wilson vainly attempted to mediate between the Allies and the Central Powers. By the end of 1915 the President was convinced both that the United States could not stay out of the war should it continue much longer, and that the prospects of an early end to hostilities were faint. As he said to Congress in December: "I assure you that there is not a day to be lost. There may be at any moment a time when I cannot preserve both the honour and peace of the United States." He gave full support to a preparedness campaign which rapidly expanded the armed services and established a Council of National Defence to co-ordinate industry for war production. Nevertheless, Wilson won the election of 1916 primarily with the slogan "He kept us out of war." An important factor in the 1916 election, however, was the adoption of several social reform planks by the Democrats, which persuaded a number of Republican Progressives, who had voted for the Bull-Moose party and the New Nationalism in 1912, to support Wilson in 1916.

In January 1917 a desperate Germany decided to risk driving the United States into war by resuming unrestricted submarine warfare in the hope of strangling France and Britain before American troops could reach Europe. Diplomatic relations with Germany were terminated immediately. During February German submarines sank more than two hundred merchant ships, many of which flew neutral flags. By early March the prospect of a German victory was very real. British morale was faltering, French troops had mutinied, and Russia was crippled by the March Revolution which overthrew the Czar's government. The last factor was doubly significant, for, as a leading Progressive noted, the

Revolution seemed to "cast the influence of a great nation in favour of true democratization of the war against merely imperialistic use of victory." The collapse of the Czarist régime seemed to make more possible the realization of Wilson's plea for a peace without victory and a League of Nations to maintain an international peace.

At the same time, there were forces at work which were less idealistic than the aims of Wilson and his supporters. In the early months of the war most American securities owned by British and French investors had been sold to Americans in order to finance purchases in the United States. For the first time the United States became a creditor nation and, in a sense, formally ceased to be a European economic colony. Of more immediate importance was the fact that the United States had increasingly financed the Allied war effort. A German victory would wipe out much of this investment. Moreover, many American businessmen were interested in the economic opportunities offered by the preparedness campaign and even more in the prospects for expansion which would inevitably follow American entry into the war. More specific events, however, were to become the immediate causes of war.

Early in March 1917 the British intercepted and decoded a message from Alfred Zimmermann, the German Foreign Secretary, to the German ambassador in Mexico, which revealed a German attempt to arrange an alliance with Japan and Mexico should the United States enter the war. Mexico was promised that Texas, Arizona and New Mexico should be restored to her as a reward. After a week's hesitation, Wilson gave the Zimmermann note to the press as a means of securing greater public support for his decision to arm American merchant ships. When American ships fell prey to the submarine campaign in March, Wilson finally felt justified in asking Congress to declare war on the side of the Allies. He had resisted longer than many statesmen would have felt able to, and although by April he had little choice, he was still painfully aware of the implications of his decision. A prominent New York journalist gave this report of an interview with the President the day before Wilson asked Congress to declare war:

> "We couldn't fight Germany and maintain the ideals of Government that all thinking men share. . . . Once lead this people into war," he said, "and they'll forget there ever was such a thing as tolerance. To fight you must be brutal and ruthless, and the spirit of ruthless brutality will enter into the very fibre of our national life, infecting Congress, the courts, the policeman on the beat, the man on the street." Conformity would be the only virtue, said the President, and every man who refused to conform would have to pay the penalty.
>
> He thought the Constitution would not survive it; that free speech and the right of assembly would go. . . .

On the following morning Wilson delivered his message to the Congress:

> With a profound sense of the solemn and even tragical character of the step I am taking. . . I advise that the Congress declare the recent course of the Imperial German Government to be in fact nothing less than war against the government and people of the United States; that it formally accept the status of belligerent which has thus been thrust upon it. . . . The world must be made safe for democracy.

On April 4, 1917 the Senate passed the declaration of war.

2. THE RESULTS OF INTERVENTION

Wilson's fears about the effects of the war upon America were only slightly exaggerated. At once the spirit of Progressivism was cast aside. Despite the President's statement that the war was not against the German people, the Committee on Public Information mobilized scholars, speakers, editors, clergymen to pound home the idea that the whole of German history showed the depravity of the Hun. The Committee's work strengthened the bigotry that lies dormant in every nation, with the result that hundreds of thousands of German-Americans went in fear, hundreds of foreigners, pacifists, socialists and liberals were maltreated, and not a few were killed by violent outbursts of "patriotism." George Creel who headed the Committee on Public Information which was established in 1917 to counter "subversive ideas" later regretted the excesses of the patriotic campaign, writing: "The chauvinists, however, managed to figure largely in the Liberty Loan drives . . . and flooded the country with posters showing 'bloody boots,' trampled children and mutilated women." In June 1917 the Espionage Act provided severe penalties for opposition to conscription for military service and in May 1918 the Sedition Act went much further. It decreed fines of $10,000 and imprisonment for twenty years for anyone hindering the sale of Liberty Bonds, discouraging recruiting, commenting adversely on the American form of government, or advocating "any curtailment of production in this country of anything necessary or essential to the prosecution of the war."

One of the most striking features of life on the domestic front was the economic boom fostered by war orders, which was accompanied by uncontrolled profiteering. Vast fortunes were made, despite higher income and corporation taxes. The War Industries Board and other government bodies, established to stimulate production, lacked the power to prevent fraudulent contracts, hoarding of scarce commodities or inflation. Property values and prices rose more rapidly than wages and salaries, which caused severe hardship for many classes. The American Federation of Labour consented to a no-strike pledge in 1918 and Samuel Gompers was appointed to the War Labour Conference Board which was established to advise the government on labour matters. The increased acreage under cultivation and a rise in prices led farm income to increase nearly thirty per cent from 1915 to 1918, although much of this gain was offset by inflation. Higher levels of direct taxation and the sale of bonds financed the war.

The United States made a major contribution to the Allied war effort. At the outset, the navy was of crucial importance. Anglo-American convoys reduced shipping losses by two-thirds between April and November 1917 and the two navies effectively countered the submarine menace by mining the North Sea route by which the submarines escaped. This reversal of German undersea fortunes came at the crucial moment for Britain and France, since the former rate of loss in merchant shipping if sustained might well have given Germany the quick victory on which she had gambled when she decided to resume unrestricted sea warfare. Curbing the submarines also meant that when the main stream of the American Expeditionary Force began to cross the Atlantic early in 1918 it did so in relative safety. Two million American soldiers eventually reached Europe, and no troop transport was sunk.

The military result was decisive. With the psychological encouragement of the American declaration of war, reduction of losses at sea, and speeding up of supplies, the Allies withstood the major offensive launched by the Germans on the Western Front in the spring of 1918, although Germany had 300,000 more soldiers than the Allies. The advantage in men was cancelled by summer, and at the end of the war in November the presence in Europe of a million and a half Americans gave the Allies a marked superiority in manpower. To raise its manpower the United States relied on the Selective Service Act of May 1917 which compelled all men between twenty-one and thirty (later between eighteen and forty-five) years of age to register for service. Conscripts were chosen by lottery from among the five classes defined in the Act. There were cases of irregularity in this method of raising an army, but there was no serious complaint about the principle of the legislation, apart from those who opposed the war itself.

By the time of the Armistice of November 11, 1918 American losses stood at 48,000 killed in action, 2,900 missing and 56,000 dead from disease. Compared to the British war dead of 947,000, the French of 1,385,000 or even the Canadian of 60,000, these losses were relatively slight. On the other hand, the experience was bitter and the cost high enough to raise a post-war isolationist feeling equal in intensity to wartime patriotic fervour.

3. WILSON AND THE PEACE SETTLEMENT

This isolationist feeling impeded and ultimately destroyed Wilson's magnificent attempt to secure a lasting peace. Before the United States entered the war he had appealed for "peace without victory," and after 1917 he had repeated that the Allies fought neither for revenge nor for territorial gain, but only to destroy autocratic government. In January 1918 he placed before Congress a programme for peace that embodied his famous Fourteen Points, which included the following: "open covenants of peace, openly arrived at"; freedom of the seas, in peace and war; the removal of economic barriers among nations; the reduction of armaments "to the lowest point consistent with domestic safety"; the adjustment of European boundaries to conform with lines of nationality; the free and autonomous development of subject peoples in Europe; an impartial adjustment of colonial claims which would take into account the interests of the peoples concerned; and a general association of nations to guarantee and protect the political independence and territorial integrity of its members. Wilson became the hero of millions of war-weary Europeans, for in his programme, it seemed, was the promise of genuine liberal democracy and peaceful internationalism.

It was, however, infinitely more difficult to implement such high aspirations than it was to state them. Acting both as a stimulant for a Wilsonian peace and as an obstacle to it was the Bolshevik Revolution in Russia in November 1917, which was headed by Lenin. The triumph of Bolshevism, with its idea of International Communism, warned the Allies that western democracy and capitalism might be destroyed if a genuine peace were not made on a lasting basis. Yet the fear of Communism led the Allied powers to launch an unsuccessful military campaign in Russia in 1918 to unseat Lenin and the Bolsheviks, even though the White Russians, whom the Allies supported, represented the kind of autocracy that Wilson had pledged himself to destroy. Moreover, while other Allied leaders applauded Wilson's sentiments, they were by no means willing to forego the fruits of victory. The desire for revenge, the demand for territorial gains, the concern for security and the promises made to each other in secret treaties all stood in the way of the implementation of the Fourteen Points.

At Paris, where representatives of the victorious Allies gathered to draw up a peace treaty, Wilson's high idealism clashed with the hard-headed realism of Lloyd George of Britain, Georges Clemenceau of France and Vittorio Orlando of Italy. Faced with their insistence on revenge, security, and territorial gains, Wilson had to compromise on one principle after another. National self-determination was sometimes sacrificed on the altar of security and compensation for the victors, as agreed earlier in a variety of secret treaties. The German empire disappeared. The German people were so humiliated by occupation of their territory and so weakened by the imposition of enormous reparations for the damage their armies had caused in Europe that the basis was laid for another German appeal to arms, less than a generation later, which almost destroyed western civilization. Freedom of trade and freedom of the seas were virtually ignored. Wilson fully realized how great were the concessions he had made, and in an attempt to console himself he wrote in September 1919: "It is a very severe settlement with Germany, but there is not anything in it that she did not earn."

The price of all Wilson's concessions was the agreement of the Allies to establish a League of Nations and include it as an essential part of the peace settlement. Wilson pinned his hopes for "a just and lasting peace" on the League. "It is a definite guarantee by word against aggression," he told his colleagues at Paris. "It is a definite guarantee against the things which have just come near bringing the whole structure of civilization into ruin." A Covenant defining the League's functions was drawn up. Under Article X, the heart of the Covenant according to Wilson, members of the

League promised "to respect and preserve as against external aggression the territorial integrity and existing political independence" of its members. The member nations were pledged to bring matters that threatened war before the League and submit them to inquiry and arbitration. Article XVI created machinery to stop an aggressor by providing for the imposition of economic and military sanctions against it. A Permanent Court of International Justice was established at The Hague under the Covenant of the League.

Although the Europeans may have been less convinced than Wilson that the League would solve all the problems of diplomacy and war, the chief opposition to the League came not from Europe but in the United States. This was due partly to political blunders by the President and partly to traditional factors in American foreign policy. In the congressional elections of October 1918, the Republicans won control of Congress, despite Wilson's appeal to the electorate to give him a mandate by electing Democrats. The appeal served only to alienate those Republicans who had supported the President's military and foreign policy, however, and Wilson's subsequent failure to take any Republicans to Paris further outraged his opponents. This last blunder was tragic, for there were many outstanding Republicans who shared his views and who would have been of great value at Paris and later in the political struggle at home.

The traditional American fear of European diplomacy further strengthened Republican opposition to Wilson. Despite an amendment to the Covenant which conceded that the Monroe Doctrine should be beyond League jurisdiction and another that permitted a member to withdraw from the League, many Americans viewed the League as an instrument of European diplomacy which would involve the United States in every European war. The principles of collective security and American isolationism were thus starkly opposed. Led by Henry Cabot Lodge, chairman of the powerful Senate Committee on Foreign Relations and a personal enemy of Wilson, a group of isolationist "irreconcilables" gathered their forces in the Senate to oppose any connection with the League. Not only did the League destroy American freedom of action, cried Senator William Borah, but as an association based on force it threatened American democracy:

> You cannot yoke a government whose fundamental maxim is liberty to a young government whose first law is force and hope to preserve the former. . . . We may become one of the four dictators of the world, but we shall no longer be master of our own spirit. And shall it profit us as a nation if we shall go forth to the domination of the earth and share with others the glory of world control and lose that fine sense of confidence in the people, the soul of democracy?

Not only the Republican isolationists were opposed to the League and the peace treaty. German-Americans felt that Wilson had too readily accepted a harsh and vindictive peace. Irish-Americans were incensed that he had not supported the movement for Irish independence. Many Democrats themselves wanted to see American obligations under the Covenant defined and reduced, while some liberals and Progressives although supporting ratification, were reluctant to endorse the harsh terms of the peace treaty.

Nevertheless, Wilson rightly believed that a majority of the people and even of the Senate favoured American membership in the League. What Wilson needed at this critical juncture was patience, flexibility, diplomacy, and above all that astute political sense which could see when small concessions would bring major gains. But these fine arts the President lacked. He refused to accept any amendments or reservations which might have conciliated enough of his opponents in the Senate to give him the necessary two-thirds majority. When the anxious French ambassador assured him that the Allies would willingly accept the amendments to secure American entry to the League, Wilson was adamant: "I shall consent to nothing. The Senate must take its medicine." Wilson felt that he had compromised too much at Paris to get the League established; now he would begin to save his soul. The days of compromise and concession were over; it would be total victory or absolute defeat.

It was absolute defeat. As the Senate debated fourteen reservations proposed by Senator Lodge, supposedly designed to limit American obligations but in fact drawn up to make American membership in the League impossible, President Wilson took his case to the people. For a month in the fall of 1919 he toured the country, as if in an election campaign, denouncing his opponents and pleading with his people to endorse the principles of collective security which might prevent another world war. Already weakened by wartime strains and the influenza he had contracted in Paris, the frail President suffered a complete physical collapse. From his bedside he appealed successfully to the Senate to reject the treaty with the Lodge reservations.

Wilson and Lodge were asked from all sides to find a basis of compromise, but both refused. In March 1920 when the treaty again came before the Senate with reservations, many Democrats disobeyed the President and supported the treaty, in an attempt to find a way out of the deadlock. But the vote of forty-nine to thirty-five was still seven short of the necessary two-thirds majority. Wilson had gambled and lost. The United States rejected the treaty and the League. Not until July 1921 did the United States formally declare that hostilities were over. Not until the bleak days of the Second World War did the United States assume that position in the world which Woodrow Wilson had fought for in 1919 and 1920 at the cost of his life.

The period of imperialism, Progressivism and war came to an end in general disillusionment: disillusionment of idealistic Progressives at the results of a war supposedly fought to make the world safe for democracy; and disillusionment of a President who believed that his justification for taking his nation into war had been stolen from him. On the other hand, the United States was entering another period of rapid economic growth, and the election of 1920 symbolized the dual mood of disillusionment and expectancy. In that election the totally undistinguished Republican

Senator Warren Gamaliel Harding of Ohio defeated the Democratic candidate James M. Cox of Ohio to become President of the United States. Cox was a Wilson supporter and his defeat seemed to endorse Harding's electoral method of standing on both sides of every question, including the treaty and the League, and allowing the party machine to provide the few speeches he delivered. Harding's own analysis of the election provided the name by which the period from 1919 to 1929 would be known: "America's present need is not heroics but healing," he said, "not nostrums but normalcy; not revolution but restoration." It was both Harding's weakness and his political strength as an "average man" that he should unwittingly employ a word unknown to the English language. The United States was about to enter a period of "normalcy."

14

Farewell to Reform

WARREN G. HARDING's ideal of "normalcy" dominated the 1920's and marked the triumph of political conservatism and *laissez-faire*. Most influential Americans now accepted the ideals of the business community without question. The government abandoned the wartime policies of economic planning and gave unrestricted free enterprise a green light. Successive Republican administrations refused to resume the prosecution of the trusts, and instead extended lavish aid to private business. Businessmen supplemented these public policies by organizing extensive and effective anti-union campaigns. Judicial decisions also reflected the triumph of "normalcy" as the courts declared unconstitutional the former Progressive measures in the field of social welfare and industrial regulation. The philosophy of "normalcy" was best expressed by Herbert Hoover, who became Republican President in 1928:

> When the war closed, the most vital of all issues . . . was whether governments should continue their wartime ownership and operation of many instrumentalities of production and distribution. We were challenged with a peacetime choice between the American system of rugged individualism and a European philosophy of diametrically opposed doctrines—doctrines of paternalism and state socialism. The acceptance of these ideas would have meant the destruction of self-government through centralization of government. It would have meant the undermining of the individual initiative and enterprise through which our people have grown to unparalleled greatness.

Ironically, Mr. Hoover delivered his "rugged individualism" speech during the election campaign of 1928, just one year before the stock-market crash touched off the Great Depression of the 1930's.

1. RADICALISM AND CONFORMITY

The " 'Twenties" have attracted the attention of an army of novelists, historians, and dramatists who have given the decade such names as the Roaring 'Twenties, The Aspirin Age, The Jazz Age, and Prosperity Decade. However, despite their profusion, none of these titles reveals the potent combination of vitality and frustration that characterized the United States in the years that followed the First World War.

A series of disturbing events heralded the new period of "normalcy." The very high cost of living at the end of the war produced serious unrest among farmers and workers. Following the Armistice of 1918, criticism of government policy mounted sharply. A wave of strikes rocked the nation's economy and thoroughly alarmed leaders in government and business. More significant were demands by mine and railway unions that the government assume the ownership and operation of their industries (as it had done with the railways during the war). To many people, such demands had an unpleasant "Bolshevist" ring that recalled the successful Russian Revolution of 1917, and the attempted Communist revolutions in eastern Europe in 1919. Linking unions, strikes, and demands for public ownership with Bolshevism, the press, business, and government used propaganda techniques developed during the war to create public fears of imminent revolution. Isolated acts of violence, exaggerated out of all proportion, were portrayed as part of a monstrous Bolshevist or anarchist plot to overthrow the government by disrupting industry. Soon known as the "Red Scare," these charges had such a profound influence on public opinion that civil liberties became as insecure during the early 1920's as they had been during the war.

In 1919 and 1920, individual anarchists committed acts

of outrage which helped to bolster the Red Scare campaign. Parcels in the mails, addressed to prominent persons, were found to contain bombs. One bomb exploded on the front lawn of Attorney-General Mitchell Palmer's home. In September 1920 a bomb exploded on Wall Street in New York killing thirty-eight people and injuring many more. Some politicians and newspapers used the tragedy to demand the eradication of radicalism from American life. Five socialist members of the New York Legislative Assembly were expelled on the ground that they could not properly swear to uphold the American Constitution. A man who shot and killed a foreign-born American citizen for saying "to hell with the United States" was swiftly exonerated in court. A kind of vigilante action by conservatives caused liberals and dissenters to live in fear of bitter criticism or actual molestation.

Thousands of people who had previously supported Progressive candidates now accepted without question the Red Scare news stories and editorials. Wilson's Attorney-General Palmer, a former Progressive, moved swiftly from Progressive principles. After issuing an injunction forbidding union leaders to organize a coal strike, Palmer ordered a nationwide roundup of foreign-born radicals. Of the more than six thousand people who were arrested, over five hundred were eventually deported. Many of those arrested were neither Communist nor foreign-born. The most notorious case of the period was that of Niccolo Sacco and Bartolomeo Vanzetti, both Italian-born philosophical anarchists, who were arrested following the hold-up and murder of two men carrying a factory payroll. Accused of the crime, Sacco and Vanzetti were found guilty in a Massachusetts court, and sentenced to death. Liberals within and outside the United States charged that the court had been influenced by the poisonous atmosphere engendered by the Red Scare and that the trial and verdict had been a gross miscarriage of justice. On the basis of new evidence, the liberals launched a campaign to obtain a retrial. The execution of Sacco and Vanzetti was delayed, but in 1927 both went to the electric chair. Many

Americans were firmly convinced of their innocence, and believed they had really been executed because they were anarchists.

In the South, the Ku Klux Klan revived with terrifying vigour and broadened purpose, and soon became an important and vicious instrument for the enforcement of conformity to the Klan's idea of Americanism. Reorganized in 1915, the Klan announced as its aim the protection of a Protestant and Anglo-Saxon United States from the multiple threat of foreign political ideas, Negroes, Jews and Roman Catholics. Fiery crosses aflame on dark Southern hilltops announced an assault on some unfortunate "un-Americans." The Klan remained an important power in Southern and Midwestern politics until revelations of widespread corruption in the late 1920's seriously damaged its already unsavoury reputation.

The pressure for religious conformity was strong in the South where Protestant fundamentalists secured state legislation to prohibit the teaching of anything that contradicted a literal interpretation of the Bible. In Tennessee, a high school teacher named John T. Scopes determined to test a state law by purposely teaching the Darwinian theory of evolution, although the law forbade mention of anything that denied "the story of the Divine creation of man as taught in the Bible."

Scopes' trial was a national event. Widely publicized as the "monkey trial" it involved some very prominent contestants. William Jennings Bryan led the state's case, and Clarence Darrow, the nation's most famous liberal lawyer, led the defence of Scopes. In the steaming Tennessee summer, with the entire court in shirtsleeves and swarming with reporters, the trial was a knock-down battle. At first Bryan insisted that it was necessary for every Christian to believe that the world was created in six days in the year 4004 B.C., because this was the accepted fundamentalist interpretation of the Bible. Since this was believed to be true, Bryan argued, the state had a duty to enforce such teaching in its public schools. Darrow reviewed the literature which questioned many of the traditional translations of Biblical sources. Then he trapped Bryan in a net of logic. In reply to Darrow's question, "Do you think the earth was made in six days?," Bryan replied, "Not six days of twenty-four hours." From this crack in the argument, Darrow forced Bryan to admit that creation might have extended over millions of years. Bryan's point about literal meaning was thus destroyed. Although the court found Scopes guilty and imposed a nominal fine, the Scopes-Darrow argument in defence of freedom of opinion and unfettered education helped to reduce pressures of conformity.

Indeed, during the most intense years of the Red Scare, liberal opinion was never silenced. Individual members of the Supreme Court, for example, dissented vigorously from majority decisions against political freedom. In a 1919 case before the Supreme Court, the noted Justice Oliver Wendell Holmes enunciated one of the most famous American definitions of civil liberties. In every case of alleged disloyalty, he declared, the question is "whether the words used are used in such circumstances and are of such nature as to create a clear and present danger that they will bring about the substantive evils that Congress has a right to prevent." The "clear and present danger" doctrine was specifically intended to limit the rights both of legislatures and of courts to restrict freedom of speech and political association.

2. THE POLITICS OF "NORMALCY"

Politically, the 1920's opened with an orgy of corruption. President Harding, the former editor of a small-town Ohio newspaper and a machine politician, was completely uninterested in moral questions. His private life was a mixture of poker and promiscuity, and his administration was riddled with dishonesty. Although he appointed some capable men to his Cabinet, he recruited most of his advisers from his old cronies of the "Ohio Gang." The most shocking of many grave scandals was the "give-away" of the Teapot Dome and Elk Hills naval oil reserve lands in Wyoming and

California. The Secretary of the Navy, Edwin Denby, and Secretary of the Interior, A. B. Fall, arranged the transfer of the oil reserve lands from the Navy Department to the Department of the Interior. Fall then leased the lands to two business groups, in return for which he received $400,000. Harding himself escaped the worst of the revelations when he died of a paralytic stroke in August 1923. Like a predecessor in the Presidency, Ulysses S. Grant, he had fallen prey to the wiles of evil friends.

Calvin Coolidge who, as Vice-President, succeeded Harding on the latter's death combined the New England virtues of thrift and business acumen. He had slowly climbed the rungs of the Massachusetts political ladder, and at the time of his nomination to the Vice-Presidency was Governor of the state. As President, Coolidge maintained Harding's *laissez-faire* policies, and is supposed to have declared that "the business of the United States is business." He refused to intervene in a major coal strike and replaced the advocates of business regulation in agencies such as the Interstate Commerce Commission with men who believed that business should be given an entirely free hand. Coolidge believed that the government should confine itself to maintaining law and order and administering essential services as inexpensively as possible.

By 1924, Progressive influence was largely eliminated from both major parties. A hastily-contrived new electoral alliance took up the name in an effort to carry on Progressive principles. This 1924 Progressive party nominated Robert LaFollette for President and Senator Burton K. Wheeler of Montana for Vice-President. Unlike the major party platforms which were non-committal on most points, the Progressive programme called for public ownership of railways, farm relief, a referendum before a declaration of war, abolition of court injunctions in labour disputes and other familiar Progressive policies. In the campaign, LaFollette received sixteen per cent of the popular vote, but since his opponents identified him with the radicalism which was so much feared at this time, he was no match for the incumbent "prosperity President" whose campaign slogan was "keep cool with Coolidge."

Four more years of prosperity left the Republicans in an equally favourable position to fight the 1928 election. Having accepted Coolidge's blunt remark that he did not "choose to run," the Republican Convention nominated Herbert Hoover, a candidate who was popular in the business world. A former Roosevelt Progressive, Hoover had served as administrator of post-war Belgian relief and later as Secretary of Commerce. In these fields he had proved himself a humane and efficient administrator. In addition, he conformed to the image of the successful businessman. Born on an Iowa farm, he had gained an engineering degree from Leland Stanford University. From engineering he moved to business promotion and soon became a wealthy man. To oppose Hoover the Democrats nominated Alfred E. Smith, the Governor of New York. A rather unpolished politician, Smith had risen from the slums of New York and had gained a reputation as a liberal.

The party platforms in 1928 did not differ significantly, and with no serious third-party threat the contest was one of personalities and interests. Hoover was billed as the "engineer in politics," the able administrator who would resist radical change and preside over unending prosperity. Smith campaigned as a man of the people, but was handicapped by "Republican prosperity," and the facts that he was a Roman Catholic and that he favoured the abolition of Prohibition. In 1918 the sale and manufacture of liquor had been prohibited in the United States. Smith stood for the repeal of the Eighteenth Amendment which had made this Prohibition a part of the Constitution. In wide areas of the South and West which were normally Democratic, Smith's opposition to Prohibition, together with deep-seated Protestant feelings on the part of the electorate, reduced his vote considerably. On the other hand, he appealed to the rising political consciousness of urban immigrants and their descendants, for Smith's own grandparents had been Irish immigrants. Nevertheless, Hoover won all but eight states in the electoral college and received 21,391,000 popular votes to Smith's 15,016,000.

3. THE ECONOMICS OF "NORMALCY"

Economic policy and social attitudes provide further clues to the nature of the 1920's. Encouraged by the absence of anti-trust suits, and with the active assistance of Herbert Hoover as Secretary of Commerce, businessmen worked effectively to minimize competition. In all fields of commerce and industry, mergers of firms swallowed up thousands of small competitors and consolidated the control of economic activity in fewer and fewer hands. In a variety of ways, government actively subsidized business. Trade missions to foreign countries multiplied. The large merchant marine created by the government during the war was sold off to private companies at nominal prices. Private shipping lines were encouraged by high mail subsidies and changes in the tariff which favoured goods imported in American ships. And although the government gave the Interstate Commerce Commission additional power to supervise railway financing, it also encouraged the railroad companies to form combinations for greater efficiency. Tax reductions for business increased the amount of money available for investment, which in turn helped to inflate stock values above their real value and thus left the market weak in the face of any decline in confidence which would lead people to sell their stocks.

Republican tariff policy further assisted the major industrialists. In 1923 the Fordney-McCumber Act restored the levels of protection that had existed prior to the tariff of 1912. The return to high tariffs hindered European recovery from the ravages of war, and other nations raised their tariffs in retaliation. Even after the stock market collapse, and despite mounting public protest, Hoover signed the Hawley-Smoot Tariff Bill which raised duties still higher, and retarded economic recovery during the Great Depression.

The Supreme Court co-operated wholeheartedly in the general trend to reduce government intervention in the economy. In 1919 Progressives in Congress had secured passage of a Child Labour Act which placed a special tax on any firm employing children under fourteen years of age. In 1922 this use of the federal taxing power was declared invalid by the Court.

The Court furthermore declared unconstitutional a law fixing minimum wages for women and children in the District of Columbia. At the same time, federal courts issued frequent injunctions against striking unions and refused to outlaw company labour spies whose job it was to discover the identity of union organizers and to try to gather incriminating evidence against them. With this judicial assistance, business launched a full-scale attack on labour unions. The National Association of Manufacturers and other business organizations sponsored advertisements promoting the "open shop" and company unions. Almost every strike was portrayed as the work of alien radicals. Although the labour force expanded steadily during the 1920's, membership in the American Federation of Labour declined by more than a million workers.

Despite the tension in industrial relations, American productivity increased rapidly. The assembly line technique, developed first by Henry Ford, spread to other industries, but nowhere was it more successful than in the automobile industry. The first conveyor belt was used in the Ford factory in Michigan in 1914, and it reduced the time taken to assemble a "Model T" from fourteen hours to an hour and a half. As production and profits rose proportionately, other manufacturers followed Ford's lead. Automobile production soared throughout the 1920's and government expenditures on highways kept pace. Other industrial developments created a whole new range of household equipment and appliances, as well as new means of entertainment. Whether as cause or result, such production materials became a part of the turning away from idealism to a scramble for excitement and material comfort. The day of the coonskin-coated college boy, of the short-skirted, boyish flapper, of the Charleston and "bathtub gin" was also the day when the gangster Al Capone and many like him could erect empires based on bootlegging, gambling and prostitution; empires which could and did corrupt hundreds of businessmen and policemen.

The Eighteenth Amendment, prohibiting the manufacture or sale of alcoholic beverages, had been ratified in 1919 almost in a fit of absentmindedness; yet it was to create national lawlessness on a quite unprecedented scale. The Volstead Act, drafted to enforce Prohibition, was passed with only scattered protests. It was not until enforcement machinery was ready that most Americans woke up to all the implications of the Amendment. There were some eighteen thousand seven hundred miles of sea and land frontiers to be guarded against smugglers. With fast automobiles and motor-boats, war-surplus machine-guns and a huge potential market, it was not difficult for criminals to organize virtual empires based on the illicit production, smuggling and distribution of all kinds of alcohol. Providing liquor and "protection" to thousands of "speakeasies," as the illegal bars came to be called, underworld gangs competed for larger and larger shares of the market. Reputable citizens patronized the trade in all its forms, until much respect for law disappeared. In Chicago, the centre of the industry, where controllers of the trade took in many millions of dollars annually, gang warfare reached its peak as Al Capone consolidated his power by such methods as the elaborately planned "massacre" of St. Valentines's Day, 1929, when his men machine-gunned seven members of the gang of his chief opposition. Touring his Chicago empire in an armoured car, Capone was as well known as any of the nation's political figures. And every city of any size had its Al Capone. Not until the Amendment and the Volstead Act were repealed was the rapidly-growing Federal Bureau of Investigation able to restore a semblance of order. Moreover, generations later, many protection rackets outside the liquor trade remained as a monument to the age.

The murderous gang warfare of Chicago and other large cities was a reflection of the public's lack of concern with the kind of political idealism for which Progressives had stood. Many people found escape in the thousands of pseudo-plush movie palaces which replaced the pre-war nickleodeons of early motion-picture days. By 1919 Mary Pickford, Charlie Chaplin and other famous screen stars were household names, and Hollywood was the seat of a heavily financed, over-glamourized industry. In 1928 *The Jazz Singer* with Al Jolson introduced "talkies" and further stimulated the film industry, which was already one of the largest industries in the country.

In the same decade, radio became a mass-communication medium and a major form of entertainment. The first commercial station opened in 1920 and by the end of the decade nearly half the American population owned radio sets. As with newspapers earlier, radio played an important role in advertising and tended to increase the acceptance of commercial values in the entertainment and cultural fields. For broadcasting political conventions, and for campaigning, the use of radio compensated to some extent for decreasing attendance at political meetings. After he became President, radio was one of the most effective devices of communication employed by Franklin Roosevelt, particularly in his famous "fireside chats."

As with earlier phases of American industrial development, much that was new in the 1920's was derived from earlier British and European inventions, which American organizers developed in mass-production factories. At the end of the war a number of important German chemical patents were appropriated by the American government and given to American companies. From this beginning, companies like DuPont and Union Carbide vastly expanded their production of plastics, explosives and other chemical-based commodities. The same years also saw a vast increase in the generation of electricity and the discovery of new means to transmit it both to and within large factories. These developments resulted in more efficient factory organization and made possible the spread of factories into areas which had hitherto been short of power. With such improvements in production came a vast expansion in the manufacture and consumption of domestic labour-saving and entertainment equipment, such as vacuum cleaners, washing machines, phonographs and radios.

The growth of aviation, stimulated by the First World War, also accelerated the pace of life in the 1920's. As with shipping, the federal government heavily subsidized the aviation industry. Tentative airmail and passenger services began in 1920, and in 1926 the Air Commerce Act granted mail subsidies to private airlines. In 1927 enthusiasm reached a peak when Charles A. Lindbergh, in the tiny monoplane, *Spirit of St. Louis*, made the pioneer solo transatlantic flight in thirty-three and a half hours.

4. THE END OF "NORMALCY"

Despite the widespread material progress and political complacency, many people were disturbed during the torrid 'twenties. They noted that "good times" were not shared equally by all regions and classes. The urban middle class was the chief beneficiary, while average working-class "real wages" rose very little. High American tariffs made it difficult for foreign nations to sell enough in the United States to enable them to purchase American surplus farm products, and this resulted in a steady decline in farm income, which was not halted until after 1933. In Congress, a farm bloc of both Republican and Democratic Senators and Representatives from Western and Southern states pressed hard for easier farm credit. The McNary-Haugen Bill, which would have enabled the government to purchase surplus farm products to be sold below market prices to other nations, was twice vetoed by President Coolidge, despite the substantial assistance given to industry in the same period. In 1929, at President Hoover's instigation, Congress passed an Agricultural Marketing Act which gave limited assistance to farmers, but neither the President nor Congress took further significant action on the farm problem until after the election of 1932.

In addition to the worsening plight of the farmers, large areas of industry failed to recover from a minor depression which had followed the end of the war. Coal-mining, leather and textile manufacturing and other basic industries were hit by changing patterns of consumption or by price-wage policies which kept the real wages of workers very low. In short, while "national income" rose spectacularly, it was unevenly distributed. In 1929, forty-two per cent of American families received less than $1,500 a year, while more than 24,000 families received more than $100,000 a year. Corporations also built up huge profits, much of which went into further investment. Many Americans came to believe that prosperity would be unending, and hundreds of thousands of people poured every dollar they had saved or could borrow into the stock market and speculation reached astronomic proportions. The boom became a bubble and the bubble burst.

Late in October 1929, stock prices dipped. People who had been buying stock "on margin," that is, without enough cash to back up their orders, began to sell. Within two weeks stocks had fallen twenty-five billion dollars in price. Despite the explanation of the most prominent bankers, businessmen and the President that there was only a failure of confidence, the declines continued. Between September 1929 and July 1932 the value of stocks listed in New York dropped from ninety billion dollars to fifteen and a half billion. By then it was evident to many people that the real reasons for the crash lay deeper than the investors' loss of faith in the market.

Many people lost their savings immediately in the stock market crash. Millions more were crushed as the shock waves reached out through banking and industry. Hundreds of businesses closed and unemployment spread rapidly. Mounting unemployment meant decreasing purchasing power and this in turn brought more unemployment. By 1932 there were more than twelve million Americans unemployed, which meant that thirty million people were without a regular source of income. Many thousands of people, no longer able to pay rent, moved into wood-and-tin shanty towns on the scarred fringes of great cities, frequently called "Hoovervilles," in derisive tribute to the President. Hundreds of thousands of men joined the straggling breadlines or "hopped freights" or "rode the rods" in a futile search for jobs. A Senate committee heard this evidence:

> One woman went along the docks and picked up vegetables that fell from wagons. Sometimes the fish vendors gave her fish at the end of the day. On two different occasions this family was without food for a day and a half. . . . Another family did not have food for two days. Then the husband went out and gathered dandelions and the family lived on them.

By far the most terrifying economic collapse ever to hit the nation, the Great Depression continued to be minimized in the statements of the President and those businessmen who managed to survive it.

The American people became increasingly critical of Hoover's apparently callous aloofness, but despite rising opposition, Hoover told reporters: "Nobody is actually starving. The hoboes, for example, are better fed than they have ever been. One hobo in New York got ten meals in one day." Despite his bad public relations, Hoover did try to curb the depression, but each of his measures was partial and none seemed to attack the root trouble. Hoover's most positive act was to obtain from Congress a law establishing the Reconstruction Finance Corporation which could "prime the economic pump" by lending money to businesses to keep them afloat when private credit had dried up. One and a half billion dollars were lent by this agency in 1932. The Reconstruction Finance Corporation was to be a potent factor in the economic recovery programme of Franklin D. Roosevelt.

Perhaps Hoover's most serious error was to refuse to allow the federal government to enter the field of unemployment relief. With millions of Americans dependent for their survival upon public relief, the inability of states and municipalities to finance relief payments brought the most dangerous kind of despair, frequently raising the question whether the American economic and political system itself was valid. By 1932 many state and city governments were virtually bankrupt and the spectre of widespread starvation began to materialize. But with his deep faith in the responsibility of the individual for his own welfare, Hoover steadfastly refused to press for federal assistance in relief payments. He argued that relief was "unearned income" which would demean its recipients, while to use federal funds for an essentially "local" problem would threaten the federal structure of the United States. By the autumn of 1932 he seemed like a man in a trance, unwilling to believe the stark evidence of mass destitution.

It was in such dark and dangerous circumstances that the election of 1932 took place. In opposition to Hoover the Democrats nominated Franklin Delano Roosevelt, a man who had been vaguely associated with the Progressive wing of the party as Wilson's Assistant Secretary of the Navy and Vice-Presidential candidate in the 1920 election. While "F.D.R." has become almost a legendary figure in American history, he was a relatively unknown quantity at the time of his election in 1932. He had won the New York State Governorship in 1928, a year of low fortunes for the Democrats, and had been re-elected handsomely in 1930. At the Democratic Convention in 1932 he was nominated over Al Smith, who bore the stigma of defeat from the last campaign. Observing his wealthy Hudson Valley background and country squire manner, left-wing Democrats were dubious about Roosevelt's qualifications. One psychological factor in his favour, however, was the triumphant struggle he had waged during the early 1920's against a crippling attack of poliomyelitis, a disease which had left him dependent upon steel braces on both legs. Related to this was a buoyant personality which radiated confidence and good cheer, symbolized by a jauntiness of attire and a broad smile. In the later days of his long Presidency, these characteristics became almost trade-marks, as did the dramatic black naval cloak he wore to wartime conferences.

In 1932 the Democratic platform was a mixture of caution and promises: a balanced budget, repeal of prohibition, lowering of tariffs on a reciprocal basis with other nations, unemployment insurance and old age pensions, reinforcement of anti-trust legislation, federal aid for state unemployment relief, planned public works, and other direct assistance to economic recovery. Emphasizing those planks which savoured of the Progressive tradition, Roosevelt promised a New Deal for the American people, vigorous executive action, and continuing concern for the "forgotten man." Without preaching a radical solution, he convinced most voters that he would bring vigour to the White House to replace the drift and hesitancy of Hoover, who confined his campaign to warning of the dire results of a Democratic victory.

The election was decisive. Carrying all but six states, Roosevelt received 22,821,000 popular votes to Hoover's 15,761,000. The Democrats also won large majorities in both House and Senate. Coolidge Prosperity had ended in Hoover Depression, and the Republicans were given credit for both false prosperity and fatal depression.

15

F.D.R. and the New Deal

AS FRANKLIN ROOSEVELT took the oath of office as President
he looked out from the steps of the Capitol upon a nation in
ruins. In his inaugural speech, he declared his intention to
restore to the United States what he considered to be its
original goals, the maintenance of human dignity and equality of opportunity. The new President left no doubt of his
determination to act strongly:

> The money-changers have fled from their high seats in
> the temple of our civilization. We may now restore that
> temple to the ancient truths . . . there must be an end
> to a conduct in banking and in business which too often
> has given to a sacred trust the likeness of callous and
> selfish wrongdoing. . . . In the event that the Congress
> shall fail [to enact the necessary measures of recovery]
> I shall ask the Congress for the one remaining instru-
> ment to meet the crisis—broad executive power that
> would be given me if we were in fact invaded by a
> foreign foe. . . . [The people] have asked for discipline
> and direction under leadership. They have made me the
> present instrument of their wishes. In the spirit of the
> gift I take it.

1. ROOSEVELT AND HIS CABINET

Some observers feared that this speech heralded a move by
the United States in the direction of dictatorship in the
manner of Hitler in Germany and Mussolini in Italy, while
others recalled the dark days of Andrew Jackson and the
rule of King Mob. Even the President's observant and

politically active wife, Eleanor Rooosevelt, recorded her anxiety at the huge demonstration accorded her husband's reference to powers ordinarily granted in wartime. Yet, despite his determination to use the executive power to its full extent, Roosevelt was equally resolved to work within American political traditions and to preserve the capitalist system. Like earlier Progressives, he believed in reforming existing institutions rather than replacing them. His own favourite description of his political method was to say that he was like a football quarterback: he called a play and if it worked he followed it up; if it did not work, he tried another. Experimentation became his watchword. He spoke from conviction when he said in his first inaugural address: "The only thing we have to fear is fear itself—nameless, unreasoning, unjustified terror which paralyzes needed efforts to convert retreat into advance."

Roosevelt's greatest asset was his liking for people. He was not of an original turn of mind, but he had the ability to dramatize ideas which he had picked up from others. He had, too, an innate understanding of politics which enabled him to work with some of the least respectable Democratic party machines, while at the same time retaining the loyalty of many friends in more idealistic circles. His Cabinet reflected this. James A. Farley, his Postmaster-General, was a professional politician who knew every nook and cranny of the party, and who dispensed patronage. Frances Perkins, Secretary of Labour, was the first woman Cabinet member in the United States; her sympathies were Progressive. The Secretary of State was Cordell Hull, a conservative Democrat from Tennessee with a Southerner's belief in low tariffs. Henry A. Wallace of Iowa, whose father had been in Republican Cabinets, became Secretary of Agriculture and proved to be one of the most radical members of the Roosevelt team. The Secretary of Commerce was Harold Ickes.

In addition to his Cabinet, Roosevelt gathered about him a group of very close advisers, which soon came to be called the Brain Trust. Some of these he appointed to special administrative posts; others he simply consulted. Harry Hopkins, a former social worker, was influential in framing unemployment relief and rehabilitation policies. Several professors from Columbia University supplied the basic ideas for new policies in banking and agriculture. Indeed, the Brain Trust produced so many ideas that Roosevelt's main task was to choose among them. Such use of academic advisers was then a novelty and provoked sharp criticism from professional politicians who resented the intervention of the amateurs into what they regarded as their special field.

2. THE HUNDRED DAYS

The new President moved with unprecedented speed to redeem his campaign promise of a "new deal for the forgotten man." Immediately after his inauguration on March 4, Roosevelt called a special session of Congress to meet on March 9, 1933. In the hundred days that followed, he set a record for both legislative and executive accomplishment.

An acute banking crisis faced the President on his first day in office. Roosevelt ordered all banks closed for four days until Congress could meet and on its first day of sitting Congress passed an Emergency Banking Act which provided the conditions within which the banks could safely be re-opened. Under this act, the government insured deposits in approved banks and the Reconstruction Finance Corporation extended credit to enable thousands of banks to resume business on a sound basis. The Banking Act of 1935 later increased federal supervision of the banking system and gave the Federal Reserve Board power to regulate rates of interest.

On March 21, 1933, Roosevelt recommended to Congress three approaches to the crucial question of relief of the unemployed: federal grants to the states for financing direct relief payments to the unemployed; a bigger programme for such traditional federal projects as roads and public buildings in order to provide more jobs; and the creation of what came to be called the Civilian Conservation Corps. The last was quickly brought into being and enrolled 300,000 single men for conservation work. Each received free board and thirty dollars a month in pay. The C.C.C. remained in being until 1941 and assisted more than two and a half million young men who accomplished impressive feats of reforestation and allied conservation work. Roosevelt's other two recommendations were likewise acted upon in that first hundred days. As time went on, however, and unemployment stubbornly persisted, the government, influenced especially by Harry Hopkins, placed more and more emphasis upon providing jobs for the unemployed as opposed to simple relief. Millions of men were put to work on projects ranging from the building of roads, airports, schools, bridges and dams to the construction of aircraft carriers. A new agency, the Works Progress Administration (W.P.A.), was set up in 1935 to co-ordinate this many-sided effort and Hopkins became its head. Stressing the importance of saving both the dignity and the skills of trained people, the W.P.A. sponsored projects in the fine arts, theatre, music and historical research as well as others of the kinds already mentioned. The W.P.A. spent over eleven billion dollars in the next six years and found work for more than eight million people. In addition, the federal government spent over four billion dollars in underwriting direct relief up to 1941.

Many tax-payers deplored the billions of dollars spent in relief and there can be no doubt that the relief measures did not solve the unemployment problem, since in 1939 there were still nine million people out of work. They did add a vast amount of public property and equipment to the nation, however, and, as one observer put it, "they placed a lift under the wings of the people's spirit." A prominent banker, answering the many harsh attacks on the New Deal made by his colleagues, remarked: "Well, if the country was willing to spend thirty billion dollars in a year's time to lick the Germans, I don't see why people should complain about its spending five or six billions to keep people from starving."

The government's emergency plan for revitalizing industry was launched with the establishment of the National Recovery Administration (N.R.A.) which was brought into being by the National Industrial Recovery Act. Designed to provide "the machinery necessary for a great co-operative movement throughout all industry," N.R.A. actually adopted much the same policy towards industry as had been followed by Herbert Hoover when he was Secretary of Commerce under Coolidge. Anti-trust laws were suspended, and industrial leaders drew up "codes of fair competition," endorsed by N.R.A. All "co-operating" firms displayed posters and window stickers bearing the device of a blue eagle under the N.R.A. initials. Although both industry and labour welcomed the plan at first, it soon became apparent that N.R.A. benefited the largest firms most because its policy fostered monopoly, price maintenance, production cutbacks and division of the market.

In the summer of 1934 a Review Board reported that N.R.A. was doing more harm than good, even to the point of hindering recovery. Consumers disliked it because one of its purposes was to keep prices up, and even Roosevelt, who had pinned high hopes on N.R.A., breathed a sigh of relief when the Supreme Court ruled N.R.A. unconstitutional in May of 1935. In the opinion of the Court, the National Industrial Recovery Act delegated legislative powers improperly to the executive branch and infringed states' rights by regulating trade within, as well as between, states.

Section 7a of the National Industrial Recovery Act had required that every code should guarantee the right of collective bargaining, and had also established maximum hours of work and minimum wages, and condemned "sweatshops" and child labour. Under the terms of this section, it was possible for labour to organize a new drive for members, and union membership rose from 2,800,000 to 3,700,000 in two years. As labour strength grew, Congress became more responsive to its interests and requests. In 1935 Congress passed the Wagner Act, creating a National Labour Relations Board (N.L.R.B.). The new Act restated the rights of collective bargaining and established tight rules against employers' coercion of employees. The N.L.R.B. was empowered to certify unions as bargaining agents whenever the union enrolled a majority of workers in a firm or industry. Despite fierce opposition by management, the N.L.R.B. was extremely effective, and the number of "company unions" declined sharply. By 1941 the Board had settled amicably seventy-five per cent of the strikes dealt with, and by that year union membership had risen to 10,480,000.

The new security given to the unions by the New Deal facilitated the organizing of industrial unions. Led by the fiery John L. Lewis, President of the United Mine Workers of America, a group of A.F. of L. unions founded a Committee for Industrial Organization (C.I.O.). The C.I.O. set itself the task of organizing all the mass-production firms on an industry-wide basis, beginning in 1936 with automobile and steel companies. Employing the drastic method of "sit-down" strikes (strikes in which the men refuse to leave a plant until their union is recognized) and mass demonstrations, the C.I.O. drive in 1937 was forcibly opposed by employers and led to widespread violence. Opposed by the craft union leadership of the A.F. of L., the C.I.O. was suspended from the American Federation of Labour in 1938 and became the Congress of Industrial Organizations. The two were finally reunited in 1955.

Despite Roosevelt's own doubts about some of the methods employed by the unions, the rising strength of labour was extremely important to him politically. The C.I.O. in particular worked hard for the "Roosevelt coalition." This coalition consisted of organized labour; Southern Democrats who supported most New Deal measures; big-city Democratic machines; and Western farmers, who were increasingly won away from the Republicans.

At the time of Roosevelt's inauguration, the western "farm-belt" was in a depressed condition which was accompanied by scenes of violence. On the Great Plains, farmers organized to prevent mortgage foreclosures, while physical assaults on sheriffs' deputies and finance-company agents were commonplace. Reduced to penury, and in daily fear of losing their homes, many farmers demanded that the government correct the market forces over which the farmers themselves had no control. Thus, at the same time as the National Industrial Recovery Act was passed, Congress enacted the Agricultural Adjustment Act, creating yet another "Administration," the A.A.A. The purpose of A.A.A. was to establish "parity" farm prices, that is, to make the prices of farm products rise until they were as high compared with other prices as they had been in 1909 to 1914. Farmers made agreements with A.A.A. to cut down the acreage sown to particular crops, in return for cash payments. The idea was to increase farm income by reducing the size of the crop and thus raising prices. It was financed by special taxes levied on firms processing farm products, such as meat-packers and flour millers. As part of the first year's production cut-back, thousands of acres already seeded were plowed under and millions of young pigs killed. This aspect of A.A.A. horrified consumers generally, and political liberals in particular, since it meant both higher prices for food and destruction of food which was desperately needed both at home and abroad. While prices of farm products rose appreciably, it was found that A.A.A. benefited large producers much more than small, especially in the South where crop reduction losses were frequently passed on to tenants and share-croppers. In January 1936, the Supreme Court declared A.A.A. unconstitutional on the ground that the controls exercised and the taxes imposed violated state jurisdiction. However, later New Deal acts firmly established the principle that farmers were entitled to government assistance and planning, to counterbalance the many kinds of help given to industry and commerce. Yet, despite the fact that widespread drought and devastating dust storms had deepened the lengthy farm depression, the New Deal farm programme was bitterly criticized by urban conservatives for its cost and because it created scarcity as a solution to the farm problem rather than expanding exports.

In this remarkable hundred days, Congress passed yet another act that broke new ground. In May 1933 the Tennessee Valley Authority (T.V.A.) was created and given power to embark on the New Deal's greatest experiment in planning. With authority to build dams, generate and sell electric power, undertake conservation and flood control measures and "to provide for the general welfare of the citizens" of the area, T.V.A. was really a regional experiment in socialism. It represented the triumph of years of campaigning by the notable Western Progressive, Senator George W. Norris. In an area of 40,000 square miles which touched seven states T.V.A. brought a section of the United States which had been in a chronic condition of economic depression into thriving activity. Huge control dams produced electric power, which was distributed through the Authority to provide rural electrification. The dams formed the basis for much new industry, saved vast areas from destruction by flood, and irrigated many more. Low-cost housing was built in many adjoining communities, co-operatives were organized, new agricultural methods developed, public health agencies established and large recreational areas created on the new lakes. David Lilienthal, one of the first T.V.A. directors, wrote:

> This is the story . . . of how waters once wasted and destructive have been controlled and now work, night and day, creating electric energy to lighten the burden of human drudgery. Here is a tale of fields grown old and barren with the years, which now are vigorous with new fertility, lying green to the sun; of forests that were hacked and despoiled, now protected and refreshed with strong young trees just starting on their slow road to maturity. It is a story of the people and how they have worked to create a new valley.

Partly because of T.V.A.'s success, private companies led a well-financed campaign to have it declared unconstitutional. Compelled to reduce their power rates, as T.V.A. showed how cheaply electricity could be distributed, the power companies supported Wendell Willkie, President of the Commonwealth and Southern Corporation, in challenging T.V.A. However, in 1936 the Supreme Court decided that T. V. A.'s powers as an interstate authority were entirely constitutional.

3. CONSOLIDATING THE NEW DEAL

The year 1935 marked a turning-point in the development of the New Deal. The plays called in 1933 had had time to show their worth. On the one hand there were distinct signs of recovery; on the other, unemployment continued to be high. Where from here? The social stress of five years of depression had by this time raised up a strange variety of prophets, each of whom believed himself possessed of the answer. Three won followings large enough to pose serious threats to Roosevelt's leadership and the Democratic hold on power. One was Father Charles Coughlin, a Michigan priest with a wide radio following, who preached a radical doctrine of semi-fascism. Although he supported Roosevelt at first, he opposed him violently after 1935. Another was Dr. Francis Townsend, an elderly California physician, who gained wide support from old people with a plan to provide everyone over sixty with an income of two hundred dollars a month. The object was to boost purchasing power and so speed recovery. Money to finance the plan was to be raised by levying a sales tax. Millions of people voiced support for Townsend despite the fact that his scheme would have cost the impossible sum of twenty billion dollars a year. The most serious threat came from the third, Senator Huey Long of Louisiana. Known in Louisiana as the "Kingfish," Senator Long controlled the state as though he owned it. Although his régime was as corrupt as any in American history, he introduced a number of popular reforms. By 1935 he had become a national figure and was securing considerable national support by a vague plan to "share the wealth." His career came to an abrupt end when he was shot by a personal enemy.

Although the Great Depression produced a Socialist political party in Canada which opposed the major parties and demanded fundamental changes in the economic system, no similar party arose in the United States. American Socialists did not believe that the New Deal was a permanent answer to the problem of the depression but they were not able to cope with the political appeal of the President. Norman Thomas, who had succeeded Eugene Debs as the Socialist candidate for President, explained the decline in Socialist voting strength in one word: "Roosevelt." At the same time, however, Roosevelt and Congress were aware of radical pressure from left-wing political elements, and took steps to offset it. In the summer of 1935, Congress passed a series of new laws that introduced permanent reforms and moved the New Deal leftward.

One such measure was the National Labour Relations Act, already noted as the Wagner Act. A Wealth Tax Act raised tax levels steeply on large personal and corporation incomes. The Public Utilities Holding Company Act provided for the break-up of trusts in public utilities if they could not prove that they passed on the savings of monopoly to consumers. However, the most signficant legislation of 1935 was the Social Security Act which provided old age pensions, unemployment insurance, and aid for dependent mothers and children. Funds for unemployment and old age insurance were raised by a payroll levy on employees, with equal contributions from employers. The cost of the other benefits was shared by the federal and state governments.

As the elections of 1936 approached, opposition to Roosevelt among Republicans, and even on the part of some Democrats, reached fever pitch. To them, the legislation just described constituted "creeping socialism." Through an organization known as the Liberty League the Republicans built up a huge anti-Roosevelt election fund. Most of the nation's newspapers were also against the President. But the economic upturn, and the undoubted benefits enjoyed by millions of Americans from New Deal legislation left no doubt about Roosevelt's renomination and little about his re-election. The Republicans nominated Governor Alfred Landon of Kansas and took as their platform the need to defend the Constitution. Roosevelt conducted a free-swinging, moderately left-wing campaign in which he castigated the country's "economic royalists" who, he declared, knew they were losing their monopoly of power and wealth. "They are," he said, "unanimous in their *hate* for *me—and I welcome their hatred.*" The election result was a landslide for Roosevelt.

Roosevelt's second inaugural address, delivered in January 1937, was perhaps bolder and more challenging than his first, and presaged a programme of further reform. "In this nation," he declared, "I see tens of millions of its citizens—a substantial part of its whole population—who at this very moment are denied the greater part of what the very lowest standards of today call the necessities of life." Ironically, the very size of the Democratic majority in Congress might tempt his followers, as Roosevelt shrewdly realized, to be freer in criticizing and opposing his proposals. A second possible stumbling-block lay in the Supreme Court which had already invalidated the N.R.A. and the A.A.A. To rally his supporters and at the same time to defeat the opposition of the Supreme Court, Roosevelt proposed to Congress a Court Reform bill which he and his Attorney-General had quietly prepared. The bill gave the President power to appoint a Supreme Court justice for each justice who failed to retire at the age of seventy. Arguing that the majority of the "nine old men" who constituted the Court were allowing conservative social views to interfere with their judgment on laws made necessary by new problems, Roosevelt said he needed power to appoint liberal men to the Court. "Little by little," he said, "new facts become blurred through old glasses fitted, as it were, for the needs of another generation."

At once conservative opinion raised a storm of protest. The Court bill was denounced as a court-packing scheme which destroyed the concept of judicial independence. A number of leading Democrats opposed the bill, some because they were irked by Roosevelt's failure to consult them in advance, some because they believed it would destroy the constitutional separation of powers. Debate in Congress and the country was long and bitter. The President's case was weakened when one justice who had frequently voted against New Deal measures suddenly changed his stand in several critical cases. The result was that the Court reversed the decision it had made in 1923 that the federal government could not outlaw child labour and then went on to uphold the constitutionality of basic New Deal legislation such as the Wagner Act, the Farm Mortgage Act of 1935, and the Social Security Act. In July the Court bill was finally shelved. Later, several conservative justices retired, enabling Roosevelt to appoint in their place liberals such as William Douglas and Felix Frankfurter. While both sides claimed victory in the Court fight, it was clear that the outcome was a "reformed" Court. On the other hand, the Democratic party had been seriously divided over the issue and Roosevelt never recovered the degree of political strength he enjoyed from 1934 to 1936.

In his second term Roosevelt obtained reforms which rounded out the New Deal. There were further measures to help farmers and to regulate business. Two acts were of outstanding importance. In 1937 the Wagner-Steagall Act established a United States Housing Authority which began a long-term programme of easy loans to state and municipal low-rental housing and slum-clearance agencies. Despite conservative Democratic opposition, Roosevelt also obtained passage of the Fair Labour Standards Act in June of 1938, under which interstate industry was required to adopt, over a four-year period, a maximum work week of forty hours and a minimum wage of forty cents an hour.

By 1939 the New Deal had lost its impetus; foreign affairs began to demand the President's primary attention. What had it accomplished? The Roosevelt programme had failed to cure the business depression or solve the unemployment problem. It had added some twenty-three billion dollars to the national debt. Federal power had been sharply increased over that of the states, and a complicated bureaucracy which administered the many new agencies appeared to have become a permanent feature of American life. On the other hand, the New Deal had demonstrated that democratic government was not helpless in the face of a supreme social crisis, and it had avoided extreme measures such as the communistic programme of Russia, or the Fascist régime in Germany. The opportunity for self-help afforded labour by the New Deal, together with the aid it gave to farmers, created what the Harvard economist J. K. Galbraith has called "countervailing powers" in the American economy. That is, organized labour and agriculture achieved sufficient power to enforce a more just distribution of incomes and this in turn helped to modify the pattern of alternating booms and depressions, so characteristic of American experience up to this time.

Like all American Presidents who may be accounted great, Roosevelt left the powers of the Presidency considerably increased. Certainly he gained the undying enmity of major sections of the business world and the middle class, but the final American judgement upon him was perhaps expressed by the fact that as the world slid more and more deeply into the Second World War, and despite sharp domestic criticism, Roosevelt was re-elected when he ran for an unprecedented third term in 1940.

Approaching that election, the Republicans hoped to capitalize on the increasingly conservative temper of the country. They nominated Wendell Willkie who, although he had been a leading opponent of T.V.A., was supported by liberals, and chose as his running mate the Progressive Senator Charles McNary of Oregon. Roosevelt broke precedent by accepting the nomination for a third time, with Henry Wallace as his nominee for Vice-President. Emphasizing the need for continuity in leadership and defending the New Deal reform record, the Democrats won thirty-eight states and retained control in Congress though with reduced majorities.

By the time of Roosevelt's third inauguration, war had broken out again in Europe and problems of neutrality and preparedness were already concerning the administration. Foreign and war policies were to be the chief concern of the

President and the nation from 1941 until Roosevelt's death in the spring of 1945.

16

From Versailles to San Francisco

STRONG expressions of isolationism were common in the two decades following the end of the First World War. A large majority of Americans returned strongly to the old faith that the United States should hold aloof from the diplomacy and wars of Europe. The inaugural address of President Harding in 1921 reflected the popular disillusionment with "European diplomacy":

> I have no unseemly comment to offer on the League [he said]. If it is serving the Old World helpfully, more power to it. But it is not for us. The Senate has so declared, the executive has so declared, the people have so declared. Nothing could be more decisively stamped with finality.

While isolationist feelings were dominant in the United States, complete detachment from Europe was to prove impossible. By 1920 the United States was the world's wealthiest nation, and ever-widening economic interests as well as older political and cultural forces drew her inescapably into world affairs.

1. THE POLICY OF ISOLATION

America never joined the League of Nations, but the State Department, which was charged with the conduct of foreign affairs, quickly realized that it could not safely ignore the League's work in many fields which were of concern to the United States. Thus the United States sent observers to sessions of the League's non-political committee in Geneva and, as some critics declared, "moved into the League through the back door."

In 1928 the policy of isolationism was further modified when Secretary of State Kellogg drew up a treaty with the French Foreign Minister, Aristide Briand. Eventually signed by sixty-two countries, the Kellogg-Briand pact contained a specific renunciation of war "as an instrument of national policy" among the signatories. The treaty included no machinery for enforcement; but the very fact that the United States participated in such diplomacy modified its isolationist position.

A more pronounced modification of American isolationism occurred in 1921. The United States, as we have seen, had a very practical interest in the Pacific; Americans began to watch with deepening suspicion the expansion of Japanese power in that area. To cut short fears that a naval race among the United States, Britain and Japan might again lead to war, President Harding invited Britain, France, Italy and Japan to confer in Washington on a plan to limit armaments. Later, other powers who had interests in the Pacific were added to the Washington Conference. A treaty among the four principal powers—the United States, Britain, Japan and France—was drawn up which agreed on a "ten-year holiday" in the construction of capital ships, and on limits on the size of capital ships which could be built. The four nations also agreed to respect each other's interests and possessions in the Pacific and to settle any disputes by conference. Another treaty signed by all nine members of the enlarged Conference in February 1922 accepted the principle of the Open Door for China.

In the late 1920's and early 1930's the United States took part in other disarmament conferences. None of these met with any success. In 1932 Germany withdrew from such discussions, protesting the injustice of retaining the limitations of arms imposed upon her in 1919; and in 1935 Japan withdrew when the United States and Britain refused to concede her demands for equality in naval tonnage. Although the disarmament conferences failed, the United

States had intimately involved itself in this world problem.

Problems in the Pacific continued to concern the United States, and in this area the members of the cabinet differed on American policy. When the Japanese seized Manchuria from China in 1931, Secretary of State Henry Stimson sent a sharp note to Japan pointing out the violation of its treaty obligations. Stimson also suggested to President Hoover that the United States co-operate with the League of Nations to impose economic sanctions on Japan. Hoover refused, on the ground that sanctions might mean war. As a result, Japan suffered no serious opposition at the outset of her campaign for conquests.

In Latin America in the 1920's, the United States continued to intervene to protect American investments. Public dislike of this policy increased steadily till in 1928 the United States signed arbitration treaties with the Latin American republics. In the following year President Hoover made a goodwill tour of Latin America, and in 1930 he lent his support to a State Department announcement which officially revoked the Roosevelt corollary to the Monroe Doctrine. When he became President, Franklin Roosevelt continued the policy of military withdrawal and made popular a phrase first used by Hoover to describe the new trend: the Good Neighbour Policy. In 1933 a Conference of American States at Montevideo drew up a pact, which was signed by the United States, declaring that "no state has the right to intervene in the internal affairs of another." In May 1934, after a revolution and the installation of a President likely to favour American business interests, Cuba was freed from the terms of the Platt Amendment, which had virtually given control of her foreign policy to the United States. But in Cuba, as in the other Latin American republics, American investments continued to grow so rapidly that, while officially the United States withdrew, unofficially, through embassies and corporation offices, Latin America remained subject to heavy American influence.

During the 1930's American isolationist feeling became even more intense. This espousal of isolationism was the result not just of post-war escapism but also of revelations made by a Congressional Committee headed by Senator Gerald P. Nye of North Dakota. In 1934 the Nye Committee investigated relations between munitions-makers and financiers on the one hand, and government departments on the other. The Committee produced considerable evidence which seemed to prove that the desire to protect investments abroad had been a principal cause of American entry into the First World War. It was also alleged that manufacturers of munitions and naval supplies and equipment still exerted considerable influence at disarmament conferences in Washington and other major capital cities. Nye himself spoke of the makers of munitions as "merchants of death" and argued that the United States could hope to stay out of the next war only if she made it illegal for American businessmen to trade with any belligerent country.

Yet, generally unnoted at the time, the United States economic relations with the rest of the world were developing in a way which would make it difficult to adhere to such a policy. The great bulk of American foreign trade came to be conducted with Britain, France, and their empires, and with China, rather than with Germany, Italy and Japan. This trade pattern materially influenced the outlook of American government and business as war loomed between the first group and the second.

The isolationist movement reached its climax in the passage of a series of Neutrality Acts between 1935 and 1937. This legislation forbade American arms shipments to any belligerent state, prohibited loans or credits to such states, and provided that any trade with a belligerent must be on a "cash and carry" basis, that is, paid for on delivery and carried in ships provided by the belligerent nation. Events in Asia, Europe and Africa intensified the drive to maintain American neutrality, as Italy seized Ethiopia, Germany reoccupied the Rhineland and began to build up new armed forces, Japan renewed her assault on China, and an armed revolt led by General Franco overthrew democratic government in Spain.

2. THE ROAD TO WAR

Although there was a growing concern in the United States about the implications of these events, most Americans endorsed a policy of neutrality for their country. Cautiously in 1937 Roosevelt began to lead public opinion away from extreme forms of isolationism. In October he delivered a speech in Chicago, quickly dubbed the "quarantine speech," in which he declared:

> When an epidemic of physical disease starts to spread, the community approves and joins in a quarantine of the patients in order to protect the health of the community. . . . War is a contagion, whether it be declared or undeclared. . . . We are adopting such measures as will minimize our risk of involvement, but we cannot have complete protection in a world of disorder in which confidence and security have broken down.

The speech was sharply criticized, yet it left little doubt about where Roosevelt's sympathies lay, as Europe moved again towards war. In April 1939 the President sent a personal appeal to Hitler and Mussolini, the dictators of Germany and Italy, to cease their aggressions. But though Americans began gradually to comprehend the nature of Nazi-Fascist inhumanity, isolationist feeling remained high in the United States. Roosevelt had to keep assuring the people that his intention to avoid involvement in any European war remained firm. An America First movement, led by such popular figures as Senator Nye and the Lone Eagle, Colonel Charles Lindbergh, the first man to fly solo across the Atlantic, was formed from a strange mixture of Irish and German Americans, midwestern Progressives, Fascist sympathizers and, until Hitler attacked Russia in June 1941, Communists.

Gradually, but to outsiders far too slowly, American public opinion moved away from isolationism. In November 1939, after war had broken out in Europe, the Neutrality Acts were amended to permit the sale of weapons to Britain and France. Opposition was led by Senator Arthur Vandenberg who declared:

> The proponents of the change vehemently insist that their steadfast purpose, like ours, is to keep America out of the war, and their sincere assurances are presented to our people. But the motive is obvious, and the inevitable interpretation of the change . . . will be that we have officially taken sides.

After the fall of France before the onslaught of the Germans, Roosevelt showed that he would assist the British Commonwealth, then standing almost alone. In August 1940 he met the Canadian Prime Minister, Mackenzie King, and agreed to form a Permanent Joint Board on Defence, between the two countries. In September of the same year, he transferred fifty old destroyers to the United Kingdom in return for long-term leases on bases in Newfoundland, Bermuda and the West Indies.

To secure support for his pro-Allied policy, Roosevelt appealed to the American people in his third inaugural address in January 1941, when he declared that America's faith in the Four Freedoms justified all aid to the Allies short of war. The Four Freedoms he defined as freedom of speech everywhere in the world, freedom of worship, freedom from want, and freedom from fear of aggression. Two months later he devised a formula for aid to the Allies to which the name of Lend-Lease was given. Using the argument that if a neighbour's house caught fire one would not hesitate to lend a garden hose to put out the fire and stop it from spreading, he asked Congress to make America an "arsenal of democracy" by "lending" arms and equipment to Britain to protect the United States. Bitter opposition to the Lend-Lease Bill in Congress revealed the lingering strength of isolationism. Senator Wheeler of Montana exclaimed that it was "the New Deal's triple A foreign policy [a reference to the Agricultural Adjustment Administration]; it will plow under every fourth American boy," a comment the President described as "the most untruthful, as well as the most dastardly,

271

unpatriotic thing that has ever been said."

But the adoption of Lend-Lease committed the United States formally to massive aid in the struggle against Germany, Italy, and Japan. Isolationist opinion declined, as more and more Americans came to see the true nature of the Fascist menace. Yet the isolationists were still too powerful to make it possible for Roosevelt to order the United States navy to convoy Lend-Lease goods through the submarine-infested North Atlantic to Britain. Instead, he adopted the doctrine of "hemispheric defence," and proclaimed the North Atlantic a neutral zone as far as Iceland. The Americans occupied Greenland, and established a base in Iceland, and United States navy vessels escorted convoys that far. Germany's answer to this policy was a promise to sink "every ship with contraband for Britain, whatever its name" and in the fall of 1941 several American ships were shot at or sunk. Roosevelt issued orders to the United States navy to retaliate should American convoys be attacked and in October Congress approved the arming of merchantmen and permitted them to sail to belligerent ports. In effect, the naval war with Germany had begun.

Meanwhile, in June 1941 American and British officers had held secret meetings to discuss strategy if the United States were to enter the war. In August came a public demonstration of Roosevelt's position when he met Winston Churchill, by then Prime Minister of Great Britain, on board ship in the misty reaches of Argentia Bay, Newfoundland. While the President refused to make any military promises at this meeting, the two statesmen signed an Atlantic Charter which called for self-determination of nations, freedom from fear and want for all peoples, freedom of the seas, disarmament, and the "destruction of the Nazi tyranny." Thus by the fall of 1941 President Roosevelt had taken his country to the brink of war, largely by executive decision and without the knowledge of the public until well after the event. Roosevelt justified this procedure on the ground that public opinion, and especially congressional opinion, was not moving as quickly as the course of events required. If this were true, events in the Far East soon transformed the situation, and produced nearly unanimous public support for war.

Japan's resumption of war against China in 1937 had heralded the beginning of a programme to establish a huge Japanese empire which would dominate all of East Asia. While American interests, policies, and even treaty obligations were all directly threatened by Japanese expansion, the United States was even slower to act in the East than in Europe. Frequent American protests about Japanese aggression were as futile as American loans to China. Even after Japan openly allied itself with Italy and Germany in September 1940, the United States hesitated to place an embargo on American trade with Japan. By mid-1941 Japanese troops were slashing their way through the jungles and rice-paddies of French Indo-China, and appeared to be well on their way to Malaya, the Dutch East Indies and Australasia. That autumn, United States negotiations with Japan revealed that Japan wanted from the United States complete cessation of American aid to China and non-interference with further Japanese expansion. These negotiations were still going on when Japan assaulted the United States' great Pacific naval base of Pearl Harbor in Hawaii.

3. AMERICA AT WAR

Although the American commanders in Hawaii had received unmistakable warnings that war might come at any moment, the warnings were disregarded. American officers, in Washington and in the Pacific, expected that the next Japanese aggression would be against the Philippines or in the East Indies. Thus, when United States intelligence reports showed suspicious Japanese ship movements early in December, and even the presence of unidentified planes near Hawaii, the reactions in Washington and at Pearl Harbor were incredibly casual. On Sunday December 7, 1941, most of the senior officers at Pearl Harbor were spending a quiet day ashore, relaxing with friends, content in the knowledge that skeleton crews were keeping watch aboard the ships at the base. In Washington the government and military strategists were away from their offices. In the early afternoon of that day Japanese planes taking off from carriers at sea moved on Hawaii and caught the base completely off-guard. Nearly all the American defensive planes were destroyed before they could leave the ground, five battleships were either sunk or shattered, and several thousand men were killed. One historian of Roosevelt's diplomacy summed up the result of Pearl Harbor thus:

> There was just one thing that [the Japanese] could do to get Roosevelt completely off the horns of the dilemma, and that is precisely what they did, at one stroke, in a manner so challenging, so insulting and enraging, that the divided and confused American people were instantly rendered unanimous and certain.

On December 8, President Roosevelt read to a stunned Congress his message asking for a declaration of war against Japan:

> Yesterday, December 7, 1941—a date which will live in infamy—the United States of America was suddenly and deliberately attacked by naval and air forces of the Empire of Japan. . . .
> I believe I interpret the will of the Congress and of the people when I assert that we will not only defend ourselves to the uttermost but will make very certain that this form of treachery shall never endanger us again.

Within an hour, Congress had responded to the President's message by declaring a state of war to exist by act of Japan. Only one dissenting vote was recorded. On December 11, Germany and Italy formally declared war upon the United States in accordance with a treaty they had signed with Japan in 1940.

Japan quickly exploited the advantage gained by her surprise attack. Her troops captured the Malay peninsula without delay, and in February 1942 the British naval base of Singapore fell to their assault. Other Japanese forces broke through to the north, cutting off the supply line from India to China and, soon after, Japanese amphibious forces overwhelmed the Dutch East Indies. While these rapid conquests were occurring, the powerful Japanese fleet carried invasion and occupation forces throughout the South Pacific, taking positions on the supply routes to New Zealand and Australia. In the north they seized Kiska and Attu on the western tip of the Aleutian Islands, thus posing a direct threat to North America itself. This disastrous phase of the war in the Pacific was climaxed by the defeat of the American forces in the Philippines, and their surrender in June 1942 of the last heroically defended fortress of Corregidor in Manila Bay. The American commander in the Philippines, General Douglas MacArthur, escaped to Australia to organize the long campaign for regaining the South Pacific.

For Europe 1942 was a year of dread. With all of Western Europe in German control, Nazi armies advanced rapidly on two fronts to capture the Near East. Marshal Rommel, Germany's Desert Fox, approached the Suez Canal through Egypt. In 1941 Germany had launched an assault on the Soviet Union which had met with initial success. In this year of Axis triumph, a German army rushed towards the Baku oil fields in southern Russia, while a heavily armoured German assault moved in on Stalingrad to the north. Around the globe the Allies, or as the term now emerged, the United Nations, faced rapid loss of territory and increasingly precarious communications and supply routes. In addition the Soviet Union, fighting for its very existence, was calling for the opening of a second front by invasion of Western Europe. Latin America, which, with the exception of Argentina, accepted a recommendation to break diplomatic relations with the Axis countries, provided little assistance. Half of the republics declared war, but their main contribution was the provision of raw materials.

In the United States the unity created by Pearl Harbor rendered mobilization of men and industry relatively easy. As in the First World War, a selective service draft was used to raise men for the armed services and its task was

275

made more effective by the enrolment of women in the army, navy and coast guard to release enlisted men for combat duty. Thanks to lessons remembered from the First World War, and ready popular acceptance of governmental regulation brought about by the New Deal, the government handled problems of production and distribution effectively. Price control and rationing of commodities in short supply held inflation in check, and ensured a more equitable sharing of hardships than had been the case in 1917-18. Both wages and profits rose steadily as production grew. Overtime work became commonplace and many billions of dollars were poured voluntarily into war bonds. The War Production Board, armed with extensive powers, rapidly converted industry to production of war materials. Congress gave even greater power in 1943 to the Office of War Mobilization, which exercised virtually total authority to plan the national economy. Despite the new controls, much industry remained outside war production. In such areas profits also rose rapidly, and numerous private fortunes were founded. Labour unions confined their right to strike to non-war industries, and demanded closer control of the firms concerned. One result of such planning was a national income of a hundred and eighty billion dollars by 1944, as compared to forty billion dollars in 1932. In association with Canadian war production, which was also climbing to undreamed-of heights, the United States produced war *matériel* in sufficient quantity to keep Britain and Russia in the battle at the height of Nazi successes.

It was the successful organization of American production and manpower that justified the major strategy worked out in January 1942 at British-American military talks. Here the leaders of the United Nations laid the foundation for much closer co-operation than was ever achieved by the Axis powers. Despite the political risks it involved, Roosevelt accepted a strategy which meant restricting the war against Japan to a holding operation while concentrating the major effort against Germany. Fortunately, this decision was made possible by an American-Australian naval victory over a Japanese fleet in the Coral Sea in the spring of 1942; and by the successful repulse of a major Japanese naval-air assault on Midway Island, the loss of which would have endangered the Pearl Harbor base.

By late 1942 the Allies had begun a new phase of the war against Germany. The invasion of North Africa provided an alternative to the opening of a second front in Western Europe which Russia was still demanding. It was Churchill's scheme to strike at the "soft underbelly of Europe" by way of the Mediterranean. At the battle of El Alamein, General Montgomery defeated Rommel's desert troops, who began their flight back toward Tunisia. In November American troops landed in North Africa and all of French North Africa fell to the Allies. The last enemy resistance in Tunisia collapsed in May 1943. In July Allied forces invaded Sicily under General Dwight D. Eisenhower as Allied Commander-in-Chief. The invasion of Italy and the fall of Mussolini's government followed rapidly. However, it took long months of hard fighting to complete the conquest of Italy. The best that can be said for the Italian campaign is that a considerable Nazi force was pinned down in Italy by the need to impede the Allied advance northward.

At the same time, in the summer of 1943, the Nazi tide was turned in Russia. In the most bloody battles of the war, Russian armies rolled back the German thrust to the Dnieper River. Reeling from these reverses, the Germans suffered even more by assaults from the air. Having gained control of the air, Allied bomber fleets raked German industrial cities in a merciless attempt to weaken morale, diminish production, and disrupt communications. Remembering the aerial Battle of Britain, the attack on Pearl Harbor, and the massive loss of life in Russian cities, Allied commanders, governments and peoples were less concerned than they might otherwise have been with the morality of attacking civilian populations. The very survival of individual and national freedom seemed to be at issue; the stakes seemed great enough to justify fighting barbarism by barbaric methods.

Behind the scenes in the United States, Britain and Ca-

nada, scientists were already working out the military application of one of science's most dramatic and lethal discoveries.
Indeed, at the beginning of the war, three refugee scientists
from Europe, led by Albert Einstein, had told President
Roosevelt that German physicists were working on the principle of atomic fission with a view to producing a revolutionary mass-destruction bomb. Allied researchers began to work
on the same problem. Throughout the war, experiments were
carried out at three universities, and in a laboratory at Los
Alamos, New Mexico.

In the meantime, the Allies had sufficiently pummelled the
Nazis to permit launching of the final stage of the war in
Europe. The American General, Dwight D. Eisenhower, was
appointed Supreme Allied Commander, and after long and
detailed planning at Eisenhower's headquarters in England,
June 6, 1944 was chosen as the day on which an assault
would be launched from England across the Channel to
Europe. The Allies invaded Western Europe from a beach-
head in Normandy. At the same time, the Russians threw
all their effort into a drive through Romania. Despite some
temporary reverses and continuing loss of life, the Allies
relentlessly pressed the Nazi divisions back upon their home-
land. On May 8, 1945 Germany surrendered unconditionally.

The impending collapse of the Nazis was quickly reflected
in the war in the Pacific. By early 1945 General MacArthur
was finishing the reconquest of the Philippines, while the
island of Iwo Jima, even closer to Japan, had fallen to
American forces. Okinawa, only four hundred miles from
the Japanese home islands, fell to the United States in July
after the costliest of the Pacific battles. By this time, the
Allied scientists had solved the problem of splitting the atom,
and had begun the manufacture of atomic bombs. The Allied
leaders, after conferring together at Potsdam, issued an
ultimatum calling upon Japan to surrender unconditionally
and warning of "utter devastation of the Japanese home-
land" if she did not. When Japan rejected the ultimatum it
was decided to use the new bomb.

In 1944 Franklin Roosevelt had been re-elected to the Presidency for an unheard-of fourth term. His principal appeal to the electorate was that the conduct of the war, the impending victory and the problem of a post-war settlement all required that there should be no break in United States leadership at that time. His candidate for the Vice-Presidency was an obscure Missouri Senator named Harry S. Truman. But Roosevelt's superhuman exertions through the years of depression and war had taken their toll of his frail body, and he died suddenly at White Springs, Georgia, on April 12, 1945. His successor was faced immediately with an appalling decision. President Truman obtained the concurrence of Winston Churchill in the decision to drop atomic bombs on Japan. Arguing that the unknown horror to be released would be justified by the saving of American lives, Truman showed no qualms about using the new weapon. The United States Chief of Staff, General George Marshall, warned that it might cost 500,000 lives to force a Japanese surrender by conventional methods of attack. Most of the scientists advising Truman's special committee recommended using the bomb. Mr. Truman has recorded in his memoirs:

> They recommended further that it should be used without specific warning, against a target that would clearly show its devastating strength. I had realized, of course, that an atomic bomb explosion would inflict damage and casualties beyond imagination. . . . It was their conclusion that no technical demonstration they might propose, such as over a deserted island, would be likely to bring the war to an end. It had to be used against an enemy target.
>
> The final decision of where and when to use the atomic bomb was up to me. Let there be no mistake about it. I regarded the bomb as a military weapon and never had any doubt that it should be used.

Such are the reflections of the President who assumed a responsibility greater than that ever assumed by another human being: the unleashing for military purposes of the very cohesive force of the universe itself.

On August 6, 1945 a single American plane dropped an atomic bomb over the Japanese city of Hiroshima. The destruction was appalling. The entire city was levelled and eighty thousand people were killed outright. Many more thousands died soon after of radiation burns, and each year since 1945 other people have died of the lingering results of the first atomic attack. Two days later Nagasaki was obliterated with a slightly more powerful bomb. On August 14 Japan surrendered, stipulating only that the Emperor should continue to rule.

4. THE END OF ISOLATION

The United States experienced the Second World War much more deeply than it had the First. Thirteen million citizens had been enlisted, compared to the first war's three million, and more than two hundred thousand were killed in battle. The cost was ten times greater than that of the war of 1917-18, and the action had been on a global scale. These facts, perhaps, explain the willingness of the country to accept membership in an international organization after the war. The united response to the Japanese attack of December 1941, and the United States entry into the war, had taken some of the vigour out of domestic political battles. Although Republicans made some gains in the 1942 mid-term congressional elections, by 1944 the war was being won, and a number of leading Republicans had been appointed to administrative posts. Even the incredible nomination of Franklin Roosevelt for a fourth term was accomplished without much fuss. Harry S. Truman, the candidate for the Vice-Presidency, who was to succeed to the Presidency on Roosevelt's death, was selected to placate the conservatives and city political bosses. His nomination followed a bitter struggle in the Convention. Truman had begun his career as a small businessman in Independence, Missouri, and had made slow progress through local politics to the Senate. He had, however, co-operated with the most powerful Democratic bosses and had gained some public attention as Chairman of a Senate committee investigating war contracts.

The Republicans nominated the urbane and ambitious Thomas E. Dewey, Governor of New York. Since Dewey had acquiesced in most of the Roosevelt policies, he had little to attack in his campaign, and Roosevelt won again with a substantial electoral college majority, but a reduced majority of the popular vote. The victory of the conservative Democrats in the Convention struggle over the Vice-Presidency assumed great importance, for Roosevelt was to survive less than three months of his fourth term. Harry S. Truman took the oath of office less than two hours after Roosevelt's death. In the cabinet meeting which followed he had to decide whether to go ahead with a conference which had been called to meet at San Francisco on April 25 for the purpose of founding the organization which came to be known as the United Nations. In his memoirs he noted:

> I did not hesitate a second. I told press secretary Early that the conference would be held as President Roosevelt had directed. There was no question in my mind that the conference had to take place. It was of supreme importance that we build an organization to help keep the future peace of the world. It was the first decision I made as President.

In 1945 any other decision would have frustrated the majority opinion of the country. This opinion had been expressed as early as September 1943. In a congressional resolution supporting the creation of an effective international organization to keep the peace, the United States had pledged active membership in such an organization. At a conference of the Allies held in Moscow in November of 1943 this policy had been accepted, and in the summer of 1944 at Dumbarton Oaks in Washington a United Nations Charter was drafted. At Yalta in February 1945, Roosevelt, Churchill, and Stalin had agreed to call a United Nations founding conference at San Francisco in April. Recalling the fate of the League of Nations at the hands of the Senate in

1919-20, Roosevelt decided that the United Nations Organization should not be connected with any peace treaty. Also, profiting by Wilson's errors, he arranged that both Republicans and Democrats should be represented in the delegation.

After eight weeks of debate at San Francisco, a Charter was adopted for the United Nations. A General Assembly provided equal representation for each member nation. The Assembly could debate any matter within the terms of the Charter. The Security Council of eleven members was given executive power to investigate disputes, plan peaceful adjustments and take any kind of agreed action against declared aggressors. The permanent members were the United States, Russia, Great Britain, France and China. The six non-permanent members were to be elected by the Assembly. The United States, Russia and Britain all agreed that Security Council decisions on disputes and similar "substantive" matters must be approved by seven members, including all of the five permanent members; thus each permanent member of the Security Council exercised a veto in such matters. An Economic and Social Council (U.N.E.S.C.O.), with other special agencies and commissions, was made responsible to the Assembly and was to gather information and to work for the removal of economic and social conditions which might be the roots of war. The Charter also provided for an International Court of Justice to which disputes might be submitted voluntarily, and a Trusteeship Council to keep check on conditions in territories held in trust by United Nations members.

The American Senate in July 1945 ratified the United Nations Charter with only two negative votes. At the same time it ratified the Bretton Woods Agreement which provided for an International Bank for Reconstruction and Development, and an International Monetary Fund. These latter institutions were designed to keep national currencies stable and to help post-war economic recovery.

Clearly the United States, as well as the other founding nations, hoped by such measures to avoid the consequences that had followed the peace settlement of 1919 in Europe. On the other hand, post-war co-operation was by no means perfect, nor were the problems of negotiating peace treaties to be easily solved. The military alliance with Russia had never been free of mutual suspicion, despite the feeling of understanding that had grown between Roosevelt and Stalin. Britain and the United States were not prepared to share the secret of atomic energy with their wartime ally and this, together with sharp competition for the control of central and eastern Europe, dissipated the basis of wartime co-operation. Even at the San Francisco Conference there were disturbing signs that the great nations were jockeying for control of the new organization. The American delegation, realizing that Latin America would normally vote with the western powers, supported the application for membership made by Argentina although Argentina had been a centre of enemy intrigue throughout the war. The United States won its point against Russian opposition, and also succeeded in barring Poland from immediate membership because Poland's government was friendly to the Soviet Union.

Nevertheless, the selection of New York City as site of the splendid new United Nations headquarters symbolized American acceptance of the unavoidable responsibilities of the immense power the United States had achieved. In the post-war world, as in previous American history, the United States gave evidence of a sense of destiny. Now its sense of mission was to become a dominant factor in international affairs.

17

From Fair Deal to Great Society

1. PROSPERITY AND URBANIZATION

THE ATOMIC age which opened in 1945 saw the United States pass through a series of crises, both domestic and foreign. It was a time of tension and quickly changing patterns of life in which the nation became, according to some, an Affluent Society, according to others, a Garrison State. Although an average of four million workers still lacked jobs, and by 1965 there could still be counted thirty million people below minimum welfare standards, more Americans were prosperous than ever before in their history. Politics reflected this affluence by resuming a generally conservative tone. Urbanization continued and by 1965 more than sixty-five per cent of the one hundred and eighty million Americans lived in urban centres, compared with forty per cent in 1900. By creating more varied economic interests in each region the spread of industry and urbanization modified the sectionalism of American politics. As a result, Republicans increased their normal voting strength in the South, while Democrats found new support in the midwestern "corn belt."

Prosperity and urbanization also brought significant cultural changes. Wide areas of life became more nearly standardized across the nation, from houses and motels to clothing and manners of speech. In business, the large corporation became even more dominant. Young men training for managerial positions in such firms commanded much larger salaries than their fathers could have hoped for at the same age. They seemed more willing than earlier generations had been to accept a prospect of slow but sure and well-paid advancement as opposed to the riskier course of launching their own small businesses. More and more, too, they adjusted their habits, the size and make of their cars, and the location of their homes to the corporation's assessment of what was appropriate to their business status. A new premium was placed upon loyalty to the corporation itself. Sociologists began to distinguish a new American type which they dubbed the Organization Man. Living in split-level suburban houses millions of such men basked in the steady accumulation of their mass-produced luxuries, only occasionally reflecting upon the pre-packaged and unadventurous patterns of life to which they and their families conformed.

In post-war America national productivity increased rapidly, while the average working day in industry was shortened to eight hours or less. As trade unions grew in size and strength real wages rose steadily. Yet the distribution of wealth was still markedly unequal. In the mid-1950's about seventeen per cent of American families still lived on earnings of less than $1,500 a year. As in other modern western democracies, the advance of automation created a need for more workers with technical training and the numbers enrolled in high schools, technical schools, colleges and universities rose rapidly. Moreover, the number of office or "white collar" employees increased sharply in relation to the number of production or "blue collar" workers. The growth of this new middle class concerned with sales, distribution, advertising, office records, office management, and laboratories has been significant politically, because, as a group, such workers have shown themselves to be conservative. Moreover, since few of them belonged to unions, they failed as a class to win proportionately as great an increase in income as did unionized labour or the executive class.

The growth of automation in industry also meant that less varied and skilled work was required of production workers, and employees tended to derive less satisfaction from their work than formerly. In addition, a very large proportion of the urban population lived in highly standardized suburbs. One result was that the increased leisure available to most people was sometimes as much a problem as a blessing. The way of life was reflected in an unwillingness to make leisure hours creative. Thus television, which burst upon the market in the late 1940's, concentrated on light entertainment. There was, too, an increasing dominance of spectator rather than participation sports.

At the same time, however, the dawning age of "mass culture," as it has been rather disdainfully called, also brought with it phenomenal sales of paperback books, both literary and academic, growing attendance at symphony concerts and increased sales of art reproductions and recorded classical music. Equally important was the preoccupation of America's intellectuals, artists and writers with self-analysis, criticism and social research. From well-endowed university faculties of graduate studies poured a stream of historical, sociological and scientific studies of the highest order. In contemporary English letters some of the greatest names are those of Americans.

Creative thought and criticism were also stirring in the churches. Total church membership rose from about forty-five per cent of the population in the 1920's to over sixty per cent in 1965. While churchmen and non-churchmen agreed that this extremely high incidence of church affiliation reflected in part mere unwillingness to be different in a society that emphasized conformity, in part it bespoke discontent with a materialistic mass society. At its best this revival of religion meant a return to an earlier American emphasis upon the dignity of the individual and upon loyalties higher than those of state, section or nation. Individual churchmen and church groups took a prominent part in many kinds of social action. Many led in the movement for nuclear disarmament, and some courageous ones faced extreme personal risks in agitating for desegregation of the races in the South.

2. THE POLITICS OF PROSPERITY

Post-war politics reflected the complexity and prosperity of

American life as well as the terrifying realities of a world power struggle in which Americans were deeply involved. President Truman, in close co-operation with Congress, permitted a rapid dismantling of the American war machine. Demobilization of the huge military forces was so swift that America's ability to occupy Axis countries was imperilled. Once home, the millions of ex-servicemen were treated with enlightened generosity. Under a series of acts popularly called the "G.I. Bill of Rights," ex-soldiers were entitled to a variety of re-establishment benefits. These included completion of education at all levels, technical training, low-rate loans for buying houses or setting up businesses, and inexpensive insurance. The purchasing power so provided gave a quick stimulus to domestic production. Business got a further boost when most of the sixteen billion dollars' worth of industrial plants constructed by the government during the war were turned over to private purchasers on nearly give-away terms. Finally, the pent-up demand of consumers for goods of all kinds unobtainable during the war—no domestic automobiles had been produced since 1942 for example—led business to invest in new plants and housing at a rate three times that of the 1920 boom years.

In these circumstances business profits, already high in war production, climbed even more steeply. Labour became restless as wages failed to keep pace with prices and profits. In late 1945 and in 1946 labour disputes became serious, with over a million and a half workers on strike in January 1946. The terms on which strikes in the automotive and electrical industries and in the coal mines were settled led to a general rise in wage rates. These increases in costs were passed on by management to the public in higher prices. Rising prices (inflation) destroyed the real value, or buying power, of the wage increases. Thus the unions fought for second and third rounds of wage increases in 1946 and 1947. Labour leaders argued for continuance of wartime price controls through the Office of Price Administration (O.P.A.), and the President himself favoured this course. But the bill to continue O.P.A. for one year was so watered down in Congress in response to business pressure that the President vetoed it and price controls ended in July 1946. Struggling with the bitter chaos of industrial relations, President Truman was compelled to put both the mines and the railways under temporary government ownership pending settlement of the most serious strikes of these two years.

In the 1946 mid-term elections Republicans won control of both Houses in the Eightieth Congress. A direct result of this resurgence of conservatism was the passage of the Taft-Hartley Act in June 1947 over President Truman's veto. The Act restricted the right to strike by requiring a sixty-day "cooling off" period before a strike could be called, allowed management to sue unions both for breach of contract and for damages resulting from jurisdictional disputes, and made illegal the "closed shop," that is to say, any provision in a labour contract requiring management to hire only men who were already union members. The Act also outlawed the practice of having employers collect dues for the union by deducting them from pay cheques of all employees whether union members or not. Unions were forbidden to make contributions to political parties and union officials were forced to swear that they were not Communists, on pain of withdrawal of recognition of the union as a properly constituted bargaining agent. Nevertheless, unions increased their membership by some two and a half million in the decade after the war. During these years, unions negotiated a growing number of contracts which included such fringe benefits as company provision of recreational facilities, longer holidays, and health insurance and retirement pension plans. The unions also circumvented the veto on their contributing to political parties out of union funds by establishing their own political education committees and placing considerable funds at their disposal. Through these committees unions continued to give important support to the Democratic party.

The Eightieth Congress made certain that no President could again serve more than two terms by sponsoring the Twenty-Second Amendment which was ratified in March

1951. Then, over the President's veto, Congress reduced taxation by nearly five billion dollars, and rejected executive-sponsored reform legislation.

By 1948, the Democratic party appeared to be severely disrupted. Conservative Southern Democrats, repelled by Truman's pro-labour attitude and by his defence of equal civil rights for Negroes, refused to support the President's renomination in the Democratic Convention. Instead they founded a States' Rights Democratic party, which was quickly dubbed the Dixiecrat party, and nominated Governor Strom Thurmond of South Carolina as their candidate for President. By this move they hoped to prevent any candidate winning a majority of electoral votes. If that happened, then (as in 1824) the House of Representatives would choose between the contenders and in the House their power as a united bloc might be decisive. At the same time many liberal and left-wing Democrats were dissatisfied with Truman's foreign policy and sceptical about his domestic policy. These dissidents formed a Progressive party and nominated Henry Wallace. Wallace had been Secretary of Agriculture under Roosevelt, and had resigned from Truman's Cabinet in 1946 in protest against what he considered to be the government's excessively hard-bitten attitude towards the Soviet Union. The Republicans nominated Governor Dewey of New York for a second time, with a stand-pat domestic platform and a foreign policy which differed little from that of the Democrats.

Eyeing the serious three-way Democratic split, all observers predicted a big Dewey victory. But Truman, in an almost single-handed whistle-stop campaign, castigated the Eightieth Congress for its reactionary policies and effectively preached a "fair deal" to the Negroes, labour unions and farmers in language reminiscent of the heyday of the New Deal. Refusing to believe anything but the predictions, and before the Western returns were in the Chicago *Tribune* printed a special election-night issue headlined: "Dewey Defeats Truman." There were red faces the next morning when it was discovered that the unassuming but tough little man from Independence had staged the nation's most startling political surprise. Truman's popular vote was 24,105,000 to Dewey's 21,969,000. The Dixiecrats carried only South Carolina, Mississippi, Alabama and Louisiana. Wallace carried no state.

Since the Democrats had also recaptured a majority in both Houses of Congress, Truman immediately launched his Fair Deal programme, which he presented as an extension of New Deal policies. After bitter debate, and despite the opposition of Southern Democrats, the President's supporters in Congress secured legislation to raise the legal minimum wage, to subsidize low-rental housing and slum clearance, to extend rent-control, to increase by ten million the number of employees covered by the Social Security Act and to provide aid to Europe in its struggle to recover from the ravages of war. Much of this legislation, however, was hobbled by amendments and inadequate provision for its financing and Congress completely rejected civil rights measures, repeal of the Taft-Hartley Act, and a bill designed to keep up farm prices.

3. THE CONSERVATIVE REACTION

In spite of the support given Truman's Fair Deal, the climate of opinion remained conservative. Tension between the United States and Russia and the knowledge after 1949 that Russia possessed the atomic bomb provided fertile soil for a new witch-hunt. In 1948, a former Communist agent named Whittaker Chambers declared that one Alger Hiss, a State Department employee, had turned over classified, or secret, documents to him. In a congressional hearing, Hiss denied the charges and later sued Chambers for slander. Chambers produced fresh evidence to support his charges, and in 1950 Hiss was finally convicted of perjury and sentenced to five years in jail. Many people felt that the trials were inconclusive, but while the outcome was pending, government agents uncovered several other Communists in administrative posts. Congress speedily passed a bill requiring all Communist action organizations and all organizations controlled by Communists ("Communist front" organizations) to register with the Attorney-General and place on file the names and addresses of their officers. The President vetoed this measure as dangerous to freedom of thought. Congress repassed it over his veto. The courts went even further. Heretofore they had held that an overt act must be proved before a person could be convicted of treason. Now the Supreme Court in 1951 upheld an act of 1940 which made it illegal even to teach doctrines of forcible revolution or to be a member of a group which taught such doctrine. As a result, the government's prosecution of eleven leading Communists succeeded and they received jail terms averaging four years each.

Seizing upon the uneasiness in the public mind, Senator Joseph McCarthy of Wisconsin delivered a sensational speech in the spring of 1950 in which he declared that the State Department was riddled with Communists and that he had a list naming two hundred and five of them. When pressed for the names, he whittled the list down to eighty-one, then to fifty-seven, and finally could not produce a single name. Falsehood and slander nevertheless carried McCarthy far. In the mid-term elections of 1950, he helped defeat Senator Tydings of Maryland, who had been chairman of a Senate committee which declared McCarthy's charges to be "a nefarious campaign of half-truths and untruths." As part of his campaign against Tydings he produced a retouched photograph which falsely suggested that Tydings was friendly with a leading Communist. McCarthy continued to produce charges that Communism was rampant in the government and to reduce Senate investigating procedures to the level of the gutter. Demagogic attacks upon the Secretary of State, General George C. Marshall, and many other distinguished Americans, alleging them to be "soft on Communism" and disloyal, culminating in a particularly irresponsible assault upon the army, finally led to the censuring of McCarthy by his fellow Senators in 1954.

Remarkably few people chose to fight McCarthy openly

in his day of power. Even Dwight Eisenhower, who as Republican Presidential candidate in 1952 was the head of McCarthy's party, failed to repudiate him. McCarthyism thus spread across the nation in the form of a vast witch-hunt. Local demagogues took up the cry and were able to force loyalty oaths on school teachers and university professors. They succeeded in removing from public and private positions thousands of people thought to be too radical in their views, and in censoring library holdings. In the end, the State Department itself suffered severely as potential public servants refused to join it and run the risk of public smearing by congressional committees, or private slander. Though McCarthy himself died in 1957 the fever had still to run its course.

As the 1952 elections approached, President Truman decided not to run again, and the Democrats nominated Governor Adlai Stevenson of Illinois. A suave and cultured politician, Stevenson appealed to literate Americans without attracting strong support from liberals, some of whom suspected him of compromising on such questions as civil rights. His outstanding wit and apt turns of phrase may even have been a disadvantage to him in appealing to the ordinary voter. The Republicans chose General Eisenhower. Popular with the army, unassuming, yet inspiring confidence with his fatherly manner, Eisenhower's political inexperience was no apparent disadvantage to him. Promising to end the Korean War, to weed out the corruption which had been revealed in Washington and to tighten internal security, Eisenhower gave conservative feeling a rallying point. Election night showed a startling Republican ability to cut deeply into the traditionally Democratic South. With Eisenhower's victory twenty years of Democratic rule came to an end.

Although Eisenhower's dramatic visit to Korea, in fulfilment of a campaign promise, did not alter the course of peace negotiations, the Korean War came to an end six months after his inauguration. In domestic affairs, programmes Truman had initiated were scaled down or reversed. The housing programme was curtailed, the budget trimmed, taxes cut and supports to farm prices lowered. Though private hydro-electric power development was favoured at the expense of further public power developments, nevertheless the Eisenhower government gained congressional consent to proceed with the long-debated project for joint Canadian-American construction of the St. Lawrence Seaway and its related power plants.

In the conservative 1950's there remained one group actively dissatisfied with things as they were, namely the Negroes. From 1914 to the 1950's hundreds of thousands of Negroes had migrated to northern cities and others had served in the armed forces. They discovered that while migration brought them greater economic advantages they still faced substantial prejudice and modified segregation. In cities like Chicago and Detroit, vast districts of Negro housing and business grew up quite separate from white districts, and race riots were the usual result where a Negro family endeavoured to break the pattern of residential segregation. Jobs invariably went first to white applicants, and Negroes found it very difficult to rise very far in the professions or business. During the Second World War, Congress established a Fair Employment Practices Committee to investigate and curb open discrimination on grounds of colour, race or creed. Although Southerners prevented this legislation from being renewed at the end of the war, many state governments in the North and West created similar committees. Truman forced some advance towards desegregation in the armed services, and the President's Committee on Civil Rights in 1946 recommended sweeping federal action against all forms of discrimination in schools, transportation, public services, housing and employment. Legislation to implement the recommendations was killed by a strong opposition from Southern Senators.

It was against this background of halting achievement, bitterness and stalemate that the Supreme Court handed down a crucial decision in 1954 which rejected the view that the Fourteenth Amendment was honoured if Negroes were provided with "separate but equal" facilities. In 1954, Chief

Justice Warren declared that separate school facilities for Negroes were "inherently unequal." Clearly, this implied that segregation in other social situations was also contrary to the Fourteenth Amendment. The Court thereupon issued orders calling for desegregation in education wherever separate schools were the rule. Declaring that this should be accomplished with "all deliberate speed," the Court recognized that its instructions demanded nothing less than a social revolution in the South, and possibly in the North also.

While some progress towards desegregation was made in Missouri, Tennessee, Maryland and Kentucky, violent resistance came in the Deep South. A notable test came in Little Rock, Arkansas, in the autumn of 1957, where Governor Orval Faubus used state troops to prevent Negro children from enrolling in a city high school. President Eisenhower, while avoiding a clear statement in support of the principle of desegregation, argued that the Court's decision was the law of the land and must be upheld; he ordered federal troops to escort the Negro children to school. The point was won, but Faubus was overwhelmingly re-elected as Governor. In the following autumn further trouble arose when the Little Rock School Board demanded more time to give effect to the Court's order. The Court, in a unanimous decision, refused, declaring that "the constitutional rights of children not to be discriminated against in school admission on grounds of race or colour declared by this Court can neither be nullified openly and directly by state legislators or state executives or judicial officers, nor nullified by them through any evasive scheme for segregation."

"Evasive schemes" were prepared in several of the Southern states, but proved too expensive to operate on a permanent basis. Resistance remained in the open. President Eisenhower appealed to all to co-operate in achieving the goal of equality between the races, but progress remained painfully slow. Meanwhile, lawyers for the National Association for the Advancement of Coloured People continued the long struggle in the courts to break down the system of segregation in all areas of life. In addition, Negroes in Southern cities such as Montgomery, Alabama, organized boycotts of segregated public services and "sit-ins" at public places such as lunch-bars. Such protests often led to violence and jail terms for the demonstrators. By 1961, groups of liberals from the North, comprising both Negroes and whites, were staging "freedom rides" by travelling in desegregated buses through the South and endeavouring to use segregated waiting rooms and restaurants. While all Americans recognized that the barriers which shored up white supremacy were crumbling around the periphery of the South, and would fall eventually, the battle still raged bitterly. In the autumn of 1962 Governor Ross Barnett of Mississippi challenged federal authority by refusing to admit a Negro to the State university. In the storm that followed, the Communist world was not slow to make the most of this serious blot on democratic practice.

President Eisenhower, although critically ill in 1955 and June of 1956 was nevertheless renominated enthusiastically by the Republicans in the summer of 1956. Once again, his personal popularity proved politically superior to the sophisticated sentences of Adlai Stevenson, and he won the 1956 election. The second Eisenhower administration was dominated even more than the first had been by problems of foreign policy. Furthermore, an economic recession began in 1957 which threatened both domestic prosperity and the economic strength which most Americans believed necessary in any kind of competition with the Soviet Union for world influence.

4. KENNEDY AND CAMELOT

While the country passed safely through the recession, the pace of economic growth was markedly reduced and the number of unemployed remained high. The Democrats concentrated public attention on the lagging economy as they prepared for what they believed was inevitable victory in 1960. The Democratic Convention in that year gave the nomination to Senator John F. Kennedy of Massachusetts. Son of a very wealthy Irish Roman Catholic family of Boston, Senator Kennedy had campaigned vigorously for some months prior to the Convention and appealed to a broader section of the party than any of his leading competitors. Liberals in the party were dismayed by Kennedy's choice of Lyndon Johnson of Texas as his running-mate, since, despite his progressive voting record they saw him as a right-wing Democrat. Others feared that religious feelings might jeopardize Kennedy's chances of election. On the Republican side, President Eisenhower gave his hesitant blessing to Richard Nixon, the Vice-President, who was duly nominated. It had been Eisenhower's policy to increase the responsibilities of the Vice-Presidency and accordingly Nixon's name had been much before the public. Yet he was not wholeheartedly endorsed either by the old guard of the party or by liberal Republicans who would have preferred a candidate less closely associated with right-wing opinion.

Thus both candidates represented the middle sections of their respective parties. Both were young and both campaigned tirelessly. A special feature of the election was the first television debate between Presidential candidates, an event which many commentators believe influenced the outcome markedly. The programmes set forth by Nixon and Kennedy did not diverge sharply either in domestic or foreign policy and the contenders discussed mostly the question of how best to "get America moving in the '60's." The outcome was the closest in American history; so close that the final victory of Kennedy was not certain for several weeks after the first counting of the ballots.

Despite his middle-of-the-road voting record in the Senate, Kennedy personified the hope that the United States could again become a vibrant, expansive society. His image of youthful dedicated vigour (the youngest man, save Teddy Roosevelt, ever to take the Presidential oath) contrasted sharply with that of the older and ailing Eisenhower, as well as that of "tricky Dickie" Nixon, who had endorsed McCarthyism and *seemed* devious. The Kennedy brothers (Robert became J.F.K.'s Attorney-General and closest political adviser) appealed to young people and to many hopeful liberals in much the way that Pierre Trudeau appealed to similar Canadians in 1968. Together with his glamorous wife, Jacqueline, Kennedy gave a distinctive style to the White House, surrounding himself with Harvard advisers such as J. K. Galbraith, A. M. Schlesinger and A. A. Berle, and a stream of guests from the worlds of film, television and the arts. People began referring to the Kennedy "court" as Camelot — suggesting the chivalry and idealism of King Arthur's Knights of the Round Table.

In his first months in office, President Kennedy prepared to advance toward what he called the New Frontier. His legislative programme included a large extension of federally-subsidized housing, federal aid to education, federally-sponsored medical care for the aged, a broad programme of urban redevelopment and considerable tariff reduction. By 1963 some cautious progress had been made in these directions, but many liberals became disillusioned by Kennedy's lukewarm support of civil rights legislation and by his failure to gain passage of much of his legislative programme. Like F. D. Roosevelt, he was basically conservative and sought both a balanced budget and action against inflation. Instead of expanding, the economy remained sluggish. By the spring of 1962 unemployment figures stood at four and a half million (over five per cent of the work force). The problem was particularly acute in key industries such as coal, aircraft, autos and textiles. Attempts to cope with unemployment by way of a Manpower Retraining Bill were of little help as long as industry generally was not expanding. Efforts to stimulate trade by agreement among the leading industrial nations to take mutual action to lower tariffs had little success in the face of an economic revival in Europe. The revival which had, ironically, been the major goal of American postwar policies, was seized upon by General Charles de Gaulle to assert a French-led Europeanism, independent of both the United States and the U.S.S.R.

Much of Kennedy's failure to implement economic growth and to chart a really "new frontier" was the result of his own conception of the problems of government and social direction. He believed that there was a "consensus" in the country, a "vital centre," and that all that was needed was expert management. In 1962 he told a Yale University convocation, "Today . . . the central problems of our time are more subtle and less simple. They do not relate to basic clashes of philosophy and ideology, but to ways and means of reaching common goals." Believing that the agreed goals were containment of Communism and stable growth fostered by firm leadership, he made enemies on the left and on the right. He alienated liberals by favouring business with large tax reductions on corporate income and by indicating that inflation and a balanced budget were more important problems than real equality for Negroes and slum-dwellers. At the same time, in one of his most decisive domestic actions, he angered big business. In 1962, hoping to curb inflation, he persuaded leaders of the United Steel Workers to agree to a contract providing slender wage increases. When the big steel companies immediately announced a price increase of 3.5 per cent, Kennedy pressured them into rescinding the increase, earning widespread disfavour in business circles.

A considerable part of Kennedy's effort to present a forward-looking image was his sudden expansion of the United States space exploration programme. Seeking a total expenditure of forty billion dollars to enable the United States to send the first man to the moon, he explained to Congress that "no single space project in this period will be more impressive to mankind." Neil Armstrong became that first man in July 1969; the event was a transitory relief from complex political problems on earth.

Despite relative prosperity in the middle class, there were large areas of potentially violent discontent within

American society. In 1963 two events made the issue of civil rights completely unavoidable. In Birmingham, Alabama, a massive non-violent demonstration against continuing segregation was organized by the Southern Christian Leadership Conference led by the brilliant Negro minister, Martin Luther King. Police dispersed the demonstrators brutally, using electric cattle-prodders, vicious dogs and fire hoses. In the process, three children were killed and the gruesome scene was broadcast on television both at home and abroad. Non-violent protest peaked in August 1963, when over 200,000 blacks and whites staged a March on Washington and heard King deliver his most famous speech before the Lincoln Memorial: "I have a dream that one day this nation will rise up and live out the true meaning of its creed: 'We hold these truths to be self-evident, that all men are created equal'. . . . I have a dream that my four little children will one day live in a nation where they will not be judged by the colour of their skin, but by the content of their character. This is our hope."

King's hope seemed dim to many. In the South, several desegregation leaders were murdered and in the North, a massive migration of black share-croppers into the industrial cities resulted in the growth of Negro ghettos and decaying inner cities as whites moved steadily to "safe" suburbs. Parallel to King's non-violent crusade for equality there arose a militant Black Muslim movement led by fiery "separatists" such as Malcolm X who warned his "soul brothers" that violence must be met with violence. Finally the President responded directly to what he called the "fires of frustration and discord . . . burning in every city, North and South." In Congress the administration strongly supported a civil rights bill designed to put an effective end to segregation in public places and in business. Immediately the long-smouldering conservative criticism of Kennedy's Ivy League liberalism burst into flame, led by Arizona's Senator Barry Goldwater and extremists of the right-wing John Birch Society. Seeking to mend political fences in the South, Kennedy toured Florida and Texas in November 1963. As he was driving through the Dallas crowds to make a speech, the wife of Texas Governor John Connally said to him, "You can't say that Dallas isn't friendly to you today." At that moment Kennedy was hit and killed by two bullets, while a third seriously wounded Connally.

The American people and the rest of the world were deeply shocked. Indeed, doubly shocked — by the fate which had overtaken the vigorous young President and by the intimations of a deep-seated climate of violence. Fears deepened when two days after the assassination the alienated gunman, Lee Harvey Oswald, was himself killed before television cameras by Jack Ruby, a Dallas nightclub owner. A riot of speculation at once broke loose: was Oswald part of a left-wing conspiracy? Was Ruby controlled by organized criminals? Were the Federal Bureau of Investigation (F.B.I.) or the Central Intelligence Agency (C.I.A.) somehow involved? A commission of inquiry headed by Chief Justice Earl Warren concluded that Oswald had acted alone. His background was one of political and psychological instability. However, unlike the assassins of Lincoln (1865), Garfield (1881) and McKinley (1901), Oswald's exact motives and connections will never be known, especially since a number of important witnesses who were not fully interrogated by the Warren Commission have since died. More recent Congressional inquiries have failed to reach a conclusive opinion on how many bullets were fired or even from what direction they came.

Taking the oath of office in the Presidential plane en route from Dallas to Washington, Vice-President Lyndon B. Johnson must have been painfully aware of the turbulent future he faced.

5. L.B.J. ALL THE WAY: THE BREAKDOWN OF DISCIPLINE

Johnson was, above all, a Texan. A big, lusty man with a colourful vocabulary, he liked to think of himself as more western than southern. He was both, as was demonstrated by his deep drawl and sprawling "L.B.J." ranch. Johnson was never at ease with the northeastern elite of Camelot. He reflected a profound shift in the internal American balance of power away from northeastern liberalism, a shift which also gave Goldwater, Nixon and future Presidential candidate Ronald Reagan rich southern and western sources of support. Although his origins were lowly — his grandfather was a populist and he himself began as an impecunious schoolteacher — he had risen far. Entering political life as a protege of Franklin Roosevelt ("He was just like a daddy to me always"), Johnson rose steadily from Congressman (1937) to Senator (1948) to majority Senate leader and then Vice-President. He had close connections with wealthy southwestern oilmen and industrialists and became the first President to be clearly representative of the increasingly populous and wealthy "sunbelt" with its burgeoning enterprises in energy, aerospace, electronics, entertainment and recreation. Yet while Johnson was a superb politician, his power was steadily eroded by forces he could not control.

The cross-currents of the sixties are among the most puzzling in American history. Perhaps the one unifying theme is that of "alienation." Major sections of the population rejected important aspects of American society such as employers' requirements of conformity, the dominance of the automobile, unrestricted pollution of the environment, standardization in education and the prefabrication of both taste and consumer "needs" through advertising. While millions of Americans enjoyed unprecedented affluence, close to twenty-five per cent lived at or below the poverty line. At the same time, long-established patterns of behaviour dissolved rapidly. Sociologists and other analysts still debate the reasons for what one of them called "the greening of America," yet certain broad trends are clear. Between 1960 and 1970 the divorce rate increased from one divorce for every four marriages to one for every three, and continued to rise in the 1970's. Increased availability of the contraceptive pill helped break down previous inhibitions about pre-marital sex, while youthful experience of sexual intercourse, together with the rising rate of family dissolution, led to casual relationships and skepticism about the validity of formal marriage.

A significant aspect of this so-called "permissive society," particularly puzzling for political and religious leaders, was a reassertion of extreme individualism. Many parents and teachers came to believe in increased freedom of expression and relaxed methods of evaluation in education, whereby common standards of achievement were frowned upon. Non-conformity became an ideal in itself and was expressed through an ostentatious disregard of any form of authority. But the liberation of alienated individuals resulted in the emergence of new kinds of group identity. Thus, those who thought they were "dropping out" of institutionalized society frequently adopted common styles of hair and clothing and distinctive expressions and styles of speech. Some set up "communes" where they could live with others who shared their values. Yet by the seventies many of these rebellious styles had become a new orthodoxy, while the communes were largely replaced by increasingly restrictive mind-bending religious and leadership cults.

The search for alternative lifestyles produced liberation and protest movements aimed at challenging customary attitudes and policies and confronting established authority. Some of these rebellious movements had historic antecedents such as the abolitionist crusade of the 1840's and the women's suffrage movement, while others were spawned by circumstances of the sixties. Demands spread for radical legal reforms to guarantee complete equality of treatment for women, Negroes, homosexuals and other groups. Mass protest marches, sit-ins and civil disobedience designed to secure changes in foreign policy, to curb the nuclear arms race or to secure strong student representation on university boards became frequent occurrences. Non-violent protest was inextricably bound up with violence in a decade scarred by ghetto warfare, assassinations, terrorist kidnapping, bombing and airplane hijacking. The general term New Left was coined to describe the enthusiasm for self-expression and participatory democracy. One group, Students for a Democratic Society (S.D.S.), provided much of the leadership for campus and foreign policy protest and symbolized the vaguely formulated aspirations of the New Left: the rejection of the traditional political parties, the decentralization of political power, the halting of pollution of the environment, and control by students and workers of the institutions in which they lived and worked. But increasingly the goal of curbing the political-social power of corporations blended with that of ending the war in Vietnam, which escalated steadily throughout the decade and ultimately defeated President Johnson.

When Johnson took up the reins of office he appeared to be in an advantageous position. Despite an ill-concealed hostility between the Johnsons and the Kennedys' circle, key Kennedy appointees continued in office. Secretary of State Dean Rusk, Defense Secretary Robert McNamara and Special Adviser on Security Affairs McGeorge Bundy provided real continuity in foreign affairs and defence, but as we shall see it was these very areas that Johnson was to find most perilous. In domestic policy Johnson's experience as a Senate leader and balancer of interests paid off. He immediately courted business support by securing a large tax cut which stimulated the economy and by 1965 unemployment had dropped below five per cent. At the same time, he induced Congress to enact a new Civil Rights Act, partly as a result of the shock-waves of violence and Kennedy's assassination. The 1964 Act sharply increased federal power to ensure Negro voting rights, speed school desegregation, and more effectively curb racial discrimination in both public and private accommodation and business. Johnson capped these successes and prepared for the 1964 election by announcing a "war on poverty" and securing legislation appropriating $900 million for job training, adult education and loans to small businesses. Despite the chasm still separating the poor from the affluent he emphasized that it was now time to move beyond the New and Fair Deals to what he called the Great Society where problems of quality rather than quantity would predominate. "For half a century," he declared, "we called upon unbounded invention and untiring industry to create an order of plenty for all our people. The challenge of the next half century is . . . to use that wealth to enrich and elevate our national life — and to advance the quality of American civilization."

Hoping for support from white supremacists and from opponents of extended welfare programmes, the Republicans nominated the right-wing Senator Barry Goldwater of Arizona. Advocating a tough line against expensive government and against Communism at home and abroad Goldwater declared that "Extremism in the defence of liberty is no vice . . . moderation in the pursuit of justice is no virtue." When he suggested the use of atomic weapons in crises, moderates in both parties became wary. Democrats, sensing the mood of caution, nominated Johnson and, as his running-mate for Vice-President, the moderate liberal Hubert Humphrey of Minnesota. In the light of later events it was ironic that Johnson appeared the "dove" on Vietnam, declaring, "we don't want to get involved . . . in a land war in Asia." Democratic confidence was justified by the vote count which gave Johnson the biggest victory in American history.

From 1965 to 1968 Johnson's administration attempted to deal with steadily mounting social unrest and urban violence by introducing city renewal plans, community action programmes for unemployed young people, increased federal aid for education, subsidized medical insurance for those over sixty-five and subsidized food for the extremely poor. However such efforts to alleviate social distress failed to reduce bitterness resulting from real inequalities and were further weakened by the sudden escalation of the war in Vietnam. As the number of men sent to fight in that war moved toward the peak figure of 594,000 (1968) it became clear that Negroes and the poor made up a disproportionate percentage of the total. Middle class youths found it easier to secure exemption from the draft — the Selective Service or conscription act which had been re-enacted in 1948. Young people who opposed the war on principle staged riotous campus protests and risked jail by burning their draft notices. Perhaps 20,000 "war resisters" found asylum in Canada. Moreover, calamitous racial tensions coincided with the spread of opposition to "Mr. Johnson's War." Four "long hot summers" following 1964 saw racial rioting, looting, killing and burning in cities across the country. The worst outbreak came in Detroit in 1967, cost forty-three lives, millions of dollars in property loss, and required federal troops to restore order. Troops were also needed to quell the waves of rioting which followed the assassination of Martin Luther King in the spring of 1968.

Not only the people directly involved saw the effects of the social malaise. Television gave instant world-wide viewing of the carnage in Vietnam and the violence across America. Against this background the general prosperity of "middle America" and the rising standard of living of middle-class Negroes became of less consequence than the discrediting of the man who seemed to be responsible for the war, and the growing concern about law and order. In March of the election year 1968, Johnson announced in a startling television broadcast that he was halting the controversial bombing in Vietnam and also declared, "I shall not seek and I will not accept the nomination of my party for another term." His declaration strengthened the campaign for that nomination already being waged by Senator Eugene McCarthy of Minnesota, who spoke for liberals and was pledged to implement Johnson's parting promise of peace negotiations. Competition for the mantle of Johnson intensified when Robert Kennedy entered the fray and attracted support from the groups to whom Mc-Carthy was appealing. In June, however, while celebrating victory in the California primary election, Kennedy was shot and killed by an Arab nationalist who saw him as pro-Israel. The Democratic convention in Chicago in August symbolized the decade's divisions and its violence. The delegates seemed to favour Vice-President Humphrey who had strongly supported all the Johnson policies and also enjoyed strong labour union support. Anticipating trouble from thousands of young war protesters, Mayor Richard Daley, a Democrat, surrounded the convention arena with barbed wire while Chicago police and some five thousand National Guardsmen "controlled" the city in what a later report termed a police riot. In this unprom-ising atmosphere Humphrey received the nomination.

Sensing a conservative reaction, the Republicans nomin-ated Richard Nixon, who chose right-wing Spiro Agnew of Maryland as his running mate. Thus both parties sought the middle ground, emphasizing the need for law and order and the desirability of ending the war, but making few specific commitments. Nixon won the election in a close vote and promised to "bring the American people together."

18

Foreign Policy in the Cold War

TWO GREAT questions confronted the United States as the Second World War moved to its close. The first was the question of what America should do to help her desperately war-battered Allies recover health and strength. The second was the problem of future relations with the Soviet Union. In 1945 American leaders approached these questions with a mixture of caution and confidence, but as time passed confidence diminished and the concern for world economic recovery gave way to an obsession with problems of security.

1. RECOVERY AND SECURITY

The basis of post-war diplomacy was laid at the wartime conferences held at Yalta and Potsdam in February and July of 1945. At Yalta, Roosevelt, Churchill and Stalin agreed to divide Germany into four occupation zones—British, American, Russian and French—and to exact reparations from Germany in work and equipment. But the western leaders could secure no guarantees from Stalin concerning the future of the Russian-occupied nations of eastern Europe except that they should have governments "broadly representative" of their people. Churchill argued for a "hard-headed" bargain with Stalin which would have divided Europe and Asia into Russian and western spheres of influence and advocated that Japan and Germany be rebuilt rapidly as strong industrial states to act as barriers against Russian expansion. Roosevelt disagreed; he preferred to think that Russia and the western Allies could co-operate through the United Nations and avoid the traditional device of military alliances that had brought on a holocaust twice in his lifetime.

By the time the Potsdam Conference met, Truman had succeeded Roosevelt as President of the United States and Clement Attlee had replaced Churchill as Prime Minister of Britain. The two new leaders agreed to administer Germany through an Allied Control Council until a peace treaty had been arranged, and to establish a Council of Foreign Ministers to draw up peace treaties with former enemy states. By the time treaties had been hammered out for Romania, Bulgaria, Hungary, Finland and Italy and signed early in 1947 so much friction had developed between the United States and Russia that, for the time being at least, there seemed no possibility of their reaching agreement on a settlement with Austria or Germany.

The kinds of situation which generated this friction are well illustrated by the cases of Greece and Turkey. In Greece an authoritarian but pro-western government was under attack by the Greek Communist party which, with Russian aid, was exploiting the misery of the people and their discontent with monarchy in a bid to win power. A similar situation existed in Turkey. In 1947 the British government advised the American State Department that Britain could no longer afford the burden of shoring up these two governments. Yet Greece and Turkey were key states; if they were to join the Communist camp Russia would gain control of all the Balkans and the Dardanelles. This President Truman was determined to prevent. He laid it down that "it must be the policy of the United States to support free peoples who are resisting attempted subjugation by armed minorities or by outside pressures." This was at once dubbed the Truman Doctrine, and in its support the United States had, by 1950, spent $659 million in stemming the advance of Communism in the eastern Mediterranean.

That same spring of 1947 the United States also came fully to grips with the question of Europe's economic recovery. Truman's Secretary of State, George C. Marshall, outlined a massive programme for lending American assistance to European programmes for recovery. The Marshall Plan, as it was called, began with an annual budget of five billion dollars. These funds were distributed by an Economic Cooperation Administration (E.C.A.) upon a plan worked out by representatives of the western European governments themselves through the newly formed Organization for European Economic Co-operation (O.E.E.C.). Technically membership in the Organization was also open to the states of eastern Europe within the Communist sphere of influence. As George Marshall declared, in announcing the plan:

> Our policy is directed not against any country or doctrine but against hunger, poverty, desperation, and chaos. Its purpose should be the revival of a working economy in the world so as to permit the emergence of political and social conditions in which free institutions can exist.

In practice, the countries within the Soviet sphere boycotted the Marshall Plan and the Soviet Union set up its own "Molotov Plan" for the economic reorganization of the eastern European states. Nevertheless, by 1951 the O.E.E.C. had spent twelve billion dollars in American aid, and the programme is usually credited with having prevented the Communists from winning power in France and Italy.

Yet, despite the evident success of the Marshall Plan in stemming Communism in western Europe, distrust of Russia led the United States to give her foreign policy an increasing military emphasis. A straw in the wind was an article in *Foreign Affairs* by George Kennan, published in the summer of 1947. Kennan was an official of the State Department who had seen service in Moscow and had concluded that the most effective policy for the United States would be one of "containment" of Russia and her Communist satellites. The United States, he argued, should support and strengthen non-Communist states around the periphery of the Communist world so as to be able to bring immediate counter-pressure to bear against any threat of Communist expansion. This would mean the acquiring and manning of suitable military bases in a kind of encirclement of the Soviet bloc.

Events in Czechoslovakia powerfully influenced public opinion to adopt this view of what American policy should be. Since 1946, Czechoslovakia had been ruled by a coalition of Communists and non-Communists. Now, in February 1948, with fresh elections impending, the Communist minority seized power. A chill ran through the West. Although Communist strength in Czechoslovakia reflected Czech fears that a revived German power might again threaten her, the West regarded the Czech coup as loss of a "Western" state. Communist success there seemed to many Western leaders to cast a long shadow westward. They began more definitely to look upon their relations with the Soviet states as a struggle for power in the nature of a war—a "Cold War" as the phrase went.

Germany inevitably became a major battleground of the Cold War. In 1946 the United States stopped the sending, as reparations, of German factory equipment to Russia from the American occupation zone. To Russia reparations in kind seemed essential to repair the devastation visited upon her industrial cities by German armies. The Western powers claimed that Russia was taking more than had been agreed upon and that the exaction of reparations on this scale would imperil German recovery. On her side, Russia saw the Western policy of rapid re-industrialization of Germany as an attempt to re-establish the power of a state particularly likely to menace Russian security.

To enforce her case Russia, in June of 1948, clamped a tight economic blockade on Berlin. Although deep inside the Soviet occupation zone Berlin was jointly occupied by the former Allies. By blocking the city's supply routes from West Germany, Russia hoped to force the British and

Americans to leave the city and modify their German policy. The Western powers responded by mounting a huge airlift to supply their zones of the city. Blockade and airlift lasted nearly a year and were ended when the Council of Foreign Ministers agreed to review the entire German question. They reached no agreement, however, and in September 1949 the West took the decisive step of creating a separate state in their zones, namely, the German Federal Republic (West Germany). The Soviet government responded by creating the German Democratic Republic (East Germany) in October. The fact of a permanently divided Germany and a truceless Cold War had emerged.

2. THE PROBLEM OF DISARMAMENT

Another factor, ominously mushroom-shaped, heightened apprehension in the West. By 1949, Russia was known to have the secret of producing atomic bombs. A nuclear arms race had been foreseen as early as 1945 and revulsion against it had prompted a long but fruitless search for agreement on arms control and disarmament. On this problem, the United States, for obvious reasons, was the chief spokesman of the West. Even before the testing of the first atomic bomb, Secretary of War Henry L. Stimson raised with President Roosevelt the problem of the future.

> I went over with him the two schools of thought that exist in respect to the future control after the war of this project, in case it is successful, one of them being the secret close-in attempted control of the project by those who control it now, and the other being the international control based upon freedom both of science and access.

By the autumn of 1945 Stimson strongly favoured the second alternative and thought the United States should agree

311

to cease bomb production and to impound existing stocks of bombs. Concerned about future Russian-American relations, he remarked:

> Those relations may be perhaps irretrievably embittered by the way in which we approach the solution of the bomb with Russia ... if we fail to approach them now and merely continue to negotiate with them, having this weapon rather ostentatiously on our hip, their suspicions and their distrust of our purposes and motives will increase.

Secretary of the Navy James Forrestal, on the other hand, argued that the United States should exercise a United Nations "trusteeship" over the new weapon, and declared that "until we have a longer record of experience with the Russians on the validity of engagements . . . it seems doubtful that we should try to buy their understanding and sympathy."

In its Atomic Energy Act, Congress accepted Forrestal's reasoning and placed tight safeguards on atomic energy information. The first American proposal on disarmament, the Baruch Plan, followed the same line in 1946. It proposed the establishment of an international agency under the United Nations which would own and operate every aspect of atomic energy production and which would have power to inspect atomic installations in any country. Once the system of close inspection was working, the United States would agree to destroy its stock of atomic weapons, ban their future production, and provide for punishment of any nation that broke the agreement. The Soviet Union turned down the Baruch Plan and offered an alternative based upon immediate ending of bomb production and destruction of existing bombs. Noting that the United States could count upon a clear majority in any United Nations body, and that the time for giving up the monopoly on the bomb was left to the discretion of the United States, Soviet spokesmen declared that Russia could not feel secure under Western control of atomic weapons. In succeeding meetings in the United Nations Disarmament Commission, the General Assembly and special disarmament committees, Russia and the United States by and large kept to the positions taken up in 1946. The United States insisted that a system of international inspection be worked out in full detail before any stage of disarmament or arms control was initiated. The Soviet Union reiterated its demand for immediate general disarmament but refused to subject itself to the type of control system deemed necessary by the West. So the arms race went on. In the United States it absorbed a growing percentage of the annual national income every year after 1945. It meant too a sharp increase in the influence of the military upon foreign policy.

It is a peculiarity of nuclear weapons that they are not usable in the sort of warfare which has, in fact, occurred in one hot spot after another since 1945. It followed that the deepening mutual fears and suspicions between East and West led each side to have recourse to the traditional device of a system of military alliances at the same time as they poured billions into the development of new nuclear weapons. The first step towards a Western alliance was taken in the spring of 1948 when, with American encouragement, a military and economic alliance was signed by Britain, France and the Benelux countries (Holland, Belgium and Luxembourgh). A further step was taken in 1949 when Senator Arthur H. Vandenberg, a one-time isolationist, moved that the United States should seek security through a series of regional military pacts. This initiative, which was strongly supported by Canada, led to the signing of the North Atlantic Treaty later in the same year, which established the North Atlantic Treaty Organization (N.A.T.O.). The original members were the United States, Britain, Canada, France, Belgium, the Netherlands, Luxembourg, Italy, Portugal, Denmark, Iceland and Norway. Joint training schemes and a N.A.T.O. army in Europe were established and each member agreed that an armed attack against one N.A.T.O. member "shall be considered an attack against them all."

In North America, integration of Canadian-American defence was tightened by a defence production sharing agreement and the establishment in 1957 of the North American Air Defence Agreement (N.O.R.A.D.). By this agreement the Canadian and United States air defence forces, including unmanned missiles and a vast radar detection system, were placed under an American commander with a Canadian as his deputy — reflecting the countries' respective contributions to costs. Pursuing the policy of containment, the United States secured the admission to N.A.T.O. of Greece and Turkey in 1951 and of a re-armed West Germany in 1955. The Soviet Union responded by bringing the East European states into the Warsaw Treaty of 1955 and uniting their military forces under a single Russian command.

3. THE COLD WAR IN ASIA

Europe was not the only region to witness a deepening conflict between the interests of East and West. In the long run, if it were poverty, misgovernment and frustrated hopes that gave Communists their following, the greatest challenge would arise in the vast, underdeveloped and poverty-stricken continents of Asia, Africa and South America. The challenge touched the United States most nearly, of course, in Latin America. In 1947 the United States and all the Latin American countries signed the Treaty of Rio under which they agreed that an attack on any of them should be considered an attack on all, and the following year set up the Organization of American States (O.A.S.) to give body to this undertaking. Further, members reaffirmed the pledge not to interfere in one another's domestic affairs.

Military alliance was supplemented with economic aid. In his inaugural address of 1949 President Truman outlined a four-point programme for his new term of office.

His fourth point was the provision of technical assistance to underdeveloped countries. The "Point Four Programme," as it came to be called, was launched with a vote of $400,000,000 and similar sums were appropriated by Congress in succeeding years. After 1950 the United States also contributed substantially to the programme of mutual assistance launched by the members of the Commonwealth and known as the Colombo Plan. Yet neither in Latin America nor elsewhere has the technical assistance and economic aid so far provided solved the immense economic problems of the peoples concerned. Indeed most of the aid money has been spent on support of right-wing régimes and for purchasing military and industrial equipment in the United States.

In Asia, the confrontation between the Western world and Communism occurred even more abruptly and starkly than it had in Europe. During the Second World War, the Chinese government of General Chiang Kai-shek had received continuous, if limited, aid from the United States. It was, however, not the only government in China. In the northwest province of Shensi the Chinese Communist party had established a separate soviet power. Even the crisis of the Japanese war had not brought these two governments to work together, and in 1945, with that war ending, overt civil war seemed likely to break out again between them. Most State Department officials distrusted Chiang's régime as corrupt; the chief American representative in China considered Chiang both reactionary and unreliable and wrote that the party he headed, the Kuomintang, was "a structure based on fear and favour in the hands of an ignorant, arbitrary, stubborn man." Yet the United States decided that the long struggle between the Kuomintang and the Communist party might best be ended and China's unity restored by heavily subsidizing Chiang's government. But the Kuomintang continued to withhold overdue reforms and to make a system of corruption; civil war recommenced and the Communists grew in strength. A crisis was reached in 1949. Thousands of

Chiang's troops deserted and many provincial governors went over to the Communists. Rapidly driven southward, what remained of Chiang's forces withdrew to Taiwan (Formosa). By the end of 1949 the Chinese Communists, under Mao Tse-tung, controlled all of China.

The conclusion was inescapable that the United States' China policy had failed. A powerful China Lobby, composed of businessmen with Far Eastern interests and a number of Republican Congressmen, preached that Mao Tse-tung must be ousted by force and Chiang reinstated as ruler of China. Their vilification of the State Department coupled with that of Senator McCarthy, intensified anti-Communist feeling in the United States. As a result, the United States refused to follow the British lead of recognizing the Communist government of China, a refusal which became more adamant as a result of the Korean War.

The general worsening in East-West relations led to tragic consequences in the Korean peninsula. In 1945 Korea had been freed from Japanese control, and pending the establishment of an independent government, the United States and the Soviet Union occupied the country, dividing it between them at the thirty-eighth parallel of latitude. In the north, a Communist régime was established, while in the south a pro-Western government was organized. When the President of South Korea declared his purpose of reuniting the peninsula by force, a North Korean army invaded South Korea in June 1950. President Truman immediately sent American naval and air support to South Korea and the Security Council requested the United Nations members to assist the South Korean government, an act that was possible only because the Soviet Union was temporarily boycotting the Security Council and failed to exercise its veto. While the Commonwealth of Nations and several other Western and pro-Western states contributed to the United Nations army, the United States provided four-fifths of the forces required during the ensuing three years of war, and an

American, General MacArthur, became commander of the U.N. forces.

The Korean War exacted a bitter price, but established firmly the principle that any United Nations military action should aim to repel aggression without altering the original political position of the contending states. Thus in October 1950 when General MacArthur succeeded in crossing the thirty-eighth parallel and began to move towards the Yalu River which forms the border between North Korea and China, he was forbidden to bomb sites in Manchuria from which Chinese men and supplies were being sent to the North Koreans. When MacArthur publicly criticized this decision President Truman dismissed him from his command. The resulting military stalemate in Korea led to truce negotiations which dragged on until 1953 when an agreement was signed which restored approximately the *status quo ante bellum*. The war cost the United States more than fifteen billion dollars and thousands of lives. Even more important, it increased American determination not to recognize the government of China, and confirmed American willingness to intervene directly in areas far beyond the sphere of influence originally proclaimed by President Monroe.

A tightening of lines followed these events in China and Korea. In 1951 the United States signed a treaty of peace with the Japanese government. Japan immediately made a defence agreement with the United States which permitted the Americans to maintain bases on the islands. In 1954 John Foster Dulles, President Eisenhower's Secretary of State, negotiated a treaty creating the South East Asia Treaty Organization (S.E.A.T.O.). It was signed by the United States, Britain, France, Australia, New Zealand, the Philippines, Pakistan and Thailand. Since important East Asian states such as India, Burma, Ceylon and Indonesia did not join it, S.E.A.T.O. was not as closely knit or as powerful as N.A.T.O., but it became an important agency of American policy. Another important link in the system of interlocking regional defence alliances was the Middle

East Treaty Organization made up of Britain, Turkey, Pakistan, Iran and Iraq and created during 1955. Although the United States did not formally join the Middle East Organization it was largely inspired by the Secretary of State, John Foster Dulles, and was heavily endowed with American funds. In 1959, as a result of nationalist tensions in the area, the United States decided to become a member, at which time the name was changed to Central Treaty Organization. The containment of the Soviet bloc had been carried far—on paper, at least.

4. THE "BALANCE OF TERROR"

As the system of alliances grew, it became more and more difficult to define what the "free world" was which it was the purpose of American policy to defend. The Cold War made some strange bedfellows. Spain and Portugal, both dictatorships, received assistance without which their governments probably could not have survived. The governments of Greece and Turkey, while technically democratic, were constantly opposed to social reform. Pakistan, Iraq and Iran all had totalitarian governments of varying sorts. In Asia, Chiang Kai-shek's régime in Formosa, which the United States continued to recognize as the government of China and which could not have survived without American support, was an outright dictatorship. In South Korea and in the states that gained their independence from France in Indochina (Laos, Cambodia and Vietnam), American aid was given to the most right-wing governments. Successive American administrations feared that left-wing governments in underdeveloped nations might elect a policy of neutrality in the Cold War, as, in fact, many states in Africa and Asia did. What then would become of the carefully constructed system of military alliances and the goal of containment?

It was possible to think of containing the Soviet bloc so far as concerned its expansion by force of conventional arms. What could not be contained was its nuclear capability. By 1953 it became clear that both the United States and the Soviet Union possessed hydrogen bombs of infinitely greater power than the first atomic bombs. No important military, scientific or political observer doubted that a major war would bring a holocaust of destruction so great as to stagger the imagination. In the absence of controlled disarmament, official American opinion held that a "balance of terror" provided the surest guarantee against such a war. The Soviet governments under Stalin, Malenkov and Krushchev, and American governments under Truman, Eisenhower and Kennedy all placed on record their intention of using nuclear weapons in the event of an assault upon any of their respective territories or major interests. Each nation endeavoured to establish the "credibility" of this policy, that is, its ability and willingness to use nuclear weapons. Each declared that it would not use such weapons in aggression and each kept its nuclear knowledge secret from the other. Both the Soviet Union and the United States supported a policy of restricting the number of nations which possessed nuclear weapons in the hope that control would thereby be made easier. Nevertheless, Britain, which co-operated in wartime atomic research, achieved its own nuclear bomb production in 1955; France tested her first atomic bomb in 1959; and China acquired similar capacity in 1964.

Critics of the policy of a "balance of terror" argued that such a balance was inherently unstable since the two sides were never likely to agree as to when a desirable balance had been reached. More specifically, the evidence available seemed clearly to show that the United States continued to possess a much greater nuclear striking power than did the Soviet Union. This led to heavy military pressure inside the Soviet Union to expand the Communist nuclear armoury and its system of launching sites to match the world-wide system developed by the United States. But if American nuclear weapons were more numerous than Russian, a chill of fear touched American imaginations when the first Russian Sputnik was launched in 1957. This

319

leap into space added a whole new dimension to the military problem, and in the conquest of space Russia evidently had stolen a march on the United States. Congress at once voted large additional appropriations for the American programme of space exploration.

In international relations, the belief that survival hung upon a balance of terror seemed to have two effects. Each new crisis inescapably raised the question: might *this* bring on nuclear war? It arose in the continuing struggle to maintain a Western sector of Berlin deep inside East Germany; the Soviet clamp-down on the revolt in Hungary in 1956-57; the ebb and flow of Communist and American influence in Indochina, with its chronic guerilla warfare; the announcement of the Eisenhower Doctrine in 1957 that the United States would intervene to support any Middle Eastern state threatened by foreign-supported internal subversion; the willingness of Dulles to go to the brink of war to support Chiang Kai-shek's control of Chinese off-shore islands; the shooting-down of an American U-2 spy plane over Russia in 1960. However, it also brought home to both the United States and the Soviet Union the imperative need for co-existence. In the early 1950's Secretary of State John Foster Dulles had spoken of an "agonizing reappraisal" of American policy which might lead to "utilizing the deterrence of massive retaliation at times and places of America's choosing." In 1954 President Eisenhower shifted ground when he declared that East and West "must find ways of living together." Yet in the same year Dulles authorized the C.I.A. to organize an invasion of Guatemala to overthrow the Arbenz government, which had seized the American-owned United Fruit Company in order to finance social reforms. When Arbenz appealed to the United Nations Security Council, Dulles exercised the United States veto to prevent U.N. action, and anti-American feeling deepened in Latin America.

Events in Cuba showed with searing clarity the nature of the problems involved in waging the Cold War under the conditions imposed by the balance of terror. Before 1959 Cuba had been ruled by a dictator, Fulgencio Batista. When a determined guerilla fighter, Fidel Castro, led a successful revolt against this régime most Americans applauded. However, when Castro announced that as part of his reform programme he would nationalize, with or without compensation, a number of key industries and services owned mostly by American investors, and would redistribute the land owned by the big American-owned sugar plantations, conservative opinion in the United States turned against him. American firms cut off oil supplies to Cuban refineries, and when Castro accepted crude oil from the Soviet Union the United States put an embargo on Cuban sugar, the island's main export. Behind the scenes and unknown to the American public or Congress, the State Department and the C.I.A. planned an invasion of Cuba with a force of pro-Batista Cubans and mercenaries. Shortly after President Kennedy came to office, he gave his consent to this pre-arranged plan. The resulting attempt at invasion in 1961 was a fiasco. The successful Cuban resistance strengthened the Castro government, sharply increasing its anti-American attitude, and cemented Cuba's ties with the Soviet Union more closely. As Cuba clearly emerged as the first Communist state in the Americas, President Kennedy and his Secretary of State, Dean Rusk, asserted the right of the United States to intervene with armed force anywhere in the Americas if such action was deemed necessary to prevent the establishment of a government incompatible with "the American system." This Kennedy Doctrine was, in fact, a greater expansion of the Monroe Doctrine than the Roosevelt Corollary had been. It also contravened the Treaty of Rio and the Charter of the O.A.S., both of which outlawed armed intervention in the affairs of any American state by any other American government. On the other hand, it was consonant with the principle of containment, and thus revealed the complexity of the problems created by emphasis on the military aspect of containment.

After the 1961 invasion, the United States began to put pressure on her allies to join the economic blockade of Cuba, but with little success. For the rest of Latin America President Kennedy announced an "Alliance for Progress" which would involve a massive increase in American financial aid to those Latin American states that showed political stability and a forthright resistance to Communism. By 1963 some efforts had been made under the new assistance plan, though a number of Latin American states were reluctant to endorse the tough policy against Cuba. The president of the Inter-American Development Bank declared that not only had economic progress not been made, there was "a greatly deteriorating situation throughout Latin America."

In October 1962, Cuba suddenly found herself the centre of the most serious international storm since the end of the Second World War. When American Intelligence planes revealed that the Soviet Union, despite her denials, had installed launching bases for nuclear missiles in Cuba, President Kennedy ordered a tight naval blockade of Cuba and announced that any ship approaching the island would be stopped and searched. Moreover, he clearly intimated that if the missile bases were not quickly dismantled, the United States would take whatever further military steps were necessary. Since the Soviet Union had publicly undertaken to defend Cuba against any act of war and since a naval blockade is usually considered an act of war, the world waited breathlessly upon the outcome. Through the mediation of U Thant, the Acting Secretary-General of the United Nations, President Kennedy agreed to lift the blockade if the Soviet Union would remove the nuclear missiles and dismantle the bases. The world passed safely through the crisis, but the experience revealed with painful clarity what little voice the allies of the United States and the Soviet Union actually had in decisions which took them all to the very brink of nuclear war. Prime Minister Diefenbaker protested vigorously when the American commander of N.O.R.A.D. put the R.C.A.F. on war alert without consulting Ottawa, and the willingness of other western countries to unquestionably support American military intervention abroad lessened perceptibly.

5. THE QUICKSAND OF VIETNAM

Like other interrelated aspects of the Cold War, the bloody struggle in Vietnam grew out of the break-up of European empires following 1945, as well as from historic local causes. While the war dangerously deepened the divisions in American society caused by questions of racial and economic inequality, it also revealed a basic continuity in foreign policy. Direct American involvement in Indochina had begun in 1950 when President Truman decided to subsidize the French, who were trying to re-establish imperial control of French Indochina following the Second World War. A Vietnam nationalist movement led by Ho Chi Minh, who had spearheaded resistance against the Japanese occupation during the war, had set up an independent capital at Hanoi in the northern part of the country. As they had done in neighbouring Laos and Cambodia, which had also been colonies of French Indochina, the French established a new government (at Saigon in the southern part of Vietnam) under a puppet ruler. Their hopes of regaining control behind the pretended independence of the Emperor Bao Dai were rudely shaken when Mao Tse-tung's Communists won power in China in 1949 and recognized Ho Chi Minh's Hanoi administration as the official government of Vietnam. Succeeding events in Asia were to show how clearly linked were the crises of the spreading Cold War — no longer really cold.

The year 1949 saw the establishment of N.A.T.O., the explosion of the first Russian atomic bomb and the triumph of Mao Tse-tung. In the following year war broke out in divided Korea, and China began sending aid to the North Koreans and to Ho Chi Minh in Vietnam. Both Mao and Ho had studied Communism in Moscow and saw their struggles as movements to liberate Asia from western imperialism. In Washington these developments were seen as aggressive Communist imperialism, controlled by Moscow, and threatening not only western ideals, but also supplies of raw materials such as rubber and oil, which were crucially important to industrialized nations. In the opinion of Truman, or Dulles, or Kennedy, it was just as important to stop leftist nationalist movements in Asia as it was to prevent them in Latin America or the Middle East. In fact in 1954 Dulles helped the Shah of Iran regain power after a leftist nationalist leader had come to power and begun to take over the huge oil resources of the region. Dulles began comparing the ex-colonial areas of the "Third World" to rows of dominoes which would successively become Communist once a leftist nationalist movement overthrew one of them. By 1954 he was also aware that the American interpretation of the Cold War was more extreme than that of either Britain or France and wrote, "If we take a position against a Communist faction within a foreign country, we have to act alone. We are confronted by an unfortunate fact — most of the countries of the world do not share our view that Communist control of any country anywhere is in itself a danger and a threat." In Vietnam the domino theory led inexorably to the loneliest war ever fought by the United States. The domestic opposition that eventually forced an end to the war seemed to arise from two central ironies: the war was never declared by Congress, and it was waged to deny that very "right of revolution" which lay at the heart of the American Declaration of Independence.

Despite American financial aid, the French army in Vietnam was defeated by Ho Chi Minh's forces at Dien Bien Phu in 1954. At Geneva an international conference worked out a truce agreement which divided Vietnam at the seventeenth parallel until nationwide elections could be held in 1956. However, President Eisenhower and Secretary Dulles believed that if such elections were to be held Ho would win eighty per cent of the vote and be able to

Indochina

establish a national government. Therefore the United States increased its financial aid to the Saigon government whose prime minister, Ngo Dinh Diem, refused to sanction the elections and relentlessly suppressed his political and religious opponents. In response, Ho Chi Minh increased his support for the Vietcong, a Communist organization in South Vietnam which was waging a steady guerilla war in the hope of undermining Diem and reunifying the country. By 1961, when John Kennedy took office, the position of Diem was precarious and Kennedy sent Vice-President Johnson to Indochina on a fact-finding mission. Johnson reported the need for further aid to Saigon, but also warned that "possibly Americans fail to appreciate fully the subtlety that recently colonial peoples would not look with favour upon governments which invited or accept the return this soon of Western troops." Nevertheless, Kennedy accepted Diem's request for more than the financial aid upon which his unpopular government depended. By the time of Kennedy's assassination there were more than 15,000 American "military advisers" in South Vietnam, although the extent of the growing military commitment was not yet widely understood.

Both Kennedy and Johnson believed deeply in the analysis of the Cold War developed under Truman and Eisenhower, and especially in the need to maintain and use military power decisively to keep secure the political-economic structure of the "free world." But they paid less attention to the unmistakable warning issued by Eisenhower in his farewell address:

> This conjunction of an immense military establishment and a . . . permanent armaments industry of vast proportions is new in the American experience. The total influence — economic, political, even spiritual — is felt in every city, every state house, every office of the federal government. . . . In the councils of government we must guard against the acquisition of unwarranted influence, whether sought or unsought, by the military-industrial complex. . . . We must never let the weight of this combination endanger our liberties or democratic processes.

Kennedy increased the military budget by fifteen per cent in his first year in office. Under Johnson a still more rapid increase helped lead to the beginnings of the inflationary spiral that plagued each of his successors. Heavy defence spending boosted wages and thus increased consumer demand which in turn led to higher prices. As the economy came to depend more and more on the contracts required by the defence budget it became apparent that defence needs might be exaggerated — for the wrong motives. Symbolizing the close integration of defence and corporate management were Eisenhower's Secretary of Defense, Charlie Wilson, former President of General Motors, and Robert McNamara, Defense Secretary under Kennedy and Johnson, and before that a top executive of the Ford Motor Company. Increasing commitment to stemming Communism in Indochina was to lead not only to social discord, but also to political and military methods which seemed to endanger traditional American liberties and democratic processes.

Late in 1963 the corrupt Diem government of Saigon, which attacked Buddhists more often than Communists, was overthrown by a military coup which was secretly encouraged by the C.I.A. Diem was executed and nine successive governments during the following five years were sustained by the growing American presence in Vietnam. The effort to stabilize an anti-Communist government which did not have mass support failed. With each change of government a "credibility gap" widened between assurances of early defeat of the Vietcong and the actual situation in Vietnam. By the summer of 1964, Vietcong forces controlled most of the countryside and were being helped by supplies and some troops sent by Hanoi over the Ho Chi Minh trail which ran through the mountains and jungles of neutral Laos. Urged by military spokesmen in his National Security Council, President Johnson had increased American ground forces in Vietnam to 25,000 and these "advisers" were now directly involved in the fighting. Still the Vietcong flourished, and Johnson sought reasons

327

to justify yet greater American involvement. Suggesting an idealistic goal he declared, "I want to leave the footprints of America there. . . . We can turn the Mekong Delta into the Tennessee Valley." On a tougher note he warned, "If we don't stop the Reds in South Vietnam, tomorrow they will be in Hawaii and next week they will be in San Francisco." To gain authority for a massive American intervention without having to ask Congress for a declaration of war, the President secured from Congress a resolution (passed with only two dissenting votes) empowering him to take "all necessary steps" to prevent "further aggression" in Indochina. Potential opponents of this almost unlimited delegation of power to the executive had been silenced by a naval report that North Vietnamese torpedo boats had fired at American ships in the Gulf of Tonkin — a report which did not mention that the United States navy had supported South Vietnamese attacks on the coast of North Vietnam.

The Gulf of Tonkin Resolution, as it was known, became the legal basis for "Americanizing" the civil war in Vietnam. From 1965 to 1967 the number of American combatants in Vietnam grew to half a million. On the ground, United States conscripts took on the bulk of an increasingly bloody effort to eliminate Vietcong sources of support. American soldiers were either embittered or brutalized as they killed six civilians for every Vietcong fighter. One of them recorded his puzzlement: ". . . these damn kids in black pajamas continue to hold out. I can't understand it. Each of them must have forty lives." The tragic fact was that mere military technology was not a match for the zealous determination of people fighting for control of their own country. This became even more evident as growing numbers of Americans at home and in Vietnam questioned the official purposes of the war.

Two further developments combined to undermine and eventually halt this very hot phase of the Cold War: the American bombing programme and the growing threat of direct confrontation with Russia and/or China. In 1965

328

Air Force General Curtis Le May persuaded the chiefs of staff that mass bombing was the key to success. Waves of B-52's immediately began dropping tons of herbicides, napalm and explosives both north and south of the seventeenth parallel. The herbicide "defoliants" were used to obliterate forest shelter used by the Vietcong, as well as to kill crops; napalm (jellied gasoline) destroyed villages suspected of harboring Vietcong in lethal firestorms; the high-explosive bombs impeded factory production in the north and damaged the supply routes by which military equipment from Russia, China and Hanoi reached the Vietcong. By the spring of 1967 the tonnage dropped by nearly invulnerable B-52's was greater than the total loosed against Germany during the Second World War. The destruction and civilian death toll of this assault seemed only to strengthen the determination of the Vietcong and Ho Chi Minh's followers, while in the United States morale cracked and protest swelled. Despite the resignation of previously hardline Secretary of Defense McNamara in the autumn of 1967, Johnson and Secretary of State Dean Rusk continued to support General Westmoreland, the American commander in Vietnam. The General still predicted victory and declared that he was prepared, if necessary, to "bomb North Vietnam back into the stone age."

By early 1968 the war was costing the United States twenty-five billion dollars a year and still the Vietcong was able to launch a devastating surprise assault in most cities of the south in the Tet offensive (named for the Chinese new year) — the first action in which Soviet planes, tanks and missiles were used. Failure to subdue the Vietcong and mounting danger of more direct Chinese and Russian intervention, combined with the peace movement at home, finally led President Johnson to propose peace negotiations. In his March 1968 declaration that he would not be a candidate in the November election he also announced that he was halting the bombing of population centres and invited Hanoi to begin a "series of mutual moves toward peace." Ho Chi Minh accepted and "pre-liminary" talks began in Paris in 1968. Initially, however, they had little effect on the war.

6. KISSINGER AND DETENTE

During Richard Nixon's Presidency (1969-74), foreign policy was dominated by Harvard professor Henry Kissinger, first as Presidential Assistant and from 1972 as Secretary of State. Discarding the doctrine of containment, which viewed all Communist states as agents of a "monolithic" imperialism directed by Moscow, Kissinger perceived differences among Communist countries, and especially between the Soviet Union and China. With a curious combination of idealism and tough personal diplomacy, he sought a "detente" in the Cold War, an accommodation of Soviet, Chinese and western interests based on a careful balancing of power and recognition of spheres of influence. Two forces, one of which was beyond his control, worked against the success of this promising new approach.

First, detente was contradicted by Nixon's continuance of the war in Vietnam. Peace negotiations dragged on in Paris; so, too, did the bloodshed in Vietnam and the violent anti-war demonstrations at home. In the spring of 1970 Nixon further widened the credibility gap by announcing the invasion of Cambodia by American forces, declaring the need to eliminate North Vietnamese bases there. The President had given no intimation of this sudden expansion of the war, and widespread student protest immediately erupted in the United States. Police and soldiers clashed with protesters, several of whom were shot and killed at Kent State University in Ohio and Jackson State University in Mississippi. Nixon ordered even heavier bombing than had Johnson, arguing that a "silent majority" in the United States agreed with him that "precipitate withdrawal" from Indochina would be unwise. With ever more civilian deaths and mutual brutality the war continued through 1972, as did the peace talks. At the close of that year, in the heaviest air-raiding of the war, fifteen B-52's were shot down by Hanoi's Soviet-built missiles and even Nixon concluded that the end must come soon. In January 1973 a peace agreement was signed in Paris providing for prisoner exchanges and withdrawal of foreign troops from South Vietnam within sixty days. Nixon's "peace with honour" was soon seen as a fiction. The United States abandoned its commitment to secure an independent South Vietnam and the agreement provided for reunification of Vietnam — the major goal of both Hanoi and the Vietcong, who already controlled most of the country.

A second, less obvious weakness in Kissinger's policy of detente was partly of his own making: continuance of extreme secrecy in government, which did nothing to lessen public mistrust of government pronouncements. That fissure in public faith was apparently justified by publication in 1971 of the Pentagon Papers. These secret government papers, "leaked" to the press by Daniel Ellsberg, a defence department researcher, revealed that the executive had given false information to the public and had concealed its real purposes during the war. A growing lack of confidence in government, and even in political parties, was the worst legacy of Vietnam. The longest war in American history, it had cost the United States more than a hundred and fifty billion dollars, 56,000 lives and the conscription of three million citizens. Such exactions, together with the failure to prevent Communist reunification of Vietnam, intensified American suspicion of secretive politicians. At the same time, the apparent futility of the exercise lessened the longstanding reluctance to co-exist with successful Communist societies.

As the war was reaching its climax Kissinger induced Nixon to try his new approach of detente—first with China. In February of 1972 the President went to Peking, and in talks with government leaders Mao Tse-tung and Chou En-lai the basis was laid for "normalization" of relations. Since 1949 Nixon had vociferously supported American recognition of Chiang Kai-shek's government on Taiwan (Formosa) as the legitimate government of China, although Britain and other western countries gave diplomatic recognition to Peking as early as 1950. Even Canada, most closely tied to the United States by trade and defence links, had recognized China in 1970. The dramatic Nixon overture was followed by secret talks between Kissinger and Chinese officials, establishment of quasi-diplomatic offices and re-opening of trade connections. Further progress toward formal diplomatic relations was made by the Carter administration in 1978 when the United States agreed to withdraw recognition of Taiwan as the government of China.

Kissinger knew well that this thaw in Sino-American relations would be viewed with deep concern by a Moscow increasingly worried by China's military power, which now included nuclear weapons. As a result, Nixon journeyed to the Soviet Union two months after his well-publicized Chinese visit. His Kremlin talks with Party Leader Brezhnev resulted in some loosening of trade restrictions and the signing of a Strategic Arms Limitation Treaty which became known as S.A.L.T. I. By this agreement, which was to be followed by further discussions aimed at curbing both expenditures on weaponry and the risk of nuclear war, both countries agreed to limit the number of their nuclear missiles and delivery systems. However, detente was mainly psychological. Expenditures on arms development and production continued to rise in both countries and, as the Vietnam war was wound down, competition between the Soviet Union and the West for influence in the Middle East, Africa, Latin America and Asia was intensified.

For Americans, some of these concerns were to be temporarily overshadowed by the scandalous aftermath of the 1972 election. Henry Kissinger expressed his fears for the future of democracy as the campaign for that election began amidst the uproar of anti-war demonstra-

tions. "If confidence in [the President] and in all institutions is systematically destroyed, we will turn into a
group that has nothing left but a physical test of strength,
and the only outcome of this is Caesarism."

19

Presidential Power and American Society

IF HENRY KISSINGER'S fears about dictatorship were extreme, they nevertheless bespoke genuine concern about the state of the union—a concern shared by the United States' friends and allies. At home, Congress and astute observers were as much worried by the steady growth of Presidential power, symbolized by the conduct of the Vietnam war, as they were by the secrecy and deviousness which seemed the hallmark of such power. Abroad, two developments produced tensions within the American system of alliances. Detente with Russia and China led to nervousness in western Europe and Japan where, with all its risks, American military power was seen as the principal protection against potential conflict with one or another of the two great Communist powers. At the same time, West Germany and Japan had moved beyond mere recovery from the Second World War to become major economic competitors of the United States. European and Japanese products — from automobiles to sophisticated electronic commodities—made serious inroads in American and foreign markets. When added to the staggering cost of the Vietnam war, the new economic relationships produced a serious deficit in the American balance of payments; much more was being spent abroad and on imports than was being received for exports. A strong demand arose in the early seventies to reduce the size of American military establishments in Europe (over 200,000 people, together with air and ground equipment, were stationed in Germany alone), and to have western

Europe bear more of the costs of N.A.T.O. In turn, some European leaders feared a reduced American commitment to their defence. France especially pursued an independent foreign-military policy. Over all hovered the darkening cloud of relations between the West and the Third World.

In these circumstances any indication of frailty in the American political system was bound to have serious repercussions.

1. WATERGATE

As the election of 1972 approached, a sharp polarization became evident in American politics. The continuing war was only one factor in the deepening right-left division. President Nixon's domestic policies and, even more, his use of power, seemed consciously designed to feed doubts and hobble opposition. Downgrading the role of his undistinguished Cabinet, the President isolated himself behind a screen of personal assistants such as H. R. Haldeman, John Ehrlichman and John Dean. His Attorney-General, John Mitchell, was his closest political adviser and the only Cabinet member (except Kissinger, after 1972) with constant access to the President. Behind this protective barrier Nixon increased the executive power beyond precedent. The power of Congress to examine the operation of myriad administrative agencies was largely taken over by an Office of Management of the Budget, responsible to the President. As a result, the role of Congress in domestic affairs was threatened in the same way it had been in military policy by the Gulf of Tonkin Resolution. In each case the legislators had consented to the power shift, but by 1973 many were beginning to describe it as a constitutional crisis.

Nixon and his White House private cabinet believed they acted for that "silent majority" that feared Communists abroad and liberals at home: the hardhats or labour unionists who despised middle-class rock fans and draft resisters; the white suburbanites who disliked high taxes, welfare programmes and the growing violence; and business people who desired government assistance more than government regulation. Nixon appealed to these people with specific domestic policies. To the Supreme Court he appointed conservative jurists who, as he remarked, "share my philosophy that we must strengthen the peace forces against the criminal forces in America." Nixon permitted a slowing of the school desegregation process, and spoke forcefully against a court decision which ordered busing of children from one district to another in order to establish racially mixed schools. Nixon's socio-economic policy sharply reduced funds for welfare, urban renewal and job-training. At the same time, in order to limit war-induced inflation, the President imposed wage and price controls. The controls lessened the rate of inflation but increased the level of unemployment to over six per cent.

Social conservatism seemed agreeable to Nixon's silent majority. Rising unemployment and regulated prices were not. The Nixon team thus took extreme measures to prevent uneasiness over economic conditions from combining with liberal anti-war sentiment to cause Nixon's defeat in 1972. Some of these measures became known only after the election; others were public and had both immediate and long-term effects. Some twelve months before the election Nixon suddenly released the economic brakes. Government spending on farm subsidies and other growth stimulants, lowered interest rates, and tax reductions led to an immense deficit, but also to a reduction in unemployment and a boom atmosphere for the middle class. The long-term effect was to strengthen inflationary pressures.

At an irresolute convention the Democrats nominated Senator George McGovern of South Dakota. McGovern was the choice of liberal delegates who were now better represented because party managers wanted to improve the bad image created by the disastrous Chicago convention of 1968. Right-wing labour leaders and other conservative Democrats were dismayed by the convention decision to run a liberal, anti-war candidate who was strongly favoured by student radicals and civil rights groups. Thus the divided party presented a perfect target for Nixon Republicans who, nevertheless, took extraordinary steps to avoid the risk of another close election.

The Republican campaign was organized by a Committee for the Re-Election of the President (C.R.E.E.P.), which spared no pains to ensure success. Republican speakers and journalists depicted McGovern as an irresponsible, even traitorous radical who would disarm the nation, accept a "dishonourable" peace, bankrupt the government with welfare spending, and tolerate lawlessness on the streets and campuses. Headed by John Mitchell, who resigned as Attorney-General to direct the campaign, the election committee was especially apprehensive that the newly ratified twenty-sixth amendment to the Constitution, which reduced the minimum voting age to eighteen, would boost Democratic strength. The committee's funds, swollen by illicit business contributions, were used not only for massive publicity but also for gathering confidential information with which to damage the reputations of leading Democrats. The "dirty tricks" of the committee's group calling itself the "plumbers" included burglary, forgery, and planting false information.

Two ironies are now apparent in what came to be called the Watergate scandal. The whole operation was directed by a President and an Attorney-General whose most insistent demands had been for a return to law and order. Even more striking, none of the cloak-and-dagger activity was either useful or necessary. Nixon's dramatic, if dangerous, changes in socio-economic policy had already confirmed his majority; he basked in the well-publicized achievements of detente; and the one person who might have cut in to his right-wing support, the white-supremacist Governor George Wallace of Alabama,

337

had been permanently paralyzed in May 1972 by a would-be assassin's bullet.

The November election results gave Nixon a huge majority—sixty-one per cent of the popular vote—but left the Democrats in control of Congress. Fearful of his Congressional opposition and an increasingly hostile press led by the vigilant *Washington Post* and *New York Times* (which had published the Pentagon Papers in 1971), Nixon became even more inaccessible. In an attempt to control the soaring cost of living which resulted from his relaxing of wage-price controls at the beginning of 1973, the President cut back government spending even from appropriations for welfare and environmental controls which had already been voted by Congress. This fed the suspicion that, by dictating spending priorities, the President was further upsetting the constitutional balance by assuming too much power for the Presidency. It was at this juncture that the revelations about C.R.E.E.P. began to suggest that the Nixon White House was guilty of more than constitutional impropriety.

Watergate is the name of the Washington hotel-office building which housed the Democratic party headquarters. In June 1972, five men were arrested after they had broken into the building intent on "bugging" the Democratic offices and photographing documents. These five, together with two others who were arrested later, made up the Watergate Seven. Five of the seven were either officials or employees of C.R.E.E.P., while two had been C.I.A. agents and another had been an agent of the F.B.I. All were convicted and given heavy sentences by federal judge John Sirica. But Sirica, correctly suspecting that he had seen only the fringe of a massive criminal-political operation, induced J. W. McCord to give further evidence by promising a reduction of his sentence. McCord's evidence before a grand jury and then an investigating committee chaired by Senator Sam Ervin was quickly supplemented by that of a series of witnesses who had been involved in the often silly crimes of C.R.E.E.P. The televised Ervin hearings, and the bit-by-bit release and publication of taped White House conversations, gradually revealed to a stunned public not only the President's passion for electronic devices and his amoral approach to political power, but also the existence of an inner Presidential guard composed of people willing to disregard both the law and the Constitution. Even worse—and this is what Watergate has come to mean—was the willingness of the President to "cover up" their original crimes with lies, suppression of evidence and unscrupulous use of executive power. The famous tapes, recording Nixon in his oval office giving instructions to his lieutenants in March 1973, sum it all up: "I don't give a shit what happens. I want you to stonewall it, let them plead the Fifth Amendment, cover up or anything else if it'll save it —save the plan." Despite Nixon's attempts to deny knowledge, to influence a judge, to edit the tapes that he was finally forced to relinquish, and to bribe witnesses, the evidence against him and his aides became overwhelming.

By the end of 1973 the Nixon men began to fall. Vice-President Spiro Agnew resigned, having admitted to evasion of income tax in order to avoid trial on more serious charges of corruption not connected with Watergate. The Senate, after lengthy debate, confirmed Nixon's choice of successor to Agnew, Gerald Ford, a stolid Michigan Congressman and unquestioning Nixon supporter. Ford, apparently naively, spoke out in Nixon's defence. In October, however, the President undercut Ford's efforts when he refused to turn over White House tapes to the Ervin committee and ordered Archibald Cox, the special prosecutor appointed by the Attorney-General, to refrain from "further attempts by judicial process to obtain tapes, notes or memoranda of presidential conversations." When Cox refused to surrender his independence Nixon had him fired, although both the Attorney-General and his deputy resigned in protest. When Nixon finally gave up the tapes to Judge Sirica it was too late to prevent a complete unravelling of his consistent and complex abuse of power. By mid-1974 nine more men had either confessed or been convicted of a series of crimes which had begun at the Watergate. John Mitchell and several others were awaiting trial. A grand jury had named Nixon an "unindicted co-conspirator," and the President was also charged with personal tax evasion and misappropriation of public money. The Judiciary Committee of the House had adopted three articles of impeachment and many newspapers were demanding Nixon's resignation. On television, as the end drew near, the President proclaimed, "I am not a crook." But it was clear that the only prospects ahead were impeachment and criminal conviction. On August 9, 1974, Nixon became the first President to resign his office and Ford the first to enter the office without having been elected either to it or to the Vice-Presidential post.

The immediate results of Watergate were clear: almost forty Nixon men, including four members of his Cabinet, his Vice-President and his chief aides were indicted on criminal charges and nearly all were convicted and sentenced to varying prison terms. On the other hand, the equally guilty ex-President was given an executive pardon by his own appointee to the White House, "full, free and absolute . . . for all offenses against the United States which he . . . has committed or may have committed" while in office. Ford declared that Nixon's pardon would heal the nation's political wounds more surely than would allowing a trial in open court. In fact the pardon cost the new President some of the esteem he had previously enjoyed as an honest, if unassuming, politician. Ford seemed to apply one measure of justice to the rich and powerful, and another to lesser mortals—including thousands of draft-dodgers and deserters from whom he withheld clemency.

Yet the most enduring scar of Watergate was seen in the further erosion of confidence in the country's political system, reflected in a steady decrease in the number of citizens who cared to exercise their right to vote. As if to complete public disillusionment with the democratic process, a Senate committee on intelligence revealed that dubious and even criminal practices had become as common in the security agencies as in the Nixon White House. Evidence showed that the F.B.I. deliberately smeared and intimidated people considered radical by Director J. Edgar Hoover, while the C.I.A. regularly employed burglary and illegal wiretapping to gather information on American citizens, as well as conspiring to give effective support to anti-government groups in other nations.

Against this sea of troubles, first President Ford and then Jimmy Carter struggled to re-establish credible government and reassert more praiseworthy American values.

2. GERALD FORD: THE NIXON LEGACY

President Ford recognized in himself the personality and beliefs of that middle American majority that had twice elected Richard Nixon. His modest speaking style and awkward manner seemed reassuring after the lengthy melodrama of C.R.E.E.P. and the plumbers. Moreover, just as doubts about the American ability to employ power in ex-colonial areas were spreading, Ford ordered a strong naval-air action to recover an American merchant vessel, the *Mayaguez*, which had been seized in May 1975 by the new Communist government of Cambodia.

Not everyone was content, however, with the cautious conservatism of a well-meaning but apparently ineffectual administration. A Democratic Congress warred steadily with the President, refusing to fund his proposals and, in turn, Ford frequently vetoed legislation initiated in Congress. The result was a deadlock in which public confidence in the Congress was weakened as much as it had been in the Presidency. At the same time the effects of Nixon's lifting of economic restraints showed themselves in an unsettling combination of inflation and swelling un-employment—for which puzzled economists coined the term "stagflation." Despite evidence that 1975 saw the most serious recession since the 1930's, with an unemploy-ment rate of about nine per cent, Ford accepted the ad-vice of business people, who insisted that inflation was the main problem, and vetoed Congressional bills to subsidize house-building, farm prices, and medical aid. The laws were passed over his vetoes and this, together with Ford's selection of the wealthy Governor Nelson Rockefeller of New York as Vice-President, seemed to re-establish a vaguely right-left distinction between Republicans and Democrats.

While the new government spending did create more jobs, prices continued to rise. This inflationary spiral was in part a result of the oil crisis of 1973-74 during which the price of the huge quantities of oil imported by the United States took its first startling leap upward. The sudden increase in oil prices had been arranged by a new cartel, the Oil Producing and Exporting Countries, (O.P.E.C.), and was to call into question long-standing American policies toward the Middle East and the Third World in general.

If differences between the parties' domestic policies were more apparent than real, their foreign policies un-derlined their similarities still more. Ford himself had been an extreme "hawk" throughout the Vietnam war as House minority leader. He retained Henry Kissinger as Secretary of State and Kissinger continued to pursue, through his shuttle diplomacy of travel and personal con-tacts, the implications of detente. While these included negotiations pointing to a further stage of strategic arms limitation (S.A.L.T. II), they also required continuous attention to areas of the world where the strategic and resource interests of the superpowers might lead to major conflict or serious imbalance of power. In Indochina, Africa, the Middle East and Latin America the so-called Nixon Doctrine was applied, with results which were to prove counterproductive in the long run. This policy rejected direct military intervention and called for reliance on regional allies to protect vital American interests. Essentially a modification of the aging Cold War alliance structure, it showed the same tendency to support "dependable" authoritarian governments that were often little concerned with either nationalist feeling or the welfare of their citizens.

In Latin America, reluctance to use armed intervention did not improve the United States' image. In the late 1950's, following military coups in Bolivia and Peru, much American business property had been confiscated. After the 1970 election of the socialist Allende government in Chile, Allende made it clear that he planned to appropriate the Chilean facilities of American corporations such as the International Telephone and Telegraph Company. The C.I.A. subsequently disbursed some eight million dollars helping right-wing forces and the army "destabilize" the government. In 1973 Allende was overthrown and murdered during a military coup. At the same time, in several turbulent areas in Africa, Kissinger's diplomacy seemed to move even closer to direct intervention. When both the Soviet Union and Cuba lent support to left-wing nationalists fighting for Angolan independence, Kissinger was only prevented from sending military supplies to pro-Western Angolans by forceful opposition in the Senate.

There seemed to be two main risks inherent in the post-Vietnam policy of detente: that support of regional allies by both superstates might lead to "proxy wars," and that such conflicts would be difficult to contain, thus leading back to direct intervention. In the Middle East, whose oil supplies were essential to the industrialized nations, these dangers were intensified by historic cultural forces and modern strategic concepts. The cultural forces of both Islam and Israel had produced strong nationalist sentiments during the gradual disintegration of western imperial control of the region following the Second World

War. These sentiments had led to the political state of Israel and to increasingly nationalist Islamic governments intent upon eliminating that state and also acquiring complete control of the production, distribution, and profits of their own oil. The oil resources of the Middle East had hitherto been managed by a cartel of western multinational companies. The interests of the American oil companies had been seen by every administration since 1943 as coinciding with the Cold War strategy of containing the Soviet Union, and this had led to the regional alliances arranged by Dulles, as well as to special relationships with such rulers as the Shah of Iran and the King of Saudi Arabia. The increasingly shaky alliance structure was most seriously threatened by the mutual hostility between Israel and the Islamic nationalists, all of whom supported the claims of Palestinian Arabs to a separate state. That state would include some land accorded to Israel when Palestine was partitioned in 1948 by the United Nations, and much more that was to be retained by Israel after 1967.

In 1967, after a long series of border clashes and one major conflict (during the Suez crisis of 1956), Israel launched a major strike against Egypt, fearing that Arab denial of the legitimacy of the Israeli state, and heavy Egyptian armament provided by Moscow, foretold a combined assault. In the Six Day War, Israel overcame the unco-ordinated forces of Egypt, Syria and Jordan and occupied considerable portions of each. Israel retained the occupied lands, defying a U.N. resolution, and insisted on firm guarantees for her security as a precondition of military withdrawal. The United States increased its military aid to Israel, supported by American public opinion, which saw Israel as representing democracy and the Jewish right to a national home state, and also as a bastion against too great Soviet influence in the Middle East. Yet as raids and counter-raids along Israel's borders continued, the danger of a larger conflict grew steadily, and both the Soviet Union and the United States enlarged their naval forces in the Mediterranean. Deep cultural antagonism was aggravated when Egypt and Syria chose the Jewish holy day of Yom Kippur in October of 1973 to re-open the conflict. Only as Israeli forces, after first being driven back, approached a second victory did Russia and the United States arrange a U.N. resolution providing for an armistice and peace negotiations.

Not only Washington and Moscow were agitated by the darkening complexity of the long Arab-Israeli struggle. As the Arab states acquired economic strength from their control of oil production they began to use their resulting political power. In addition to price increases, they threatened to withhold oil supplies from any nation supporting Israel and even to compel western companies wishing to share in profitable new business with Arab states to boycott Israel. The threat of an oil embargo was especially worrisome to N.A.T.O. countries and Japan, who, except for the United States, all depended on the Middle East for more than seventy per cent of their oil requirements. Not surprisingly, the United States' allies were deeply disturbed by the heavy American support of Israel. Moreover, while only twelve per cent of American oil imports came from the Middle East, any serious disruption of that supply would be crucial.

Resolution of these problems would become the top priority for Ford's successor, for both ideological and economic reasons.

3. JIMMY CARTER: THE POLITICS OF INNOCENCE

In 1976 there appeared to be a double challenge: to tackle outstanding American foreign and domestic problems and, perhaps more difficult, to convince Americans that their traditional political institutions *could* be cleansed and made effective. Indeed, the 1970's saw a very low point in democratic participation in party politics. Fewer than twelve per cent of those qualified to vote elected

Mayor Koch of New York in 1977, President Carter was to be elected by twenty-eight per cent of the qualified voters, and in the 1978 Congressional elections two out of three voters did not go to the polls. Anxious analysts offered tentative explanations. The violence of the sixties, capped by unbridled amorality in the Nixon years, had produced disillusionment and cynicism. Some social historians saw this as the expression of a "narcissistic" generation, a generation intent upon self-contemplation and the problems of purely personal fulfillment. Whether or not this was what Jefferson had meant by "the pursuit of happiness," it led to an increase in the role of pressure groups and what came to be called "single-issue" politics —groups using their influence on legislators to secure laws for particular ends such as environmental protection, health insurance, aid or concessions to particular economic interests and even balanced government budgets.

In fact, the apparent weakening of the role of political parties was not new. George Washington had seen parties as "baneful" and in 1885 Professor Woodrow Wilson wrote that in Congress there were as many parties as there were subjects of legislation. But Wilson had seen this as dangerous because disciplined parties and strong leadership were necessary to ensure responsibility for policies. The fact that only a direct threat of impeachment had been able to bring Richard Nixon to account and that most Republicans had been unaware of his more nefarious activities seemed to underline the futility of looking to parties for the restoration of democracy.

James Earl Carter, Jr., an idealistic Baptist and native of Plains, Georgia, was deeply concerned about the condition of his country. His decision to offer himself as Democratic Presidential candidate for 1976 seemed implausible, yet he moved himself methodically from the relative obscurity of state politics and business in the deep South to the limelight of the White House. Trained as an engineer, and a graduate of the Naval Academy, Carter had managed a prosperous family peanut business. In

1967, he was, to use the southern Baptist expression, "born again" in his Christian faith. Entering politics as a state legislator he rose to become Governor in 1971. In 1976 he campaigned vigorously in every state primary election. By that year the system of primaries operated in three-quarters of the states. (The "direct primary" originated as a demand of the progressive era and was designed to minimize the power of party "bosses." The primary method allows delegates to national party leadership conventions to be chosen in state-wide elections rather than by party meetings or caucuses.) By summertime Carter had won a majority of delegates to the Democratic convention. To complete a mildly reformist ticket he selected Senator Walter Mondale of Minnesota as his running mate. In contrast, the Republican convention witnessed a sharp struggle for the nomination between Gerald Ford and Ronald Reagan, an ex-movie-actor, ex-Governor of California and extreme conservative. With inherent Presidential advantage Ford won the nomination and chose Senator Robert Dole of Kansas to balance the Republican ticket.

The two candidates in 1976 did little to enlarge voter participation. Ford's stiff and apparently ill-informed speeches, and Carter's transparently sincere appeals for honesty, economy and efficient administration were equally unprepossessing in style. If those who did vote, fifty-one per cent favoured Carter, forty-eight per cent Ford. To the White House an unassuming Carter brought a disarming candour, a strong emphasis on morality and a faith that good intentions and an honest regard for human rights were what was most needed. Few people questioned his purposes although many doubted his ability to offer strong leadership or consistent policies.

The "new foundation" of Carter's administration, despite the voting support of blacks and northern liberals, was to be both cautious and traditional. Southerners rejoiced that for the first time the country had a President "without an accent," and many Georgians found high positions in Washington. While this trend, once again, reflected the growing economic strength of the sun-belt, Carter's personal loyalties proved a mixed blessing. As director of the key Office of Management and the Budget, Carter chose his close friend and principal adviser, Bert Lance. An Atlanta banker, Lance had helped Carter with business financing, but had also engaged in dubious financial activities of his own. While under Senate investigation shortly after taking office Lance gave his resignation to his saddened, but still supportive, President. Other Carter appointments, however, revealed Carter's sense of continuity with previous administrations and an unexpected intimacy with many Washington insiders. Some of these appointees, like the President himself, were members of an elite Washington organization funded by the Chase Manhattan Bank and known as the Trilateral Commission. Prestigious but little publicized, the Commission had engaged for some years in non-partisan analysis of policy options in domestic and international affairs. It included economic and military experts from other industrialized countries concerned with the socio-economic stability of the West. Indicative of Carter's inherent conservatism was his appointment of a noted Cold Warrior, Zbigniew Brzezinski, as his national security adviser, and James Schlesinger, former Republican Defense Secretary, as Director of Energy Planning.

Despite his emphasis on managerial efficiency and personal relationships, Carter's political difficulties seemed to lie in these areas. While his own party possessed large majorities in both houses of Congress, his modest legislative proposals were obstructed there and his inability to "control" Congress led to doubts about the quality of his leadership. Yet the problems Carter confronted were structural as much as psychological. There was a clear need for leadership, but there also appeared to be tight limits to Carter's range of options, limits imposed by strong centres of power both at home and abroad. "In such a world," he observed, "we seek not to stifle inevitable change, but to influence its course in helpful and constructive ways that enhance our values, and national interests, and the cause of peace." At home, both unemployment and inflation rates increased, and Carter refused to initiate a comprehensive medical insurance scheme such as existed in every other western democracy. He also found it difficult to deal with a massive shift in the market structure of manufacturing. Despite the fact that most semi-monopoly firms maintained high prices, they found their profits cut by heavy competition from abroad and, in response, many of them established branch plants in Taiwan, Korea and other countries where labour was cheap. Without the imposition of tough controls on multinational corporations, such basic economic changes were beyond Carter's influence. Nonetheless, by mid-1979 the President had gained confidence from his experience in office. Moreover, his failure to command either Congress or the Democratic party was balanced by considerable foreign policy achievement.

In foreign policy, Carter's successes included re-opening diplomatic relations with Cuba and, despite heavy Republican opposition, two treaties with Panama by which the United States agreed to relinquish gradually all its administrative rights in the Canal Zone, thus allaying the threat of renewed anti-American violence in Panama. Negotiation of the S.A.L.T. II treaty was completed, but its complicated definition of how Russia and the United States would further limit their nuclear weapons systems ran into serious bipartisan opposition in the Senate. Such opposition was intensified when the administration admitted that the C.I.A. had confirmed the presence in Cuba of some three thousand Russian combat troops. Although Moscow and many American defence analysts observed that the Soviet soldiers had been in Cuba for at least fifteen years and that their role was to train Cubans, the President feared that another "Cuban crisis" might arise. Carter responded at first by giving a tough warning that expanded Soviet military power in Cuba was unacceptable, by increasing American surveillance over Cuba, and by sending additional American troops to the Guantanamo naval base. But he followed such actions with a clear statement that there was no threat to American security.

Carter's dramatic sponsorship of meetings between Egyptian President Sadat and Israeli Prime Minister Begin resulted in an Egyptian-Israeli peace treaty, although the objective of a more general settlement in the region was heavily shadowed by the inability to satisfy the claim of displaced Palestinian Arabs and an intensification of Islamic nationalism throughout the Middle East.

4. THE ENERGY OF DESTINY

As the 1970's drew to a close, questions of energy sources dominated American political and social life. Despite a critical fuel shortage resulting from the Arab embargo of 1973-74, and a still more critical situation in 1979, neither the oil companies nor Congress had responded to Presidential proposals for a general energy programme designed to curb wasteful fuel consumption and develop alternative energy sources. In large part the reluctance to accept rigorous measures was itself the result of long-term structural changes in American society. Those changes had produced a society whose way of life was totally dependent on an ever-increasing consumption of energy. The huge interstate highway programme, begun under President Eisenhower, had made Americans more mobile than ever and had further stimulated suburban growth, including vast shopping plazas, commuter dependence on the automobile and the multiplication of energy-consuming devices. As the car became the central means of locomotion, railway and other mass-transportation systems either decayed or failed to develop. Viewing this vast, interlocking dependence upon ever-growing imports of oil, Carter warned of a "spiritual crisis" in American society.

As O.P.E.C. steadily increased the price of its oil exports, and the rate of inflation in the United States moved into double digits, the oil companies lobbied for "deregulation" of the domestic oil market, in which the selling price to consumers had been kept the lowest in the world. Carter declared that the companies sought the "biggest rip-off in history." By the summer of 1979 he appeared determined to reassert the full authority of the Presidency. He made changes in both his Cabinet and his personal staff and pre-empted prime television time to appeal to the people to counter the oil lobby by direct pressure on Representatives and Senators to vote for his proposed comprehensive energy legislation.

The impending 1980 election, a precariously low rating in opinion polls and mounting criticism from Senator Edward Kennedy for refusing to support health insurance only partially explained Carter's vigorous initiatives. Solution of the deepening energy crisis involved every aspect of American political-social beliefs, and also Carter's personal interpretation of the United States' role in the world. Moreover, the policy choices were narrowed not only by a Congress responsive to interest group pressures but also by events abroad. At home, near disaster at a nuclear generator of electric power in Pennsylvania sharply increased environmentalist opposition to further use of nuclear energy. In the Middle East the process of "stabilization" represented by the Israeli-Egyptian peace treaty was rudely disrupted in 1979 when the Shah of Iran was overthrown in a revolution led by the Ayatollah Khomeini, a puritanical exponent of Islamic religious nationalism and an opponent of Israel. The new Iranian government announced its full support of the Palestine Liberation Organization and immediately ended agreements by which the United States had maintained close to the Soviet Union its most effective electronic listening posts, which monitored Soviet aircraft and missile activity. Security of oil supplies for the United States, and also for its allies, could no longer rest upon the regional alliance network established by Dulles. But what would replace that policy while the United States and other industrial nations sought feverishly for alternatives?

At the end of the seventies, energy and destiny were intertwined in a pattern that would have seemed familiar to Jefferson, Polk or Theodore Roosevelt. Democratic ideals were still enmeshed with problems of growth and national power. President Carter, speaking to the United Nations on human rights in 1977, had declared "Thus, no member of the United Nations can claim that mistreatment of its citizens is solely its own business . . . ." His public criticism of Communist and other authoritarian states in this respect was shadowed by continuing revelations of unsavoury C.I.A. operations inside and outside the United States. Again, progress toward the second S.A.L.T. treaty seemed to be counterbalanced by the extent to which the country's economy had come to depend upon military production. In 1979 the fourteen billion dollars of American military exports about equalled the defence department's own procurements. And while the post-Vietnam United States was reluctant to endorse a policy of direct intervention in other countries, there was little doubt that such action, as a final resort, had not been ruled out completely. In mid-1979, Zbigniew Brzezinski and Defense Secretary Harold Brown announced the creation of a 110,000-man Unilateral Corps, a mobile strike force composed of Air Force, Navy and Marine units. The Corps, with no obligations to N.A.T.O., was designed to intervene wherever the flow of oil to the West was seriously threatened. A senior Carter adviser said the new approach "avoids the extremes of Vietnam, where we tried to do everything for ourselves, and the post-Vietnam period when we couldn't do anything . . . . We are not talking about permanent bases or formal alliances in the Gulf [of Arabia] but we have to be able to protect our interests in a region far more vital to us than Vietnam ever was." The Unilateral Corps appeared to some to be the foundation of a Carter Doctrine for the Middle East.

As in the earliest days of the republic, ideals and self-interest ran in tandem at home and in foreign relations. The American dream of democracy, equality of all citizens before the law and tenacious regard for individualism still competed with special interest groups, corporate power and extremes of economic inequality. Yet no matter how fiercely the elements of that dream may be in conflict within the country, there is agreement among many Americans that their dream is still the wave of the future and that the world must be made safe for its continuing manifestation.

American History as a Debate:
Suggested Readings

1. General

There are many collections of articles, excerpts from
books and primary sources suggesting differing
interpretations of important events, crises and developments. Among the best of these collections are the
following:

a) Edwin C. Rozwenc (ed.), *Problems in American
   Civilization*, D.C. Heath and Company. A long
   and still growing series of short paperbacks, each
   compiled and introduced by a specialist. Probably
   the most comprehensive available.

b) Gerald Grob and George Billias (eds.), *Interpretations of American History*, Collier-
   Macmillan Canada. In two paperback volumes
   the editors present a full set of differing views.

c) Allen Davis and Harold Woodman (eds.), *Conflict
   and Consensus in Early American History*
   and *Conflict and Consensus in Modern American
   History*, D.C. Heath and Company. An alternative two-volume paperback compilation.

d) Howard Quint, Milton Cantor, Dean Albertson
   (eds.), *Main Problems in American History*,
   Irwin-Dorsey Ltd. An excellent selection, in two
   paperback volumes, of contemporary views and

primary sources. Good editorial introductions to the material.

The above references cover virtually all the controversial issues in American history in a concise manner. The following sections 2 to 12 are for teachers and for student essayists who wish to read in greater depth on selected topics.

2. Revolution or War of Independence?

Historians continue to differ sharply on the nature, purpose and causes of the "American Revolution." J.F. Jameson, *The American Revolution Considered as a Social Movement* (1926) is the classic argument that the war set loose a social, democratic revolution. Bernard Bailyn, *The Ideological Origins of the American Revolution* (1967) stresses ideas and constitutional problems rather than social conflict. L.H. Gipson, *The Coming of the Revolution 1763-75* (1954) sees the struggle as a civil war within the British Empire. Merrill Jensen, *The Founding of a Nation* (1968) emphasizes the differing interests in the various colonies. W.H. Nelson, *The American Tory* (1961) is the best account of the role of the Loyalists, from an American viewpoint.

3. The Constitution: Democratic or Reactionary?

The notion that the Articles of Confederation were too weak and that economic depression required a stronger central government was generally accepted until Charles Beard wrote *An Economic Interpretation of the Constitution of the United States* (1913). His argument that the Constitution was a counter-revolution by propertied interests has been attacked by Robert E. Brown, *Charles Beard and the Constitution* (1956), and

Forrest McDonald, *E Pluribus Unum: The Formation of the American Republic* (1965). An interesting defence of the Articles is Merrill Jensen, *The New Nation* (1950). The best one-volume constitutional history is Alfred Kelly and Winfred Harbison, *The American Constitution* (1948 and later editions).

4. Hamilton vs. Jefferson

The debate about "true Americanism" often starts with these two towering figures: Hamilton as the father of strong, conservative centralized government and industrialization; Jefferson the defender of states' rights, suspicious of cities and factories and proponent of the rights of man. The debate involves the origins, also, of the party system and American foreign policy. Sympathetic to Jefferson are M.D. Peterson, *Thomas Jefferson and the New Nation* (1970) and Bernard Bailyn, *Origins of American Politics* (1969). Supportive of Hamilton are J.C. Miller, *The Federalist Era, 1789-1801* (1960) and Leonard White, *The Federalists* (1948). The best single-volume history of American foreign policy is Alexander DeConde, *A History of American Foreign Policy* (1963). For a stimulating paperback analysis of American expansionism see Richard Van Alstyne, *The Rising American Empire* (1960).

5. 1812: Maritime Rights or Frontier Expansion? Victory or Defeat?

The role of expansionist war hawks is stressed by Julius Pratt, *Expansionists of 1812* (1926). Reginald Horsman, *The War of 1812* (1969) and Norman Risjord, *The Old Republicans* (1965) emphasize impressment and trade, as does A.L. Burt in the classic *The United States, Great Britain and British North America* (1940).

6. Andrew Jackson: Nationalist Tyrant or People's Tribune?

Most nineteenth century historians frowned on Jackson as an uncouth westerner. Revision of this "northeastern view" began in 1893 with Frederick Jackson Turner's important essay "The Significance of the Frontier in American History." Approval of Jackson, with emphasis on urban workers and democracy, is found in A.M.S. Schlesinger, *The Age of Jackson* (1945). R.V. Remini, *Andrew Jackson and the Bank War* (1967) is critical, but balanced. Lee Benson, *The Concept of Jacksonian Democracy* (1961) describes a party of mixed interests, similar to the anti-Jackson whigs. Richard Hofstadter, *The American Political Tradition* (1948), shows a Jackson supported by "entrepreneurs" and also provides excellent thumbnail political portraits for this and other periods. Edward Pessen, *Jacksonian America* (1970) is an excellent brief overview.

7. Could the Civil War have been avoided?

The debate about the "irrepressible conflict" still rages and the literature is overwhelming. The best approach is through three excellent paperback collections of contemporary and later analyses: Kenneth Stampp (ed.), *The Causes of the Civil War* (1974); Thomas Pressly (ed.), *Americans Interpret their Civil War* (1954); C. Rozwenc (ed.), *The Causes of the American Civil War* (1972). Slavery and expansionism, as major causes, are each issues in themselves. A.K. Weinberg, *Manifest Destiny* (1935) emphasizes the idea of mission. Frederick Merk, *Manifest Destiny and Mission in American History* (1963) links slavery and expansion. Lloyd Gardner et al., *Creation of the American Empire* (1973) relates the Monroe Doctrine and the sphere-of-influence idea to later expansionism. A thorough, more traditional view of the Doctrine is Dexter Perkins, *The Monroe Doctrine* (1927). The best single volume paperback on slavery is Kenneth Stampp, *The Peculiar Institution* (1956). The best short history of the blacks in America is John Franklin, *From Slavery to Freedom* (1974).

8. The Robber Barons and their Critics

Sympathetic to the "industrial statesmen" of the post-Civil War era are Allan Nevins, *The Emergence of Modern America* (1927), Edward Kirkland, *Dream and Thought in the Business Community 1860-1900* (1956) and *Industry Comes of Age: Business, Labour and Public Policy 1860-1897* (1961). The best short analysis, stimulating but balanced, is Samuel Hays, *The Response to Industrialism* (1957). The classic criticism of businessmen and "their" politicians is Matthew Josephson, *The Robber Barons* (1934). Strongly sympathetic toward the Populists are Norman Pollack, *The Populist Response to Industrial America* (1962) and L. Goodwyn, *Democratic Promise: The Populist Movement in America* (1976). The best paperback histories of labour and socialism are Henry Pelling, *American Labour* (1959), David Shannon, *The Socialist Party of America* (1955), and John Laslett, *Labour and the Left. . . 1881-1924* (1970).

9. Was Progressivism really Conservative?

Progressivism as a democratic reform movement in the interests of the common people and against trusts and corruption was a standard view for many years. That view is represented in H.U. Faulkner, *The Quest for Social Justice* (1931). Three books present opposite versions, suggesting a dominant role for business-minded leaders: Gabriel Kolko, *The Triumph of*

Conservatism (1963); Robert Wiebe, *Businessmen and Reform* (1962); and James Weinstein, *The Corporate Ideal in the Liberal State, 1900-1918* (1968). A good paperback collection of contemporary analyses with an excellent interpretative introduction is Carl Resek, *The Progressives* (1967). On Wilson and the First World War a good paperback collection of interpretations is Herbert Bass (ed.), *America's Entry into World War One* (1964).

10. The New Deal: Radical Reform or Preservation of Capitalism?

The temptation to periodize American history is strong: the progressive era, Republican Normalcy, the New Deal Decade, etc. This can be seen in most textbooks, many of which have been patterned on Charles and Mary Beard, *The Rise of American Civilization* (1927 and later editions). Useful antidotes, stressing continuity from different viewpoints, are William Leuchtenburg, *The Perils of Prosperity, 1914-32* (1958) and William A. Williams, *The Contours of American History* (1961). For an unusually sympathetic treatment of Harding see Robert Murray, *The Harding Era* (1969). Very critical of the New Deal are E.E. Robinson, *The Roosevelt Leadership, 1933-45* (1955), which sees it as communistic, and Howard Zinn, *New Deal Thought* (1966) which sees it as a right-wing support of the capitalist system. The best paperback overview is Paul Conkin, *The New Deal* (1967) and, for F.D.R., James M. Burns, *Roosevelt, the Lion and the Fox* (1956). A fascinating account of a great woman in public life is Joseph P. Lash, *Eleanor and Franklin* (1970). A good paperback collection of interpretations is Morton Keller (ed.), *The New Deal: What was it?* (1963).

11. Who started the Cold War?

John Gaddis, *The United States and the Origins of the Cold War* (1972) gives the most reasoned defence of American policy during the Second World War and through the Marshall Plan. Much more critical of Truman (and Eisenhower and Kennedy) are Walter La Feber, *America, Russia and the Cold War* (1967), I.F. Stone, *Hidden History of the Korean War* (1952), and Barton Bernstein, *The Atom Bomb: The Critical Issues* (1976). Susan Hartmann, *Truman and the 80th Congress* (1971) relates, critically, Truman's domestic and foreign policies as does Richard Freeland, *The Truman Doctrine and the Origins of McCarthyism* (1972). Herbert Parmet, *Eisenhower and the American Crusades* (1972) and Emmet Hughes, *The Ordeal of Power* (1963), are sympathetic to Ike.

12. America and the Free World: Vietnam, Civil Rights and Watergate

Confidence in modern American democracy is shown by John K. Galbraith, *American Capitalism* (1952) and *The New Industrial State* (1971), Daniel Boorstin, *The Genius of American Politics* (1952), James L. Sundquist, *Politics and Policy: The Eisenhower, Kennedy and Johnson Years* (1968), and Raymond Vernon, *Sovereignty at Bay: The Multinational Spread of U.S. Enterprises* (1971) which is of particular interest to Canadian students. Theodore Sorensen, *Kennedy* (1965), is sympathetic, but more recent writing, both on foreign policy and civil rights, is increasingly critical of both Kennedy and Johnson: Arthur M. Schlesinger, *The Bitter Heritage: Vietnam and American Democracy, 1941-66* (1967); Henry Brandon, *Anatomy of Error: The Inside Story of the Asian War on the Potomac* (1969) and *Retreat of American Power* (1973); H.Y. Schandler, *The Unmaking of a President: Lyndon*

Johnson and Vietnam (1977). On protest in the 'new left' sixties: Howard Zinn, *SNCC: The New Abolitionists* (1964); A. Pinkney, *Red, Black and Green: Black Nationalism in the U.S.* (1976); Kenneth Keniston, *Young Radicals* (1968); Kirkpatrick Sale, *SDS* (1973); and William H. Chafe, *American Women* (1972). On the eve of the Watergate scandal Daniel Bell, *The Coming of Post-Industrial Society* (1973) was still optimistic. The evidence compiled by Carl Bernstein and Bob Woodward in *All the President's Men* (1974) and *The Final Days* (1976) was less encouraging.

INDEX